Successful Shyness

Successful Shyness

*Building Confidence
and Effective Social Skills*

Marc D. Skelton,
PhD, PsyD, ABPP

PALMETTO
PUBLISHING
Charleston, SC
www.PalmettoPublishing.com

Paperback ISBN: 979-8-8229-2645-5
eBook ISBN: 979-8-8229-2646-2

Notice

All the case vignettes or histories in this book are based on actual clinical experience. Various demographic characteristics, including names, ages, locations, and occupations, have been changed. Also, certain clinical details have been altered to protect the confidentiality and anonymity of clients, as well as any of their family members or friends. In some instances, the case vignettes or histories are composites of clinical issues, problems, and situations. The terms counseling, therapy, and psychotherapy are used interchangeably in *Successful Shyness*. Further, a licensed mental health professional should be consulted for any psychological assessment or treatment needs. As primarily a self-help book, general clinical information will be provided with an emphasis on strategies and techniques that can be learned to effectively manage shyness.

Dedication

This book is dedicated to the memory of my parents, Ben and June,
and to everyone who works toward effectively managing shyness,
as well as those who help in their efforts toward success.

Acknowledgments

I would like to acknowledge the consistent support I received from my wife, Veronica, and daughter, Mackenzie, as well as her husband, Luke. They helped me to make *Shyness Successful* a reality by listening to my evolving thoughts and comments about shyness with characteristic patience. I also received kind attention and feedback from many colleagues, particularly George Condas, Ph.D., Thomas Geisz, Ph.D. and Mary Pat Kelly, Ph.D. Phillip Cecchini, MD provided valuable input on the Medication chapter of this book. My longtime friend, Geoff Parks, kept me focused and on track as *Successful Shyness* took shape over a period of years. Thanks also to Judi Heidel who provided valuable editing services throughout. Finally, I'm grateful to the staff of Palmetto Publishing for their expertise through all stages of this book's production.

Epigraph

Let me assert my firm belief that the only
thing we have to fear is fear itself.
—FDR

Contents

Part 1
Identifying and Understanding Shyness

Part 2
Developing and Maintaining Successful Shyness

Introduction

I am writing this book because I would like readers to learn ways to become successfully shy. It is important to recognize that shyness is a common and perfectly natural personality feature. It is basically a trait or temperament that an estimated 30 to 40 percent of the world's population possesses. While shyness is often considered a negative trait, shyness can in fact be a very positive asset. For example, many shy individuals are known to listen well to others and have a good sense of humor. At times, however, being shy can also be painful and problematic. Shyness is universal. Experiencing emotional pain or discomfort in social interactions, particularly in new situations or with unfamiliar people, is so common that almost everyone can relate. Shyness can range from slight to significant and can vary for the individual, based on circumstances. This book focuses on developing successful shyness. Successful shyness involves learning to be effective in social situations and in new or unfamiliar circumstances. Like all skills, it takes practice.

A shorthand description of shyness includes experiencing discomfort or emotional pain during social interactions. What type of emotional pain? Basically, the shy person may feel self-conscious, awkward, or simply anxious when interacting with others, depending on the situation. What drives this type of reaction is usually fear of social judgment, concern about being evaluated in general, and the effects of these painful prompts on self-esteem. When self-esteem is lowered, retreat from a variety of social situations may not be far behind. By avoiding interactions with others, less discomfort is experienced, at least in the short run. Over the long run, shyness can result in significant social isolation.

Thus, shyness becomes a problem when we suffer from it. Its erosion of self-esteem occurs when we don't follow through in a way that we would like socially, especially in unfamiliar situations. Shyness itself has been described by prominent social psychologist Philip Zimbardo, PhD, as a "self-imposed psychological prison." In this regard, a main problematic aspect of shyness can be its tendency to foster loneliness. That is, shy people can become lonely because they want to be with others and interact, but their self-consciousness and avoidance can keep them apart. In other words, the shy person can end up paying a price for their discomfort in getting to know people as social isolation can occur due to their strong pattern of avoiding contact.

The main purpose of this book is to help those who are shy learn how to lower their discomfort by being more effective in a variety of social situations, as well as in new or unfamiliar circumstances. A shy person doesn't need to overcome their shyness, but instead learn to focus on managing their shyness in order to be successfully shy. The benefits of learning to be successfully shy can have a positive effect for years to come. Fortunately, both positive empathy for others and an ability to control our impulses develop as we get to know others and socialize. That is, shy individuals can learn to care for and be cared for by others in their daily social lives. Further, the shy can learn to control their impulses, which allows them to walk away or avoid contact with others, and they can learn to stay with a particular social activity, thereby benefiting from interacting.

By staying in conversations with others, self-confidence will build. Shyness involves not only the individual but also all their interpersonal relationships and the community at large. Thus, another purpose of writing this book is to share psychological concepts and research on shyness with the public at large. Importantly, more outgoing people can learn to help the shy learn to effectively interact socially. In turn, shy people can help the more outgoing learn to enjoy solitary activities.

Shyness includes a set of behaviors that are learned from experiences in everyday life. Individuals who have a more inhibited temperament or response style are likely to be more predisposed or vulnerable to the development of shyness early on. Importantly, whereas shyness itself can be viewed as problematic at times, it is certainly not a mental health or psychiatric disorder. Shyness is simply a normal response style, sometimes problematic, set in the context of a broad and unique personality trait.

According to shyness expert Bernardo Carducci, PhD, shyness has been recognized in cultures all around the world. Its rate varies substantially, with up to 30 percent of individuals in Israel reporting experiencing shyness, while in Japan the rate is a much higher 57 percent. Survey participants in various United States studies, as researched by Dr. Zimbardo, reflect up to 50 percent of the self-reported shy individuals in the population. According to the Shyness Research Institute at Indiana University Southeast, which Dr. Carducci led, shyness is viewed as very common, with 40 to 60 percent of adults in the United States considered shy. Clearly, the 50 percent estimate from Dr. Zimbardo's research would be right in the middle and no doubt highly accurate.

Research with babies has shown differences between "social" and "shy" infants that can be inferred as present within the first two months of life. According to psychologist Jerome Kagan, PhD, fair-skinned children, and especially those with blue eyes, tend to be shyer and more inhibited than dark-eyed children. Further, the blue-eyed children, possibly more characteristic in males than females, tend to have greater hesitancy in new situations. These shy children are also more cautious when approaching someone, oftentimes remaining quiet with a new person, and more likely to stay close to their mothers. Another psychologist, Steve Bressert, PhD, has conjectured that some of the withdrawal associated with shyness may begin with inhibitions in infancy, which then correlate with a relatively shy stance early in life.

Psychologist Dr. Ward Swallow has viewed shyness as quite common in very young children, as well as in older children who develop shyness before adulthood. Finally, at least one study has indicated that a physical reaction, namely blushing, may be an important marker of shyness and social anxiety.

As mentioned, shyness involves a tendency to avoid or withdraw from social interactions. This type of pulling back behavior occurs not only in anticipation of a social encounter but also with new or unfamiliar situations and circumstances. In general, shy individuals may want to be more social but feel self-conscious about how to come across effectively. Inhibition in a shy person can be directly observed in their tendency to pull back and stay away from people. While shyness itself may be more difficult to observe, it is often sensed by others, leading to commonly heard prompts such as, "Don't be shy" or "He's just shy." Thoughts that stem from self-consciousness regarding performance can turn negative. An example is a shy person saying to themselves, "I just can't speak up in public." A downward spiral oftentimes occurs with feelings related to low self-esteem, anxiety, and sometimes depression to complete the cycle.

Fortunately, there are many ways to work with the very common trait of shyness in order to become successfully shy. In fact, if you are shy, you're in excellent company. Millions of Americans consider themselves to be shy. Further, shyness is universal with millions, if not billions, of more people around the world who would likely acknowledge some degree of shyness.

The following prominent or popularly recognized individuals from a variety of occupations have been reported to be shy (in alphabetical order):

Johnny Carson	Entertainer
Theodor Geisel (Dr. Seuss)	Children's books Author
Steffi Graf	Athlete
Elton John	Musician
Nicole Kidman	Actor
Abraham Lincoln	President, United States
Rosa Parks	Equal Rights Activist
Eleanor Roosevelt	First Lady, United States
Steven Spielberg	Director
Mark Zuckerberg	Facebook Founder

And the list goes on. Why include a list of well-known shy individuals? The main reason is that many popular or famous people are more familiar to us than, say, a shy neighbor who lives nearby. When we learn about those who are widely visible to the public and who are reported to be shy, we can relate. They relate to a degree, that is, because many of these individuals actually appear to be more extroverted or use an outgoing skill set in public. This is important because it demonstrates that there are shy extroverts and that such outgoing interpersonal behaviors can be learned. It remains even better news that virtually anyone can learn to be successfully shy. Ultimately, you will then be known as shy and successful, managing this unique and multi-dimensional personal trait effectively.

Shyness can be considered a perfectly normal response style for an individual, sometimes showing up in just a few situations. Other times, it is a reflection of a broader personality feature or trait. If shyness becomes severe and anxiety enters the picture wherein an individual has a tough time with everyday functioning in social areas, there are two different psychological disorders that may come into play and are addressed below.

First, there is a significant form of interpersonal anxiety, akin to extreme shyness, and more consistent with intense, lifestyle-interfering avoidance behavior termed social anxiety disorder (SAD). This psychological disorder has previously been referred to as social phobia. Based on data from the National Comorbidity Survey Replication, SAD is far less common than shyness and affects about 7 percent of the population. An individual with SAD is likely to distance themselves from or avoid meeting new people. Worse, this same person may, for example, not even follow through with a job application because of their fear of social judgment. Other examples of significant disruption in one's social behavior include not wanting to talk on the telephone, meet new people, or use a public restroom. Thus, daily functioning in a number of activities is oftentimes negatively impacted for someone with SAD.

Second, in terms of severity, there is a more enduring, characterological disorder named avoidant personality disorder (APD). APD is notable in that it involves a long track record of an individual being socially inhibited, but also feeling inadequate, with low self-esteem becoming chronic. To summarize, shyness is a trait with biological and environmental influences contributing to a pulling back in social behavior. SAD is considered a disorder because it negatively impacts the individual's daily functioning in the social world. APD is regarded as more severe because it involves more extreme avoidance of social situations over time and includes feelings of inadequacy and hypersensitivity.

If you are shy, you recognize that you are likely to have a quieter temperament than those who are more outgoing, but that you also have a valuable set of assets. For example, a definite strength of shyness is the ability to listen as well as to reflect quietly while in a noisy environment and in the bustling everyday world. Being shy also translates into being a careful observer, although this may in fact sometimes be a sign of scanning for social safety cues. That is, shy people may look for easier or more comfortable social situations rather than ones that appear challenging. Shy individuals can be quite hesitant and would likely change the popular phrase "Just do it" to "Let's just think about it."

Thus, it is important for children and adolescents to begin to develop appropriate and effective social skills early on and to build friendships with others. Shy individuals can learn to cultivate, foster, and maintain positive social relationships, especially if given enough encouragement to do so. The result is often healthy bonding as well as higher self-esteem and confidence.

At the same time, it's important to recognize that shy individuals can be undervalued, especially by those who miss their unspoken assets. Herbert Blumer, PhD, a prominent sociologist, once conjectured that pugnaciousness is one of humankind's major adaptive traits. That is, outgoing and aggressive individuals may take over the decision-making process, but not necessarily for the good. Shy, quiet, and reflective individuals do have the capacity to make very good leaders. Their careful and cooperative leadership gives them the ability to react evenly after carefully weighing the facts and circumstances. Thus, let us be thankful for all the shy among us, as getting along with others in this world of over seven billion people is an important adaptive trait.

The main purpose of this book is to help shy people develop effective social interactions and respond well to new and unfamiliar situations. This process will help build self-confidence for shy and inhibited individuals so that they are able to participate more actively in our everyday world. Expanding opportunities for interpersonal connection and thereby giving and receiving social support can be life enhancing. *Successful Shyness* offers suggestions, techniques, and practical advice to help shy people learn to be more socially effective in their everyday lives. Important questions will be addressed, including how shy individuals can interact with others in a positive way. We will also address how others can interact with a shy individual for mutual satisfaction and benefit. Basically, a shy person doesn't need to overcome their shyness but instead focus on learning to successfully manage their shyness.

In this regard, well-researched, evidence-based approaches to shyness are included in the assessment and treatment chapters of *Successful Shyness*. For example, one main approach that will be detailed is, at its core, a social-effectiveness model. The components include social skills training, practice opportunities, direct action, and self-reinforcement. Cognitive-behavioral and interpersonal psychotherapy strategies will be discussed throughout using a strength-based, compassion-focused approach to effectively managing shyness.

Speaking of self-reinforcement, which can include simply supplying your own verbal reward for a task well done, I am reminded of the Ego Box. Many might remember the Laugh Box, a small handheld bag with a plastic box inside from which, when you pulled the string, major laughter would sound out. The Ego Box, although less popular, was similar in design, but when you pulled the string, positive comments would blare out of the small speaker within the bag. Representative verbal rewards such as "Great job; you're fantastic" or "Excellent, keep going" came forth as soon as you pulled the string. I'm not sure this is exactly what a shy person needs, but the funny gag gift approach has the unusual merit of providing instant feedback in your direction (the pull of a string). I suppose, in keeping with a cognitive approach, you can just think of positive, encouraging thoughts as meaningful self-reward or praise without the need for an external device.

The overall approach used in this book draws on various well-researched psychological methods to assess and treat the troubles shyness can bring but will not focus on one method of help or intervention exclusively. Nor is this book anchored to one particular theoretical approach. There are many ways to intervene in helping with shyness; thus, different therapeutic perspectives can be applied. To summarize, Successful Shyness has as its clinical foundational framework a multimodal, integrative theoretical and practice approach.

As mentioned, cognitive-behavioral techniques and interpersonal (systems-based) therapy strategies will be highlighted. Following assessment, issues including identification of your major personality or response style, options for dealing with shyness and inhibition, and how to manage specific situations will be offered. A major focus in Successful Shyness will be on improving social interaction skills, with effective responding in a variety of situations as the goal.

Let's take a look at the two main personality traits or response styles of introversion and extroversion, because many people wonder where shyness fits in. Many researchers and clinicians, including author Susan Cain in her book *Quiet*, have commented that introverts, demonstrating a more inward orientation, struggle in an extroverted or more outgoing world. Many introverts may lack interest in extensive socializing but are not necessarily shy. Many extroverts, while outgoing, can fear socializing if concerned about how others may react and can, in fact, be a little shy to very shy at times. A sizable number of self-help books on shyness offer assignments, exercises, or homework that are often complex, long, and too general in design. That is, even though well-meaning, these assignments do not typically adjust their purpose or strategy to the individual's preferred response style. For example, an introverted yet shy individual may benefit from an activity or exercise that helps them observe others first, then decide if they would like to engage in conversation after a warm-up period. A shy, extroverted individual could be helped by an activity or exercise that is tailored to their usual outgoing stance, but perhaps it helps to lower their anxiety by having them wait for the other person to initiate conversation.

Clearly, there are combinations of the two predominant personality traits, or major styles, of introversion and extroversion. I would describe myself, for example, as an introverted extrovert. That is, I'm basically an introvert, yet over the years I have learned a more outgoing, extroverted skill set, especially in my clinical training, in order to reach out more and be open with others. Interestingly, there is the term "ambivert," which describes someone who has a balance of introvert and extrovert tendencies. The term ambivert to describe an individual's psychological functioning sounds a bit odd, but it is akin to or analogous to someone being described as ambidextrous physically.

Successful Shyness is for all those who want to learn ways in which to effectively manage their shyness. It is also intended for individuals who are not shy to follow the various tips offered to help the shy reach their social interaction goals. Specifically, a major goal of this book is to help outgoing people, who are generally action-oriented, understand the more cautious and deliberate thinking style shy people use in their outlook or approach to everyday life.

Thus, if you are shy, this book offers suggestions and strategies that can help you be more effective socially. If you are not shy, this book can supply insights for you to better understand, help, and befriend those who are shy. Shy or not shy, or somewhere in-between, this book is designed to help you clarify and succeed with your own personal response style. *Successful Shyness* does not rely on lists and exercises alone. Instead, considering the importance of different individual response styles, this book uses a broader scope in approaching such a large, dimensionally complex personality trait such as shyness. That is, once your main personality style is identified, whether it be quieter (introverted) or more outgoing (extroverted), you can more easily learn how the individualized features of these two main response styles impact how your shyness is likely to be expressed.

There are major benefits to learning to be successfully shy, including the following:

1. Improved social skills
2. More social connections
3. A decrease in avoiding or withdrawing from social activities
4. An increase in overall daily functioning and happiness
5. Improved self-talk and self-compassion
6. Calmer physiological arousal—for example, decreased blushing or sweating

Learning to effectively manage shyness is a process, not simply a point in time. As a result, it will take practice. There are many books on shyness, yet they sometimes have a narrow focus. The central theme of these books has been describing the various types of shyness, then launching into how to lessen its negative aspects. Fair enough. *Successful Shyness* uses a different, broader scope and addresses several main personality response styles first. We can then better understand how major personality attributes and features impact both the experience and expression of shyness.

One major goal that is often talked about with shy people is developing social skills. What are some reasons and benefits for developing better social skills?

1. New social skills can improve your daily interactions with others.
2. Positive relationships developed through improved social skills will increase your self-confidence.
3. By using effective social skills, you will place yourself in a position to receive more emotional support from others.

Another important goal is to address the more severe end of the continuum for shyness, which can include significant distress in daily interactions with others—sometimes leading to social anxiety disorder (SAD). This book will include strategies along with associated *practice opportunities* that address problems associated with both shyness and SAD, as well as avoidant personality disorder (APD).

Also, for all those concerned with internet use in the world today, it remains an open question whether shy people will be able to embrace social media technology effectively. It can be done while also making strides to include more face-to-face interactions. This book will use a permissive (non-rigid) approach to the various suggestions, strategies, and exercises that, together, will lead to successful shyness responding.. In fact, the phrase chosen for many of these tasks—practice opportunities—is purposely meant to convey flexibility and sound less like school and homework. By the way, I'm not surprised that the word homework itself draws such a negative reaction in that it sometimes interfered with having fun after school for so many of us. Also, all the work in *Successful Shyness* is recommended yet optional; it is a choice—to be accomplished at your own pace, with nothing to turn in. In fact, most of the practice opportunities offered are to be done outside of the home, thus not "home" or "work."

An example of a straightforward, representative practice opportunity is as follows: Go to a public place—nearly anywhere really—a shopping mall or restaurant, maybe a local park. Next, sit down somewhere and watch people interact for a few minutes. Leave, collect your thoughts and impressions, and then write down three or four things you liked about how certain individuals interacted. You may have been impressed with how someone used friendly gestures when they talked or how a child was able to ask for a drink themselves. This simple or easy practice opportunity can teach you something important—observing others provides you with useful social information and at the same time takes the focus off yourself in order to notice the social world around you.

There are several main reasons why I've decided to use a more choice-based, permissive approach to the practice opportunities included in this book. First, by working on a particular goal that interests you, selecting a specific practice opportunity that best fits your preference for getting to that goal is the way to go. Second, the order of practice opportunities listed is not nearly as important as which one appeals to you in the moment to try out. Starting with easier practice opportunities is preferred by many, rather than beginning with challenging ones that can be accomplished when ready.

Finally, as I've leafed through the many used shyness workbooks at various libraries, a curious trend has emerged. Basically, I've found that most of the workbooks had entries wherein the reader had completed only a few of the assignments designed to help with their shyness. Apparently, they then put the book down for good and ultimately ended up donating it. One reason for this, at least in my clinical opinion, is that there was a certain (sometimes rigid) order in which the assignments or exercises were to be completed, and it turned the reader off.

Therefore, given the above reasoning, I've used the term practice opportunities, not assignments, exercises, or homework. By making the practice opportunities available to you, I'm confident you'll know which ones you would like to start with. Of course, as mentioned, beginning with easier practice opportunities will bring more initial success than struggling with a difficult or challenging one from the get-go. I suppose you could call this a menu approach, because if you don't happen to like one practice opportunity, you can try another, then circle back to those that are more difficult or challenging.

Other books on shyness tend to promote a sequential exercise or assignment order that, in theory, is meant to build on basic to advanced principles. This type of structured approach is logical and valid. Unfortunately, if someone doesn't succeed in the sequence, they sometimes just put the book down and forget about it. This book is not without structure but simply promotes flexibility in its use. By reviewing the various practice opportunities offered in *Successful Shyness*, it will be easy to choose the ones that appeal to your individual needs and interests at a particular moment in time, making the completion of the tasks involved easier. I've also decided to use relevant sayings throughout this book, along with some humor here and there, to focus or maintain attention. Sayings and humor can have a way of saying a lot in only a few words, collective wisdom of the years, I suppose.

The overall aim of this book is to help you understand yourself better, recognize important dimensions of your shyness, and learn how shyness can be an asset. Managing shyness effectively can be achieved. Expressed as a phrase, the final goal is to become successfully shy. For those who are not shy, going through the content of these pages will help you understand and thereby be able to support the efforts of those learning to effectively manage their shyness.

In summary, the good news is that humans have a natural forward developmental motion. We are evolutionarily prepared to follow a path of increased competence, effective functioning, and ultimately happiness. To help you along your journey to achieving successful shyness, this book will provide several important therapeutic strategies, with detailed Practice Opportunities to implement them. It may not be realistic for you to learn to handle every social interaction with disarming ease, but more effective responding is within the reach of all of us.

Part 1

Identifying and Understanding Shyness

Chapter 1

Shyness and Social Anxiety

This book uses a broad-spectrum, strengths-based approach to provide strategies and techniques to effectively manage shyness. Both the main assessment and treatment sections concentrate on how to improve your thoughts, feelings, and behavior to effectively manage shyness.

Shyness Features

Shyness happens to all of us, at varying times and in a wide range of intensities. Approximately 40 percent of Americans consider themselves shy. Sixty percent of those who are shy say that their shyness is a serious problem. Children who have shyness experience it lessening as they age, most likely due to gaining some measure of social skills. In adulthood, shyness frequency is about the same in men and women. Interestingly, there are gender differences that, through socialization, affect how males and females relate to each other. For example, in terms of communication, men usually focus on providing information about a topic and are quick to respond to any fight-or-flight demands. Women tend to be more relaxed conversationally, engaging in more relationship talk or a tend-and-befriend interpersonal style. Regardless, shyness is not a disorder. It is a personality feature or trait that can affect how the shy respond to others and in unfamiliar situations.

Common social fears:

1. Speaking in public
2. Eating in front of others
3. Hand trembling when writing in front of others
4. Using public restrooms
5. Dealing with new situations or circumstances

Anticipatory anxiety or expecting they will be anxious in the above situations can create even more stress for the shy. Fortunately, as will be discussed in the treatment section of *Successful Shyness*, one way to reduce this *fear of fear* is to focus on something else. Notice that if you've ever mistakenly hit your thumb with a hammer, you probably thought about little else for a while. This is a rough analogy, but the point is that because we amplify what we are focused on, by concentrating on something outside yourself, your anxiety and discomfort will lessen. Further, because problems associated with shyness are often endured silently, it is a good idea to talk with others to shift the focus. In broad terms, shyness can be defined as an internal reaction, such as discomfort from an external situation—namely, social activity. Shy people can become self-conscious over their concern about being evaluated or judged by others. One main cause of shyness is likely to stem indirectly from shy individuals having a high level of inhibition combined with interpersonal sensitivity. For example, if placed in a bustling social situation, a shy child may become embarrassed because they aren't sure how to respond. Self-consciousness can result, with the child learning that by avoiding such future interactions, discomfort is not experienced. The avoidance behavior can then maintain the inhibition and heightened sensitivity of the shy individual. What happens in the end is that the shy learn to consistently pull back from social contact. For many, new and unfamiliar circumstances seem to consistently result in shy responses, namely inhibition. *Successful Shyness* contains strategies to improve and manage shyness effectively.

Anxiety disorders in general are very prevalent in the United States. Based on several well-structured surveys, 20 percent or more individuals experience some form of anxiety disorder. While there is no shyness gene, from a biological basis, the shy among us may have a more reactive nervous system. For example, prominent American psychologist Dr. Jerome Kagan has studied the physical symptoms of so-called timid and bold children. His research found a neural circuitry that is highly reactive to even mild stress in the timid ones.

Social Anxiety Disorder

Significantly increased reactivity to the social environment, accompanied by high anxiety in various interpersonal interactions, can lead to social anxiety disorder (SAD). SAD can be considered a severe form of shyness and is also common. Specific symptoms associated with SAD include the experience of significant worry and distress in situations that involve public speaking, meeting new people, dating, or even going to work and school at times. Physical reactions, including blushing, trembling, excessive sweating, and stomach trouble, can occur. On a behavioral basis, those with SAD are likely to avoid situations, whereas shy individuals will oftentimes try to be brave through social activities. Basically, when problems associated with shyness become more significant and start to interfere with daily functioning, the SAD range or realm needs to be considered.

Avoidant Personality Disorder

An even more pervasive disorder than SAD, which highlights significant withdrawal and detachment from others, is avoidant personality disorder (APD). People with APD tend to have low self-esteem, are socially inhibited, and are very sensitive to criticism. Social isolation is another hallmark of APD and can negatively impact important areas of functioning, including family and friend relationships as well as education or job performance. Those with APD tend to be hypersensitive to criticism and rejection. By remaining isolated, a shield from negative interactions is formed, but it can lead to loneliness. Similar to the shy and socially anxious, but more extreme, those with APD tend to prefer to be somewhat social on occasion, yet inhibition or pulling back interpersonally remains strong. The features of APD tend to be persistent throughout adult life, which can result in feelings of depression and inadequacy. The good news is that treatment in the form of individual counseling or psychotherapy can be very helpful. An individual with APD can learn to accentuate their positive features, which usually involve *going-along-to-get-along* and steering around controversial subjects when relating to others. Further, those with APD can be good listeners and offer constructive feedback to family and friends once mutual trust is established.

In summary, the sequence is shyness (a trait) and, with more severe symptoms of social anxiety, the possibility of a social anxiety disorder (SAD). Finally, if significant chronic social anxiety is experienced, the type that negatively impacts daily life and functioning, avoidant personality disorder (APD) should be considered.

A Brief Summary of Treatment Approaches

Fortunately, there are several evidence-based psychological treatments that can help with shyness, social anxiety, and significant avoidance. Cognitive-behavioral therapy (CBT) assists people who are socially anxious to change dysfunctional ways of thinking, while improving patterns of behavior. The underlying assumption of CBT is that problems develop because people can sometimes view themselves and their world in biased, usually unnecessarily negative ways. To point out the most extreme example of thinking too negatively, I recall reading about a wiseman in Bali, Indonesia, whose reference to a colleague was chilling: "He became old looking because he's been eaten by his thoughts." Clearly, this colleague, assuming his thoughts must have been exceedingly negative, could have benefited from some comprehensive CBT intervention.

Interpersonal psychotherapy (IPT) focuses on relationships and works well to improve social responding. With IPT, life transitions and role changes are a productive focus. For example, the recent spread of the COVID-19 virus resulted in pandemic-related isolation. Predictably, many millions of people, including the shy, became less social, the result of which was a sort of "detachment fatigue." Ironically, it was healthy behavior to keep one's distance during this unique time. As an aside, consider what Dr. Lucy Jones, a California seismologist, wanted people to think about. Her prompt was: "Don't share your air." This was a positive message as people became more sensitive and understanding of the need to wear a mask during a largely airborne viral spread. During this extreme social life curtailment phase in society, shy people have been able to sit things out yet develop their social relationships with those close to them, including family members and a few long-term friends. On the other hand, those who are more outgoing found themselves climbing the walls and needed to learn how to curb major socializing until self-quarantining could end.

This book focuses on CBT and IPT strategies to address problematic shyness responding, offered in a strength and compassion-based format. Importantly, shyness has its assets, which include active listening and careful thinking. These will be discussed in detail. To recognize how common shyness is, simply ask those you know if they've ever been shy. Many people acknowledge shyness, particularly when they were younger. These individuals can relate well to the emotional pain shyness sometimes brings, but they also talk about how others see them as cooperative and good to get along with—given the chance.

As a personality feature or style of hesitatingly relating, we do not need to overcome shyness but learn to manage it. If a child becomes routinely shy, social difficulties and communication problems will likely surface. The issue is sometimes how to distinguish shyness itself from the more uncomfortable form of shyness. If it is hard to relate to uncomfortable shyness, or how an individual might experience this type of discomfort, imagine the following. Picture yourself being called up to sing the national anthem, solo, in front of a large audience. Another way to relate to the experience of shyness is to think of what it's like to enter a large courthouse. The shy person's social inhibition, even intimidation, becomes relatable. Even before entering the building, there are many wide steps leading to large columns, then huge doors. Once inside, you're greeted by polished marble everywhere and high, vaulted ceilings. People in courthouses often talk in serious tones; the hint of authority is immediately apparent in the seriousness of their voices. Feel wary yet? Wanting to proceed cautiously? If so, this is how the shy person feels when facing most social situations. As a side note, a reasonable assumption would be that courthouses are purposely constructed to be larger than life to encourage compliance (if not intimidation) by everyone involved.

In children, teachers have commented that young ones in the classroom can be humorously categorized as either anonymous or notorious. One aim of this book would be to have the shy student placed in the middle of these two opposites—as in, simply, it is good to be noticed. Shy individuals are acutely aware of others and social situations, and they may try to assess potential interactions from every angle before engaging. In a way, this can be an adaptive shy personality trait. That is, the shy person is trying to mentally check off all the boxes that constitute a positive social interaction before they proceed. While this problem-solving style for social situations may seem extra careful, there is a lower probability of offending anyone if you're not being too loud, impulsive, or conversationally domineering. In this regard, the age-old Japanese proverb seems apt: "The nail that stands out is pounded down."

One can assess for broad and specific signs of shyness. Shy individuals indeed shy away, as many put it, from a variety of social situations. This is particularly true for those times when they feel that possible scrutiny will come their way from others. You may have heard the expression "He's just shy," which is not accurate to the extent that shyness isn't a problem much of the time, certainly not a mental health disorder, and often a desirable personality trait. Perhaps derisively, shy people have sometimes been referred to as shoe gazers, meaning that they may be looking downward versus establishing more eye-to-eye contact. Problematic shyness does exist, and that is especially true if an individual would like to be more social. *Successful Shyness* will use the various Practice Opportunities offered to better manage problems typically associated with shyness.

In general, a major concern for people who experience shyness is that their actions or behavior may result in embarrassment or humiliation. Self-critical thoughts can follow. Psychologist Dr. Alfred Adler has explained how negative thinking combined with avoidant behavior can result in restricted living. Let's break that down:

1. Negative thinking: If a shy person does not want to make a presentation in front of others, they may think to themselves, "This isn't going to go well. I'm not going to be able to do a good job." This is usually not accurate, and with such a negative self-appraisal, it has the person wanting to stop before they've even started.
2. Avoidant behavior: After thinking they won't do well, the shy tend to scoot away or avoid the entire task at hand by failing to follow through. They may experience emotional and physical symptoms (likely real due to high stress levels), which can make it even harder to "avoid their avoidance."

It is not that shy individuals want to remain isolated from others; they would like to have social contact, but their own self-consciousness about being scrutinized can stop them in their tracks. There are broad difficulties that can result from problematic shy behavior, including impaired social lives, trouble with occupational advancement, and difficulty with romantic (intimate) relationships. How do shy individuals end up coping in social situations? On the positive side, those who are shy are known to listen well to others. They feel more comfortable using self-descriptors such as "I'm reserved" or "I'm thoughtful," which can then help them to move forward in social activities. On the negative side, too much pre-event anxiety can result in habitual alcohol or drug use as a way to relax socially. Many of the practice opportunities in *Successful Shyness* are geared toward learning positive, constructive ways in which to relax oneself in order to be more effective in social situations.

My Personal Story of Shyness

I was a shy child, very shy at times. As an example, one experience stands out. Our family of five moved from Michigan to Illinois when I was seven years old. We arrived in a Chicago suburb where, as my parents informed us, the schools were said to be excellent. It was Christmas break, and I would be attending the second half of the school year, coincidentally enough, in the second grade.

As all the students filed in on a cold, blustery January morning, we were immediately instructed to take our seats. The teacher, Mrs. Hopper, said to the class, "I have a surprise for us today." Young as I was, I gained the immediate suspicion that I was going to be the surprise. Shy individuals come equipped with or learn an interpersonal vigilance stance early on. Sure enough, Mrs. Hopper excitedly announced, "We have a new student in our class." Something about all eyes on you is kind of scary for most young children; the shy child, with no other options, exercises embarrassed endurance.

The new school environment itself had already made me anxious enough. Other children paying attention to the new kid wasn't something I was excited about. Later I learned that many different social situations or circumstances can rattle the shy; fortunately, there are strategies that can result in calmer responses, as will be detailed in the treatment section of Successful Shyness. Anyway, I did feel that classmates were paying close attention to me, and it was something that made me uncomfortable at the time. I felt that their penetrating glances were sure to detect my being-on-the-spot self-consciousness. Another thing I didn't learn until later was that the average attention span of a second grader is about eight seconds, or approximately the same as a goldfish, which clocks in at nine seconds.

In time, I settled into the classroom routine—from the early morning obligatory Pledge of Allegiance to the end of the school day when we waited for the time for Mrs. Hopper to pleasantly declare, "Class dismissed." Weeks later, the familiar cadence of a grade school routine was, for me, shockingly disrupted. Enter Mrs. Cavanaugh. She was a tall, medium-built, authoritarian, elderly woman. Elderly from a second grader's perspective, that is. Looking back, I would now estimate her to have been between forty-five and fifty-five years old. She was old enough to have acquired that detached, stern demeanor with a rigid posture. I've often wondered what power was to be gained by intimidating seven-year-old children, but perhaps I was reading too much into her behavior.

Mrs. Cavanaugh announced with firmness that she was from the testing department and that the class was to now take an achievement test. This was a set of circumstances that few second graders seemed to grasp, let alone care about. She came equipped with her materials, including thirty or so achievement test booklets in a large, white cardboard box with official labeling. I recall the box itself, probably another reflection of a shy child's hypervigilance. I almost forgot to mention that she wore those black-rimmed, pointed-at-the-ends glasses—no doubt meant to add to her air of authority or gravitas. I sensed danger ahead and was wary of any intrusion on my self-insulated stance in the classroom. I didn't want any potential social criticism or embarrassment, yet somehow, I anticipated something along those lines was coming.

There was no way out for me that day as Mrs. Cavanaugh passed out an achievement test at each desk. She paused long enough at the side of each student to make sure she commanded instant respect, if not fear. Again, I may have been reading into her behavior way beyond what was objectively the case, but I don't think so. She then walked to the front of the room and began with, "Write your name where it is to go at the upper left-hand top of your test," or some such curt verbiage. There was a line for your first and last name, the standard procedure that we've all become accustomed to. I wrote down my first name. She must have noticed me, as I had frozen in place at this juncture. She semi-marched right up to the side of my desk, stating, "Go ahead. Write your last name."

The fact was, at this school, on this day, I had to acknowledge to Mrs. Cavanaugh that I didn't know how to write my last name yet. In hindsight, I've surmised that Michigan schools, at least in the late '50s and early '60s, were far behind Illinois suburban ones. So, what does she do? Mrs. Cavanaugh chose this dilemma to loudly ask, "You don't know how to even spell your last name?" A few giggles arose from neighboring students, but it was not too bad overall. I, however, felt total embarrassment, even humiliation. I may have even been slightly tearful and upset, yet I did my best to hide it. Would this have been so troublesome for most of the kids if it happened to them? Maybe, especially if they were shy. As an elementary school student, it wasn't easy for me to be anything but frustrated and a little angry with what had occurred. Now, looking back, I view Mrs. Cavanaugh as a likely casualty in the administratively burdened Chicagoland school system. She probably had to run from school to school with her load of achievement tests and was likely frustrated at times herself.

Shy children, adolescents, and adults maintain a worrisome stance toward any type of perceived social judgment and can be unusually sensitive to criticism or rejection. Oftentimes, shy children simply do not roll with the punches when it comes to even slight or small criticisms. The good news is that shy individuals can and do work through the problematic aspects of their shyness with success. At the same time, the shy can take stock in the fact that a quieter, deliberative, more reserved personality style is what we need more of in this world, which has become altogether too loud. As an aside, anyone of us can probably be quieter than a particular situation calls for. Perhaps surprising to some (or not), in working with shy individuals, I've gotten irritated with others (even though I know they're shy) if they just won't talk. We all remember our mothers, or like parental figures, remarking, "Has the cat got your tongue?" Clinically, I will sometimes catch my frustration and just let the person know that at times it is hard for me to patiently wait out the silence. By the way, I looked up the cat phrase because it struck me as so odd. Apparently, its origin appears to be light-hearted imagery that was or is directed at children to get them to speak up.

Is there any follow-up to this particular negative early school authority-initiated event? Not really; I got through it as we all have, referencing early difficult social situations. I've forgiven, while clearly not forgotten, what was a "small-large" slight. May we all learn to, as they say, "Move on." Although now, as an experienced clinical psychologist, I do find myself suggesting to parents and anyone else interested that it is usually always a good idea to "praise in public, punish in private." This axiom is especially applicable when dealing with children, as they are more vulnerable than adults when faced with difficult interpersonal situations.

One other school story comes to mind, which I'm assuming many can relate to. I was the kind of kid who was excited about each new school year. Once I was able to get my pens, pencils, and lined paper purchased, I was ready to go. The teachers in elementary school usually start the first day by telling the class some form of, "You all begin with an 'A' grade." This proverbial remark, I assume, was meant for students to be able to start off on the right foot. For me, it was a time for things to turn sketchy. With early shyness in place, I was happy to sit quietly and not interact much but daydream instead. My teachers would typically remark during parent-teacher conferences that "Marc, tends to drift off and daydream during class, especially when he should be on task." Oh well. Like many of you, I've gotten better over the years, but I still like daydreaming occasionally. Who doesn't?

Common Shyness Remarks

Talking about my own early shyness and considering the shyness of millions of other people prompted me to write down some common expressions that I've heard over the years regarding shyness and shyness-related sayings:

"She's just shy."

"Don't be shy."

"He is painfully shy."

"Scared stiff."

"Dying of embarrassment."

"He's afraid of his own shadow."

"Hide in your shell."

"She's socially awkward."

"Lively in private, but clearly uncomfortable in public."

The last one, I think, I read somewhere. People can detect shyness in others and describe it, but I'm not so sure the accuracy is always high or spot on. That is, someone may appear shy, although they are simply being quiet in a particular situation. Conversely, an individual might look confident and even be talkative with others while internally feeling discomforted and even embarrassed about how they're coming across. This book has many strategies and techniques to help you feel more comfortable in your own skin while learning to manage shyness. It's odd, though; come to think of it, you don't hear many people say, "He's just outgoing." I suppose this one-way stance of shyness being regarded differently than other personality features may in part be culturally bound. "Just do it" implies action, at least in America and other western civilizations. At the same time, there are many societies around the world that highly value a more reflective approach to daily life for the shy and non-shy alike. Extremes in either direction are a universally curious phenomena. Consider the outspoken Texan, whom others describe as "all hat and no cattle." Or for the overly avoidant and detached, "There are no happy hermits." In our emotional development, we all have the opportunity to learn more about our personality functioning, which can help us to make constructive choices and take positive actions.

Using a Permissive Approach

Successful Shyness takes a more permissive approach to rehearsing social interactions or taking part in what I've termed self-directed practice opportunities. Many other books on shyness and anxiety tend to prescribe exercises, done in a certain sequence. This stepwise approach is logical as well as valuable, but many readers may simply put down the book or stop their forward progress when they falter on a particular assignment. The suggestions for practice in this book do follow a sensible, helpful trajectory, but they can be done in any order, with breaks in the process encouraged as needed. Basically, you have full control over what practice opportunities you want to try out and when. Speaking of basic, some of the practice opportunities may seem fairly basic or simple, and they are. Yet it is good to start with the easier practice opportunities to help build your social skills' confidence. I recall a time many years ago when I took drum lessons. The instructor began the first lesson by stating, "These are drumsticks." Elementary and odd, I thought, even at twelve years old, but I never ended up calling them turkey legs. Fortunately, being basic and simple often leads to complex and deep understanding, as well as ability.

In *Successful Shyness*, I will generally use the term or phrase "direct-action" instead of exposure. I also use the term "avoidance prevention" instead of response prevention. The standard phrases of exposure and response prevention, sometimes referred to as simply ERP, are fine, yet the phrasing I've come up with seems more descriptive as to what is actually taking place. Taking direct action clearly means that you're going to become engaged in an activity, not simply exposed to one. Avoidance prevention better defines blocking or steering away from a social situation than the broader "response prevention" phraseology. Also, I will use the term practice opportunity as it is a more neutral descriptor than the sometimes-dreaded labels exercises or homework.

The positive feature of entering social situations that concern you and taking direct action is that you're acting as if you know what to do. The "fake it until you make it" can work in that what you're really doing is practicing or rehearsing effective social responses in live situations. This approach builds confidence and enables you to know what to do sooner rather than later, because of practice. This is the main rationale as to why I've called the structured work in *Successful Shyness* practice opportunities. By the way, the best model is not "practice makes perfect." Let's replace it with "practice makes progress." By being kind to ourselves and appreciating our own progress toward a goal, good things will happen. At the same time, we can more easily move forward, unburdened by needing to be perfect or, as the analogy goes, "not waiting for the river to run dry before crossing."

Speaking of practice opportunities, I was going to identify each one by a simple rating such as easy, difficult, or challenging but decided against it. My reasoning has been that what might be considered an easy practice opportunity by one person could be viewed as challenging by another. For example, I saw a shy young adult who explained that talking in front of a group would cause him significant anxiety. He was willing to rehearse his talks beforehand in a practice opportunity he deemed difficult. Another young adult I treated only a week later for essentially the same problem, namely public speaking, felt differently. She said that talking in front of others caused her only "a little tension," thus she considered the practice opportunity to include rehearsing her lines easy. Another shy client I saw, a middle-aged family law attorney named Jordan, said that he didn't get all that socially anxious. Then he said, "You know there are only two realistic fears in life." Curious, I asked, "And what are they?" Jordan said, "The IRS and Carny people." I responded, "interesting," and went on to explain that in my training as a clinical psychologist, we are taught that newborns are innately afraid of only loud noises and loss of balance. During our session, Jordan did acknowledge that he has always been highly anxious regarding public speaking and would like to work on it. I suggested a practice opportunity that would allow him to learn how to relax before entering a public speaking activity, then to try out his new skill in smaller venues first. A variety of relaxation procedures that are particularly effective with social anxiety and tension are included in the treatment section of *Successful Shyness*.

One way to decide whether you want to proceed with a given practice opportunity is to consider the readiness factor. You can be ready when you feel like the next practice opportunity you would like to complete is within your reach, or it's doable with some effort. Success or failure on any given task is not an essential ingredient. That is, you can attempt a new social skill, and if you succeed, great. If you don't accomplish what you wanted to, simply evaluate where things went wrong and try again. It's the old "That's why pencils have erasers" notion. Also, if you don't finish a practice opportunity to your complete satisfaction, go for partial success—it is a useful step in your overall progress. And, of course, as mentioned, you can go back to the practice opportunity you're trying out any time and give it another whirl.

Practice opportunities provide a way to work toward your personal and social goals because you're taking action steps. When you review what you've accomplished, you're able to gain insight. Both action and insight are ways to improve how you operate on an everyday basis. When you think about it, one good working definition of intelligence, or I.Q., is the overall competency or capacity one has available to comprehend and cope with their world. Action and insight will help get you there. It is okay to mildly confront yourself for not meeting a specific goal as long as you remember to encourage yourself for the effort taken. The goal in this regard is to balance the personal behavior-shaping qualities of constructive self-confrontation and self-encouragement.

Shyness and Alcohol

Regarding alcohol specifically, research has shown that those who have significant social anxiety are at a higher risk for developing an alcohol use disorder. Unfortunately, as social anxiety rises over time, social skills may decrease due to the self-imposed lack of interpersonal interaction or even contact. An important side note in this regard is that introverted individuals may not necessarily be shy, but if they remain too isolated from others, their social skills may erode. One particularly vulnerable group is college students. Going off to college involves unique anxiety-provoking situations, including making new friends and settling into new living arrangements, all while being away from the creature comforts of home. Social anxiety can spike during times of stressful transitions, and alcohol-drinking behaviors often increase in social contexts, like bars and parties.

Alcohol has been termed *liquid extroversion*. Shy individuals may be more prone to drink because alcohol can lower anxiety and inhibition enough to make a person more comfortable socially. The problem that can occur is that it is dose related. That is, if the shy individual drinks a little, it may help, but too much, and others may notice the person's interactions are really alcohol influenced. Also, it can be logically argued that by using alcohol as a social relaxant, it can leave the individual not able to comfortably respond in those social situations where alcohol use would be inappropriate. For example, the interpersonal situation inherent in a job interview would not call for someone to show up having had a few drinks.

Also, if shy or socially anxious individuals use alcohol to reduce anxiety in a variety of interpersonal situations, other more adaptive coping strategies will need to be learned. As will be discussed in the treatment chapters of this book, social skills training, including real-life direct-action (oftentimes referred to as exposure) can be immensely helpful. Dr. Philip Zimbardo has described shy individuals as being in their own social prison, with the goal obviously to learn ways to break out. Being successfully shy, as described and detailed in this book, is an effective way out and into the social world on one's own terms.

Shyness and Behavioral Withdrawal

At times, the shy individual may want to keep the world at bay, as if to be at least temporarily impenetrable from possibly demanding social interactions. It is important to assess the type of behavioral withdrawal a shy person is experiencing. For example, if a shy young adult is simply withdrawing from having been in too many social situations over the past week, their pulling back can be viewed as a healthy way to seek balance. On the more problematic side of the equation, withdrawing or isolating can sometimes be a symptom of depression. For example, by keeping things in, wanting to be social but too cautious to proceed, a depressed mood can result from such internalizing difficulties.

What is the relationship between shyness and withdrawn behavior?

A. An individual may be shy yet not withdrawn. For example, a teenage girl may attend many of the social activities at her high school, usually feeling anxious and hesitant to join in, but she is there or present with no behavioral withdrawal occurring. On a physiological level, the area of the brain called the amygdala often acts as a smoke detector. This automatic function finds us immediately aware of our surroundings but also anxious and worried. Thus, the teenage girl may feel shy and hesitant to join in, but fortunately another area of our brain, the prefrontal cortex, can engage to help regulate our decision-making. In this case, the teenage girl may be able to tell herself, "Yes, I'm anxious, but it seems okay to hang in here for a while."

B. An individual may be withdrawn, but not shy. In this set of circumstances, a young adult man, for example, could be busy at his desk working. Others around him may wonder why he's being so quiet. But for his intense task engagement, he would otherwise be social.

C. An individual may be both shy and withdrawn. This is quite common, as most shy people are likely to report that because social interactions are at times difficult for them, withdrawing from people and unfamiliar settings can provide short-term relief. However, there is a price to pay in that it makes it harder to learn effective social skills if you're not in the game.

D. Regarding internalizing problems versus externalizing problems, the pivot point is how an individual may cope with difficulties. An internalizing problem solver may tend to see a difficulty as their own doing or believe that they were somehow responsible, thus blaming themselves and sometimes withdrawing. With an externalizing problem solver, the individual may see difficulties as outside of themselves and blame others. Clearly, shy and socially anxious people are more likely to be internalizers, perhaps due to heightened sensitivity in interpersonal situations and a tendency to ruminate if problems arise.

In children and adolescents, teasing seems to be an unfortunate rite of passage. With males, physical taunting seems to be the main modality. With females, teasing seems to take a more relational form in that gossip and rumors tend to be used more than any physical interaction. The relevance to young shy people is that if they tend to internalize problems, then teasing can be taken quite personally and become a very painful set of experiences over time.

In evaluating your own shyness level, try to look into and understand the subtleties and complexities of the daily interactions you engage in. Increasing your own self-awareness of how you're coming across to others and self-monitoring the effect your efforts are having on others will help you learn to effectively manage your shyness. Be aware that social anxiety can negatively impact interactions with others. It seems that several of the difficult conversation patterns stem from the shy and socially anxious individual being silent for long periods and doing too much subtle fidgeting.

The good news is that learning improved general conversation skills can go a long way in facilitating interactions with others. Also, asking for and receiving feedback from empathic and supportive family members or friends can help a shy, socially anxious person become more self-aware. With self-awareness, it is easier to understand or at least accurately sense how you are coming across to others.

Practice Opportunity
Family History and Shyness
Can you identify anyone in your family history as being shy? What were they like? How did you view them growing up? What did you hear about them from other family members? For example, my paternal grandfather, Ralph, was quiet and didn't seem to venture much out of the house he shared with my grandmother. On the few occasions each year when our family would travel to visit them, I did notice that when we went out for dinner, he seemed anxious, tended to look down, and almost seemed spooked by it all. In retrospect, I think he was shy and avoidant. Perplexing in that he was a nice person but didn't seem to share much information or ask how others were doing. I do recall that he frequently smoked cigarettes and infrequently trimmed his nails, but to my knowledge, those aren't necessarily shyness-specific behaviors.

Relative	Shy Characteristics
Paternal Grandfather	Quiet, reserved, and anxious in social situations

As an example, I've placed my grandfather's shyness characteristics above. Use the lines below to list any shy characteristics you've noticed in your relatives.

Relative   Shy Characteristics

_____   _____

_____   _____

_____   _____

_____   _____

If there are few problems with overall intelligence quotient (I.Q.) functioning, a productive focus can be on developing the emotional quotient (E.Q.) in the shy individual. Dr. Daniel Goleman, a prominent psychologist, has worked on the broad concept of emotional intelligence for years and has made important contributions through detailed research. Below, in summary form, are five key elements or skills to foster an increase in one's E.Q.:

1. Self-awareness: recognizing your emotional impact on others
2. Self-regulation: controlling your own impulses
3. Self-motivation: discovering your purpose in positive pursuits
4. Empathy: recognizing and understanding other people's feelings
5. Social Skills: building rapport and communication with other people.

More on Shyness and Social Anxiety Disorder

Shyness involves personal discomfort when relating socially. This occurs in large part due to concern or fear of harsh social evaluation and judgment. When anxiety increases a shy individual's discomfort, it can begin to affect functioning. For example, the shy may not engage in daily communication with others as often as they would like due to a rise in anxiety related to a concern over social rejection. Their social activities in general may become limited, with their everyday world becoming narrower in focus. As a result, and if symptoms persist and significantly worsen, social anxiety disorder (SAD) may develop. The central feature of SAD is behavioral inhibition, including the avoidance of anxiety-producing social situations. Also, the anxiety experienced can become excessive and out of proportion to the situation. Finally, the anxiety and distress that are endured interfere with daily living.

In general, there is also a strong self-focus, with hypersensitivity present in individuals diagnosed with SAD. Both shyness and SAD have in common tension, anxiety, and associated discomfort over social-evaluative judgment from others. Corresponding coping skill deficits can occur due to withdrawing from social interactions. That is, when social skills don't get used or practiced, deficits in skill development can occur. To become successfully shy and thereby less socially anxious, it is first important to assess the level of distress you experience in different social situations. Also, look at what ways your distress, be it anxiety or tension, has disrupted your ability to function in different social situations and circumstances.

It is also important to reiterate that SAD is more significant and severe in scope and form than shyness. Most shy individuals can cope reasonably well without crossing the line into the more persistent, intense anxiety characteristics of SAD. Also, any of us can become socially anxious in a number of different situations, and this does not equate to a disorder. The disorder classification comes from long-lasting socially anxious behavior significantly impairing daily functioning, such as not going to school, work, or missing other obligations. Fortunately, SAD is treatable, and with a combination of individual psychotherapy, oftentimes cognitive behavioral therapy (CBT) and interpersonal psychotherapy (IPT), and (if indicated) medication, much can be gained therapeutically.

Shy individuals tend to internalize or take in problems that occur socially but do not discuss them with others. Interpersonal sensitivity, emotional restriction, and social discomfort are characteristic features of chronic shyness. The anxiety and inhibition that often accompany shyness tend to have a genetic component, or runs in families, as does a tendency to be highly reactive. Whereas there is no shyness gene, shy children have been found to have a propensity toward high resting arousal. This means that if you see a shy child sitting in the company of others, they may look calm, but internally they are active and no doubt quick to scan their environment.

Certainly, learning and conditioning throughout childhood and beyond, especially for a shy person, can cause problematic shyness to take hold. The shy may learn to retreat from life experiences as a form of self-protection after experiencing negative social interactions, such as bullying or being harshly criticized. Signs of shyness can be seen in an individual who has strong emotional reactions to a social situation while also experiencing a corresponding physical response. For example, a shy young adult may be embarrassed by slightly stuttering during a conversation with a prospective date and then be told "You're blushing," a physical expression. Social avoidance may result. Too much avoidance behavior at a young age may make it difficult for a shy individual to engage in enough social opportunities to learn helpful social skills.

Many shy individuals suffer in silence while others may view the shy as just quiet, or worse—aloof. A quiet person may be deep in thought, or perhaps just in the mood to relax for a while. The inventive singer and songwriter Courtney Barnett titled one of her albums *Sometimes I Sit and Think, and Sometimes I Just Sit*. Also, there are millions of people who are shy and reserved, with others simply being reserved, although not shy. Importantly, there is a potential interpersonal problem when a shy person is seen by others as standoffish. When people view the shy person's quietness as something more, let's say, negative, such as perceived standoffishness, they sometimes respond with frustration or irritation toward that individual. Interestingly, regarding Courtney Barnett, if her thinking was realistic and her sitting "present focused," you have a natural cognitive-behavioral and mindfulness-practicing adult.

Unfortunately, as mentioned above, shy individuals can rub people the wrong way or be annoying to others when they are viewed as being distant or aloof. Most everyone can relate to the experience of being frustrated with someone with whom conversation may be like pulling teeth. This type of response by other people can occur even though the shy person is simply being quiet, possibly socially anxious, but quiet. Shy individuals seem to notice that if they're feeling discomfort when interacting with others and becoming tense, in time they may experience a decrease in social confidence. In other words, if you are shy, it is likely that you've recognized times when your inhibition has pulled you back from communicating more with others. Because you are socially withdrawing in these situations, your reaction of lowered self-confidence is now understandable. Basically, you did not interact in a way that you preferred, because of shyness. The good news is that learning to interact effectively in social situations, that is, becoming successfully shy, is highly related to improved well-being. For example, being more aware of how you're coming across to others will allow you to adjust away from a stance that somehow portrays aloofness. The practice opportunities in this book will help you gain self-awareness and confidence in dealing with others in a variety of social situations.

In working with shyness, it can be helpful to identify common triggers that can occur in social situations. For example, many shy individuals become more hesitant if asked to join a conversation with people who are not familiar to them. Another common shyness trigger is being asked to respond to a difficult question while being observed by others. Finally, not knowing what to say in a particular conversation has resulted in many shy (and non-shy) people pulling back further.

Case Vignette
Shyness Triggers

Adam came to counseling because he was being asked to broaden his communication skills at work, and he was anxious about it. At twenty-six years old, Adam had grown comfortable talking with his friends and various peers but would become almost mute in the company of unfamiliar people. He explained that he had been shy from a young age and talking with others he didn't know caused him to question how he was coming across. Adam wanted to keep his job, which occasionally involved talking with new clients who would come into the design center's office. I asked him if he had heard of *Toastmasters* as a way to get comfortable in front of others, and he said, "I thought *Toastmasters* was a cooking show," which I believe he meant as humor. It was best to start easy and go slow, which Adam agreed to do as we discussed engaging in a practice opportunity.

As further background, Adam also had an increase in self-consciousness anytime he wasn't sure of what to say in a given work conversation. To deal with these common shyness triggers directly, Adam agreed to plunge ahead and converse more with others, yet he recognized that he could remain brief in his comments if his anxiety was rising too rapidly. This strategy worked for all three of the related shyness triggers Adam dealt with as detailed in the following practice opportunity offered. For Adam, getting out of the all-or-nothing mode, and in this case, it was "If I can't communicate well, I don't want to communicate at all," seemed to help his responding most when he could keep it short with others while being conversant.

Practice Opportunity
Dealing with Shyness Triggers
As an example, here are Adam's responses to common shyness triggers and responses that he dealt with in social situations:

1. Trigger: Being asked to join a conversation with unfamiliar people.
   Response: "I can go ahead but keep my comments brief."
2. Trigger: Responding to a difficult question while being observed by others.
   Response: "I'll think about it first, then respond."
3. Trigger: Not knowing what to say in a particular conversation.
   Response: "Maybe I can ask the person to elaborate, then I'll respond."

If any of these shyness triggers have occurred in your everyday social situations, write down a response you've made (or would like to make) that will make communicating easier.

1. Trigger: Being asked to join a conversation with unfamiliar people.
   Response: _____
2. Trigger: Responding to a difficult question while being observed by others.
   Response: _____
3. Trigger: Not knowing what to say in a particular conversation.
   Response: _____

Shy individuals can oftentimes be sensitive and careful observers. In general, people do care about how they think or view themselves, but surprisingly, sometimes seem to care much more strongly about what others think of them. Hesitating to approach others to talk can be considered a missed opportunity. *Successful Shyness* has several practice opportunities that focus on learning to manage discomfort so that you will go ahead and meet people whom you find interesting and seem willing to talk. In other words, discomfort when approaching a person and starting a conversation can be worked through. One way to look at it is that confidence follows mastery. Thus, if you haven't mastered a task yet, don't worry too much about not being fully competent. As I've mentioned, you don't need to go by practice makes perfect; instead, shooting for practice makes improvement, and mastery often follows.

The practice opportunities in this book will help you explore effective ways in which to reach out to others. For example, by learning to read social cues, activities like dating, job interviews, or going out with new friends can become much easier. Referencing dating, specifically, research has pointed toward adolescents experiencing less dating anxiety when they have close friendships. Thus, the challenge of dating can likely become easier if a young person first cultivates friendships that can provide mutual support and encouragement. Speaking of social cues, I observed one unique example when I was working at an adolescent inpatient hospital treatment program for adolescents. The unit for the teenagers housed anywhere from twenty to twenty-two males and females at any given time, aging between thirteen and eighteen years old. This assessment and treatment unit could get quite loud at times, with many teens doing their best to demonstrate their rebellious side. One evening, the entire group went on a supervised outing to the movies, which I attended along with other staff. The movie was better than something like *Count Dracula Joins the Navy*, but what I observed was just short of astonishing. These normally rowdy teens were quiet throughout the film. Upon returning to the unit, I asked one of the males, usually notorious, how they were all able to be so respectful. His answer was succinct: "You're supposed to be quiet at the movies." Now that's quite an example of the power social cues can command.

Differences in Shyness, Social Anxiety, and Avoidant Personality

Individuals who are shy can be, without a doubt, interpersonally sensitive. That is, shy people are very aware and reactive, at least internally, to what those around them say and do. Shyness often has a corollary, which is worry. Basically, the sensitive and shy person may become preoccupied and overthink social situations. They may ponder how they can possibly communicate socially without becoming anxious, which ironically usually produces more anxiety. If shy individuals allow themselves a warm-up period, a strategy that will be discussed in the treatment sections of this book, a calmer presentation will result, and more casual conversation can take place.

Whereas shyness can clearly involve discomfort and anxiety in social situations, what is the difference between experiencing some social anxiety and having a social anxiety disorder (SAD)? One main difference between shyness and SAD is that shyness is considered a facet of personality or characteristic. Social anxiety often occurs in the shy but doesn't stop participation in routine functioning or lifestyle. In SAD, the anxiety experienced can rise rapidly, or go through the roof, with disruption in daily socially based activities occurring. Another difference between shyness and SAD is that anxiousness in a shy individual is likely to subside when the situation or circumstances become more familiar. In SAD, the distress, unfortunately, seems to have more staying power. It essentially sticks around and, on its own, can become worse at times.

A third difference is that shy people may likely avoid some situations where they can't easily relax. For the individual who has SAD, there are too many social situations in which they find themselves anxious and tense, and then they want to avoid them entirely. Surprisingly, shy people can sometimes get frustrated with other shy individuals for not speaking up! You would think that there might be more empathy, but it probably simply reflects that we want to hear more of what someone has to say, as communication is a good thing across the board.

Shy people as well as those with SAD may be quiet socially, but they are certainly able to form meaningful relationships. The kind of relationships that are forged through time and mutual trust seem to take longer with the shier among us, but consistently loyal responses are characteristic.

As discussed, it is common to have more than one problem in life, sometimes even a set of big or significant problems at the same time. Similarly, if shyness turns severe, a person may meet the criteria of social anxiety disorder (SAD) while also experiencing significant depression. When two psychological disorders are present at the same time, they are referred to as co-occurring. For example, panic and depression can occur along with SAD, and if untreated, a personality disorder, namely avoidant personality disorder (APD), can develop. The same is true with physical disorders. When a patient has a cold, there might also be a complaint of joints aching or arthritis and the possibility of pneumonia. Of course, we may want to step back a little in that it is important to recognize that we all feel anxious or depressed, and, yes, shy at times. I've phrased everyone's occasional low mood as the "normative depression of life" as in—it's hard out there. The positive therapeutic news is that we can all increase our happiness quotient by making sure we incorporate positive experiences into our lifestyle.

Overall, as mentioned, shyness is much more common than SAD or APD, and all three can be managed in a range of ways from self-help strategies to effective counseling and various psychotherapies. Whenever we look at assessing co-occurring problems or disorders such as significant anxiety coupled with depressive responding, we want to ask ourselves: "Are these conditions affecting my functioning on the job, or in any other daily activities?" Focusing on how multiple (and simultaneous) difficulties affect our lives help in figuring out what to do about them, all of which will be discussed in the main treatment chapters. The emphasis of self-help strategies in Successful Shyness will be on how to deal effectively with everyday social activities and new and unfamiliar situations to better manage shy behaviors.

More on Social Anxiety Disorder (SAD) and Avoidant Personality Disorder (APD)

Most everyone can list times when they have felt shy, even to the extent that they have avoided interacting with others. Importantly, a shy individual may not always be that socially anxious. It's safe to say that many or most individuals with shyness report rising anxiety in different social situations. Also, as previously discussed, someone with a social anxiety disorder (SAD), which is considered a severe form of shyness, will usually report significant anxiety. Individuals with SAD are also likely to be not only shy but inhibited, as well as extremely uncomfortable in a variety of social situations. Those with SAD often have remarkably high self-focus, can overthink things, and often overestimate the probability of having a negative social event. Further, those with severe social anxiety can become depressed because of its unrelenting demand on the nervous system. That is, they can get into freeze, flight, or fight mode too often, which is physically taxing. Depression can follow and is painful, both emotionally and physically, making it important to assess for it whenever social anxiety is at the forefront.

The good news is that chronic social anxiety can be identified and, when it is a contributor to depressive responding, treated with counseling and medication if needed. One way I like to approach therapy with people at appropriate junctures is to simply ask, "Is your behavior getting in the way of how you want to live?" Socially shy and anxious individuals usually respond yes, saying that they would like to reach out more to others. The treatment section of *Successful Shyness* will offer many ways in which to connect more with others with the behavior that's usually in the way is avoidance. This book has strategies that include "avoiding avoidance" a somewhat awkward expression I use. How though? Through practice opportunities that focus on taking more direct action in a variety of situations and circumstances.

Avoidant personality disorder (APD) is described in detail in various diagnostic manuals, including the *Diagnostic and Statistical Manual of Mental Disorders* (5th ed.; text rev. DSM-5-TR; American Psychiatric Association, 2022). One major feature of this personality disorder is pervasive avoidance, a type of individual response that has been characterized by significant isolation over time due to avoidance of social contact. Feelings of inadequacy and low self-esteem are often present. Thus, as mentioned above in different contexts, it is important to make some distinctions regarding shyness. Basically, shyness is a trait that has its advantages but can be problematic from time to time. Social anxiety disorder (SAD) can be accurately conceptualized as a severe form of shyness, and avoidant personality disorder (APD) is a characterological pattern of major social avoidance.

For a cinematic example of dramatic social avoidance, think of Boo Radley in *To Kill a Mockingbird*. Boo avoids everything and everyone and hangs out alone in the bedroom of his house. Nevertheless, he possesses a truly kind heart and disposition, which he sadly keeps to himself. He secretly places little prizes in the knothole of a tree, which childhood neighbors Jeb and Scout are thrilled to find. At the end of the movie, he comes out briefly to subdue an attacker of the two children. As he stands in the corner of a room in their home, Jeb and Scout ask about him. It is their father who announces it was Boo, who is practically hiding and looking pale and shy, who had likely saved their lives. He is a withdrawn, shy, and avoidant man, but he has a finely tuned moral compass and is demonstrably compassionate.

To summarize, individuals with APD tend to be extremely inhibited socially. They can be hypersensitive to both criticism and rejection. Those with APD experience the pain of isolation or loneliness because they desire to be at least somewhat social but pull back due to excessive self-consciousness. They suffer in ways that are not easily visible to others as social interaction remains low. Social skills can lag, leaving an individual anxious, tense, and depressed. Shyness and insecurity, as well as low self-esteem, are common in highly avoidant individuals. Fortunately, many of the symptoms associated with APD can be improved with diligent effort. The case vignette below will shine a light on how progress can be made by targeting significant avoidance.

Case Vignette
Avoidance Behavior

Evan described himself as always shy. "Ever since I was a little kid," he once divulged. His shyness extended to situations away from home, including at the university he attended. He was particularly shy while playing sports and with friends whom he was just getting to know. Now, twenty-two years old, Evan frequently remarked that he would like to reach out to others and communicate more, but something stops him short. "It's like I'm in my own shell," he explained. In working with Evan, it became clear that, while highly intelligent, he lacked social awareness cues. For example, when others would look away from him, even if only briefly during conversation, he assumed that they didn't like him. Or, if he saw someone turn their attention to someone else who was approaching them, he took it to mean they didn't want to talk with him. Clearly, he was sensitive to any possible social judgment or scrutiny, which is a hallmark of shyness.

Often retreating to his college dorm, Evan felt that he could work on improving his social awareness cues by watching how actors responded to one another on various TV shows that he liked. Unfortunately, this led to his viewing a seemingly endless number of old sitcom reruns, all while simultaneously upping his junk food intake substantially. We discussed the merits of his engaging in observational learning, as it is certainly beneficial to watch how others socially interact effectively. The downside of his minimal efforts at home became obvious. Upon recognizing this, Evan commented, "I guess by watching all this stuff and gaining weight, I'm not getting out there to actually interact with others more."

Evan's avoidance of real-life social situations had become chronic. Fortunately, with good insight developing, Evan began to move in the direction that practice makes perfect. He found himself slowly engaging more with others. Was he anxious about doing so? Of course. Evan was indeed somewhat uptight in initial conversations with just about anyone and everyone, but the anxiety became manageable as he learned that shyness can be lowered with his own efforts. He had learned that even though he knew his avoiding situations helped ease tension in the short run, they had a lasting negative impact. By forging ahead, even though meeting and talking with others created anxiety and restlessness, Evan appreciated the fact that he was becoming more social with others. He also learned that they were more engaging with him.

Clinically, Evan looked like he was on his way to either a serious social anxiety or avoidant personality set of problems, but he turned the corner. He was able to acknowledge shy behavior while disrupting his own anxiety long enough to engage with others and break some of his avoidance patterns. Evan did well, and by reaching out in counseling for help with his shyness, social anxiety, and avoidance, he ultimately found several rewarding relationships by learning to communicate more actively and spending time with others.

Most shy individuals dislike being shy or don't like certain behaviors that are commonly associated with shyness. For example, many shy people would rather be in a variety of social situations but hold themselves back. Those who are publicly shy report feeling awkward and sometimes passive during social activities. The privately shy person has developed a skill set or learned how to act more outgoing, yet still experiences internal arousal and discomfort. In what ways has shyness been a problem for you? By assessing how shyness operates and is experienced in different ways, this practice opportunity can help you narrow things down. Basically, there are different types of shyness with avoidance seeming to be the most consistent behavior running through them all. Listed below are four main shyness domains that involve avoidance, directly or indirectly. They include public performance deficits, subjective discomfort, concern over behavioral deficits, and avoiders.

Practice Opportunity
Dealing with Significant Avoidance
Take a look at the client examples given for each of the four shyness domains related to avoidance. Next, describe a current situation of your own for any of the four domains by writing them down. Then, indicate what the outcome was. This will allow you to gain self-awareness and insight. The treatment section of *Successful Shyness* will guide you through how to improve on any or all of the four shyness domains with which you may be concerned. The general goal for each shyness domain is to move from avoidance to more comfortable social engagement.

1. Public performance deficits: there can be awkward behavior or even a failure to respond.
   Patrice's response:
   A) Situation: Patrice was very talkative with her friends yet had a hard time giving even a short presentation in her college class.
   B) Outcome: Sometimes Patrice would simply not follow through or else give the shortest presentation possible.

   Your response:
   A) Situation: _____
   _____
   B) Outcome: _____
   _____

2. Subjective discomfort: a strong focus on internal discomfort and concern over negative evaluation prevails.
   Elijah's response:
   A) Situation: Elijah, a young adult, felt "knots in his stomach" as he prepared to play a pickup game of basketball with his coworkers.
   B) Outcome: Elijah was worried that he would be judged for any lack of coordination. He played a short while then left.

   Your response:
   A) Situation: _____

   _____

   B) Outcome: _____

   _____

3. Concern over behavioral deficits: oftentimes a heightened concern over being negatively evaluated, which results in a failure to proceed.
   Olivia's response:
   A) Situation: Olivia, a forty-year-old lab tech, felt dread when her manager asked her to perform certain work tasks. "She can be like the Wicked Witch of the East and raises her voice way too often."
   B) Outcome: Olivia said she froze when her manager asked her why she hadn't finished an assignment that was late. She finally came up with a response, delivered in a quiet voice, explaining that she had had a brief emergency the day before.

   Your response:
   A) Situation: _____

   _____

   B) Outcome: _____

   _____

4. Avoiders: the broadest type of shyness behavior and can refer to avoiding social activities as well as new and unfamiliar situations.
   Jin's response:
   A) Situation: Jin was a freshman in college when he became tense and uptight about joining a fraternity after he was invited.
   B) Outcome: He chose to avoid an open house, missing an opportunity to meet many of the other students who were also considering joining.

Your response:
A) Situation: _____

_____

B) Outcome: _____

_____

More on Avoidance Behavior

Because avoidance behavior is so prevalent for all of us from time to time, and particularly for the shy in different areas, we will consider when it can be modified to a more direct type of responding. In fact, avoidance behavior does work, but usually only in the short run. The benefit is that you can get out of, or move around, a social interaction or activity that is causing anxiety and tension. Unfortunately, you do not then learn how to hang in there with a particular interaction, recognize that you made it through, and that it was likely not as bad as you had anticipated.

Thus, by way of self-assessment, you can view whatever social avoidance behavior you may have used and simply ask yourself: Is this avoidance behavior getting in the way of how I want to live? Another way to bring the point home is to list what you may have missed out on because of being shy and avoidant. Representative areas of functioning include family, friends, school or work, and hobbies.

Practice Opportunity

Identify what avoidance behaviors you may have used in the four areas listed below and how this type of coping caused you to miss out on an opportunity to interact with others socially.

1. Family (e.g., Nicholas didn't want to go to his sister's recital. Later, he felt like he missed out because other family members came in from out of town.)
   A) Avoidance behavior _____
   B) Consequence _____
2. Friends (e.g., Amira decided to skip the dance because she felt awkward out on the floor. She stayed home but felt frustrated that she had missed some fun.)
   A)_____
   B)_____
3. School or work (e.g., Chaquille was behind in his schoolwork, but avoided his tutor because he felt that he wouldn't be able to communicate easily.)
   A)_____
   B)_____
4. Hobbies (e.g., Grace wanted to play soccer with her friends, but couldn't bring herself to attend practices due to the concern that she would look clumsy.)
   A)_____
   B)_____

As will be detailed in the treatment section of this book, consider at this time a major shyness and social anxiety goal: Get out there and have some face-to-face interactions. Keep the activities with others short and simple. They should feel relatively safe at the beginning. These activities will puncture your avoidance to a significant degree over time. During a pandemic or other difficult external circumstances, social media can be used more often to enjoy online interactions from the comfort of your home. Of course, you'll want to access quality social media sites that provide constructive feedback and support.

Skelton Shyness Survey (S.S.S.)

I've created an informal survey, the Skelton Shyness Survey (S.S.S.) that is meant to help you identify various features of shyness you may have. In creating items for this survey, I want to be clear that they have not yet been systematically researched or validated. I've assigned my name to the S.S.S. mainly to take responsibility for the survey's content and encourage any feedback, including not only positives but also constructive criticism on how it can be improved. The S.S.S. is an emerging effort on my part to get at what shyness essentially involves in terms of identifying shyness characteristics (Skelton, 2022).

Circle true (T) or false (F) to the numbered statements. If the statement is not always true or always false, consider which applies best—if mostly true, circle (T) or mostly false, circle (F)

Statements 1 through 11 mainly refer to how you view yourself.
1. T or F My social life has been limited due to shyness.
2. T or F I lack self-confidence due to shyness.
3. T or F I consider myself to be a sensitive person.
4. T or F I get embarrassed easily.
5. T or F I don't feel comfortable talking with people I don't know well.
6. T or F I wanted to have more friends growing up.
7. T or F I usually prefer that people speak to me first.
8. T or F I was bullied or severely teased in school.
9. T or F I feel anxious or uncomfortable in social situations.
10. T or F Shyness sometimes stops me from getting to know someone.
11. T or F My shyness sometimes leads to loneliness.

Statements 12 through 22 generally focus on how you relate to others and your social world.
12. T or F I generally hesitate to initiate a conversation with others.
13. T or F I become anxious or stressed when anticipating social situations.
14. T or F I often become preoccupied with being criticized in social situations.
15. T or F I will often avoid social situations due to concern about being judged.
16. T or F I often regret that I haven't spoken up in social situations.
17. T or F I have taken a drink or drinks to help relax and express myself.
18. T or F I worry about appearing tense or anxious to others.

19. T or F I generally have a hard time coming up with the right kind of things to say.
20. T or F I usually try to avoid a large group of people.
21. T or F I hesitate to go into a room where others have already gathered.
22. T or F I become inhibited when I'm suddenly the center of attention.

Scoring estimates: The more statements you circled true, the more shyness characteristics you are likely to have, at least at the present time. Feel free to take this self-report survey again after reading *Successful Shyness* and completing a number of the practice opportunities. Your number of statements answered as true will likely be lower.

Chapter 2

Shyness in Children and Adolescents

An Overview of Shyness in Children

On the physical aspects of shyness, Dr. Kagan, a prominent psychologist, professor, and re-searcher, has found that many young children show shy, timid behavior early on. Interestingly, blue-eyed children, especially boys with a thinner body build, tend to be more inhibited and less social (at least those from European ancestry samples studied). Shy children, in contrast to their darker-eyed peers, are more likely to be cautious in new situations and quiet when with others. Indeed, shy children with blue eyes are more likely to stay close to their mothers. Brown-eyed children tend to be bolder. If one or both parents tend to be detached, it will be harder for the shy child to learn ways to connect with others. How detached is detached? A dramatic but real example occurred when a mom asked me if I knew any Big Brother type programs that her shy and withdrawn son could become involved in. I was taken aback and asked, "Aren't you married?" The forlorn mom simply responded, "My husband stays in his home office most of the time."

Research by psychologist Dr. Joseph Himle also points to shyness and social anxiety start-ing relatively early. Children can become sensitive to being scrutinized or perceiving negative social judgment. Concern over being rejected socially can lead to even very young children wondering what they may have done wrong. Overthinking or ruminating over a difficult social interaction can occur. A cascade of vulnerability develops wherein a shy child or teen can become more avoidant, essentially pulling back from social interactions to eliminate the possibility of being judged. Young people with social anxiety can begin to experience interfer-ence in basic or core areas of functioning. For example, one shy child complained of worrying about "messing up," which made for increased self-consciousness while eating or drinking in public and even writing in front of others.

Shyness can manifest in feelings of tension and hesitancy in new situations. Self-consciousness and embarrassment can occur when a shy child feels that they are being eval-uated. Shyness tends to be stable. Shyness isn't something that someone needs to grow out of, but rather it needs to be effectively managed so that social opportunities are not missed. Children can learn coping skills at a young age to be able to engage in activities they want to do, such as making friends or speaking up in social interactions. A shy child may recognize they are being cautious yet learn to engage with others. A shy child can develop an "I can do this" mentality, which will slowly build confidence.

Social skills deficits can emerge without our even being aware. For example, there are adolescent rules, adult rules, and cultural rules for a behavior as basic as how close we should stand next to someone. When we aren't sure of how we should respond in our social world, discomfort can result. Shy individuals are acutely aware and self-conscious about the possibility of not responding well enough regarding the various roles we must play in our daily social lives. In fact, as soon as children attend preschool or kindergarten, they are confronted with numerous social guidelines to follow. When shy, children may pull back from mildly demanding social situations due to rising internal discomfort or anxiety over performance.

Mistrust, avoidance, and general wariness of others can stem from difficulties in attachment during the early years of childhood. As children develop, prosocial skills are learned. Thus, secure attachment and parental role modeling of social skills are important. Further, feeling connected to others, particularly with school peers, becomes a major plus. Conversely, difficult peer relationships or peer victimization can negatively impact social skills. Evidence shows that learning such important social skills translates into better academic performance and later job competence. Success at school and then work are important milestones as the transition from child to adolescent and adult takes place. Conversely, social withdrawal and peer exclusion in childhood can make academic and job responsibilities somewhat harder in the transition to adulthood. Based on parent reports of their children in potentially stressful social situations, the following social skills could be beneficially targeted early on: starting or joining conversations, attending and engaging in group meetings, and speaking to new or unfamiliar people. Long-term social competence, especially for shy and socially anxious individuals, is a valuable goal and an important component of becoming successfully shy.

An Overview of Shyness in Adolescence

Shyness in teens can be a problem when an individual avoids or withdraws from a social activities they would like to be involved in. In this regard, shyness becomes an emotionally painful experience. Outcome studies from well-validated research have shown that interventions for shy children and adolescents have had generally beneficial effects. One example includes social skills training for young individuals who are shy. Getting kids to talk with others and loosen up while feeling support from adults is particularly helpful.

When parenting a shy adolescent, ask if your son or daughter has had any difficulty maintaining relationships. For example:

1. Do they reject friends while preferring to stay at home?
2. Do they find excuses not to take part in school and family events?
3. Does your teen talk about being rejected by peers or treated unfairly?

Adolescents can be quite sensitive to criticism and rejection. The following short list includes major contributors to rejection-sensitivity:

1. Parental influences. For example, children of emotionally or physically abusive, neglectful, or critical parents tend to become extremely sensitive to rebuffs.
2. A teen's innate level of reactivity to stress. For example, genetic predisposition or premature birth may set the nervous system on the skittish side. This set of circumstances may result in a child who is hypersensitive to rejection, which can sometimes worsen during adolescence.
3. Significant peer rejection in childhood or adolescence. For example, a youth who is taunted or teased on a frequent basis by classmates or peers is likely to develop some measure of rejection sensitivity.

Ultimately, the shy teen may pull back and withdraw in the face of rejection, avoiding intimacy altogether. Detachment in young people can result in losing out on finding acceptance, or at least support. Thus, the possibility of loneliness and depression is not far behind.

Shyness Expression in Children and Adolescents

To assess shyness and social anxiety in children or teens, it is important to look at what might be developmentally appropriate. For example, a child might understandably be quite anxious if asked to recite a poem that is beyond their reading level, but they should be able to talk with a friend about how their day went. Shyness and social anxiety tend to increase in adolescence because attention to others and how people are coming across intensifies. There is often a desire to be involved with peers, but if one is too shy or socially anxious to do so, fear of missing out (FOMO), can occur. FOMO can dramatically increase a shy person's subjective or internal distress level.

Troublesome as it can be, one extension of wanting to join in or belong includes teens who learn to drink or take drugs to relax. In fact, alcohol has been humorously termed liquid extroversion, social lubricant, or even liquid courage because of its ability to loosen anxiety, tension, and inhibitions. Shy individuals are likely to be interpersonally sensitive with inhibition due to fear of rejection, timidity, and an unspoken need for approval all quite possible. Thus, the circumstances of entering a new or unfamiliar social situation can be intimidating. Alcohol use can oftentimes increase someone's ability to enter and engage in social interaction, but at what cost? One problem is that if someone drinks a little too much, they are no longer able to communicate with ease, but are instead alcohol or drug affected. A second concern is that, while taking an external agent to relax can provide some temporary relief from being uptight in social situations, there is a downside. The individual who indulges does not learn more effective (and sober) techniques to relate to others, which would better enhance their confidence. The focus of *Successful Shyness* is how to build that confidence and, particularly for children and teens, learn effective social responding.

From being a self-perceived social outcast to becoming (almost) the life of the party, how do you get there? In assessing a child, teen, or adult for shyness, it is important to look at how much control the individual seems to want or need. For those who are shy but careful to maintain control of their situation, providing support while allowing for the ventilation of positive and negative emotions can be helpful. For example, if you find yourself resisting reaching out to be with others or socializing more, you could instead allow a warm-up period and ease into brief interactions first. One major goal in the assessment of your own shyness level is to ask yourself how much social interaction is comfortable for you at present and how much social isolation you can currently tolerate. Basically, you do not want to develop a feeling or sense of social homelessness but to work toward or strive for human connection on your own terms.

In general, do shy people lack confidence? The shy may be quite confident in non-social situations and circumstances. In contrast, it is those situations that involve a social component that can result in shy people becoming too avoidant, withdrawn, and isolated. The net effect of pulling back socially can be lowered confidence. Further, if you are shy and withdrawn and isolative behavior occurs, you may develop increased psychological as well as physical distress. Not to worry (too much)—reaching out to another person, a family member, or friend, for example, can lower your distress level. Also, many of the practice opportunities in *Successful Shyness*, particularly the ones that involve developing positive thoughts that are realistic and relaxation exercises that are calming, can help you along your way to manage shyness and social anxiety effectively.

Main Parenting Styles, Child and Teen Temperaments, and Developmental Trajectory

The next section explores four main parenting styles, three main child and teen temperaments, and how to incorporate a child or teens' developmental trajectory.

Main Parenting Styles

1. Authoritarian parenting. A restrictive, even punitive style in which the child is to simply follow all the parents' directions. Firm limits and controls are placed on the child, with little verbal exchange allowed. This style is associated with the child having difficulty initiating activities and sometimes exhibiting poor communication skills.
2. Authoritative parenting. This style encourages children to be independent but still places limits and controls on their actions. Extensive verbal give-and-take is allowed. Parents are warm and nurturing toward their children. The child or children of authoritative parents tend to be self-reliant and socially responsible.
3. Detached parenting. A style in which one or both parents are relatively uninvolved or detached from their child. Unfortunately, this parenting stance can result in a child demonstrating a lack of control as well as socially awkward behavior.
4. Indulgent parenting. A highly involved style wherein parents interact at every opportunity with their child, yet few demands or controls are placed on behavior. Regrettably,

although these parents are attempting to be warmly comforting, the child may lack the ability to interact with others in a negotiating capacity and lack self-control.

Importantly, the second parenting style, authoritative parenting, offers the best option for optimal child development. You can't go wrong using a constructive compromise and negotiation style with a child or teen while maintaining the final authority as parents.

Three Main Child and Teen Temperaments

1. Compliant or easy. These children and teens are described by others as willing to cooperate and tend to go-along-to-get-along. They are likely to be polite and respectful, earning parental praise along the way. Many of these young individuals, including the shy, have garnered large amounts of admiration from adults. One unintended effect of such praise is that they are sometimes surprised when their peers treat them with the same crankiness or disrespect they would deliver to any other of their acquaintances or friends.
2. Non-compliant or difficult. Children and teens who tend to be non-compliant do not always follow rules that are commonplace at school or in the home. Some ask if the prognosis for non-compliant youth is different from those who are compliant. It really depends, although some insight may be gained from the ranks of the wealthiest adults in the world. It would appear as though well-known personalities such as Elon Musk, Bill Gates, and Mark Zuckerberg, who are highly non-compliant at times (e.g., all dropped out of college), have demonstrated a fierce independent streak with arguably wildly successful results.
3. Withdrawn. There are many shy children and teens who are behaviorally withdrawn, but certainly not all individuals with shy personality features demonstrate this characteristic. In fact, some children and teens are simply withdrawn and seem to remain this way into adulthood. These individuals may be described by others as quiet and preferring isolation to meaningful social interaction. The saying "still water runs deep" interpreted as it applies to withdrawn youth, refers to their being careful thinkers who are insightful and generally reserved.

Developmental Trajectory

Once you assess your own temperament as it once was as a child, teen, or even now as an adult, pay close attention to your developmental trajectory. That is, if you are parenting a child or teen, whether they are compliant, non-compliant, or withdrawn, you would want to interact with a six-year-old differently than a sixteen-year-old. For example, if you want a six-year-old to clean up their room (whether compliant, non-compliant, or withdrawn), you could simply offer an encouraging participatory statement such as, "Let's clean up your room together." This same approach would come off poorly to a teen but requires only a small adjustment: "Please clean up your room."

Chapter 3

Shyness and Your Personality Response Style

First, to increase self-knowledge, you can learn to become more aware of and understand your main personality style. Once you are able to self-reflect on your personality dynamics, you can then match this important psychological information to what self-help strategies and Practice Opportunities may work best for you. In other words, to improve effective shy responses in social situations, a careful look at your main personality style and its features or components is a great starting point.

Viewing personality style broadly, some people are more to themselves or introverted. Others tend to be more broadly socially engaged or extroverted. Interestingly, and possibly surprising to many, you can be shy and introverted, or shy and extroverted. Why the surprise? We often think of extroverts as outgoing and at ease socially, but this is not always the case. Many extroverted individuals report wanting to socialize more and yet find themselves getting anxious and turning quiet if they aren't in familiar social territory. Just as an outgoing person can be shy at times, an introverted individual can sometimes be unusually open and socially engaged. It is helpful to focus on shyness when responding by first looking at the introversion-to-extroversion continuum (you can have a mixture of introvert and extrovert qualities). Once you've determined yourself to be more introverted or extroverted, or a blend, then it is easier to learn how your main personality style along the dimension of introversion-extroversion shapes the expression of shyness.

Introversion, Extroversion, and Shyness

It is helpful to explore the two main personality styles or temperaments of introversion and extroversion in more detail, as understanding them is important to the goal of successful shyness. First, a description of predominant introvert and extrovert characteristics should help frame our topic and how these main styles affect how shyness is expressed.

Predominant characteristics of introverts:
1. Introverts enjoy having a small group of close friends.
2. Introverts are generally very self-aware and able to be reflective.
3. Introverts feel comfortable being alone with less interpersonal attention.
4. Introverts benefit from a quiet environment in which to concentrate.

Predominant characteristics of extroverts:
1. Extroverts may experience more positive emotions than introverts in both social and solitary situations.
2. Extroverts are more sensitive to rewards in their environment (reward sensitivity), particularly the desire for positive attention.
3. Extroversion may represent a high-intensity strategy for gaining attention.
4. Extroverts tend to be more enthusiastic and assertive.

Introverts enjoy time alone; spending a lot of time with others can be emotionally draining for individuals with this personality temperament. By contrast, a shy individual may not want to spend a lot of time alone but end up doing so because of their hesitancy to interact with others. The consensus is that shy people recoil at the prospect of negative social judgment or possibly being ridiculed. Introverts, by contrast, with energy directed inward, have less concern when being social yet have more of a preference for quiet, minimally stimulating external environments. Importantly, it is safe to say that because an introvert can be shy, there is quite an overlap.

Another way to view the introvert-extrovert continuum is to look at the different ways in which each uses their energy. Introverts tend to be more to themselves and review matters in-depth; their energy is gained by ideas, impressions, and emotions. An extrovert generally has a more outward approach and seeks the breadth of issues over depth; their energy is gained by people, places, and activities. Regarding personality temperament, extroversion has even been purported to be a "happiness facilitator." I would speculate that the extroversive individual may experience more happiness in part because they do not mull over things or ruminate as much as a more introversive person is likely to do.

Because a key component of being shy involves experiencing discomfort in social situations due to concern about being evaluated or judged, both introverts and extroverts can be shy. The surprise is that extroverts, because of their attraction to people and interactions, may be spared the worst aspects of shyness symptoms. This is not always the case, as it may be harder for the extrovert who is shy than the introvert who is shy, because the extrovert would love to interact more socially but feels the pain of their shyness pulling them back. The shy introvert can also experience significant distress when anticipating social interaction but, unlike the extrovert, may not mind being alone or apart from others as much.

Introverted children do like spending time alone and are sometimes happier to curl up with a book or build a Lego tower than to join the neighborhood kids in a game of tag. At least

30 percent of children are estimated to be introverted. An introverted child who is not shy is usually found to have good social skills but does need some quiet time to process what is going on. Behaviorally inhibited or shy children, on the other hand, may crave social interaction. The problem is, those very interactions are also a source of stress, largely due to the shy child's concern over how others may react to their social performance. The introverted, non-shy child may roll with the daily social interactions that take place a little more easily than a shy child, introverted or not, who feels the need to avoid socializing.

Shyness is not the same as introversion, although, as mentioned, many introverts are shy. To explain further, the introvert may likely prefer quiet time and less interpersonal interaction, but they will not necessarily feel uncomfortable when socializing. Shy individuals do experience discomfort in many different social activities. Just as someone can be an introvert or an extrovert, there exists a middle ground on the continuum. That is, as discussed, the ambivert, who shares both introvert and extrovert features in their personality temperament. To understand the term ambivert, which sounds more like a reptile description, just think ambidextrous, or someone who can use both left and right-handedness depending on the task.

Extroverts, that is, those who are outgoing, can also be shy, even though much of their energy is directed outward. Extroverts like to socialize, but if they are shy, they may feel the emotional pain of being hesitant to proceed because of perceived harsh social judgment. Interestingly, many outgoing adults describe being shy as children or during adolescence. It may be that shyness has more in common with extroversion than introversion at times. This is because the shy individual would like to interact with others but is held back. Introverts may simply prefer more solitude but are not necessarily shy when interacting with others.

In terms of cognitive or thinking style, introverts tend to be more reflective or ponder things often. By contrast, extroverts have a more action-oriented way of considering issues. These contrasting styles each have their advantages and form a characteristic way in which introverts and extroverts problem solve and attempt to resolve conflicts. In general, introverts prefer a quiet, minimally stimulating environment. Extroverts prefer seeking out and engaging in social interactions. Introverted or extroverted individuals can be shy with the same common factor operating, mainly deeply felt concern and reaction to the possibility of negative social judgment.

To summarize, an introvert or extrovert can be shy. It is surprising to many that an extrovert or outgoing person can be shy, but it is common. These extroverted individuals are sometimes referred to as shy extroverts. As an example of extroverted bravado in an otherwise oftentimes detached entrepreneur, J. Paul Getty is said to have remarked, "According to the Bible, the meek shall inherit the Earth, but I would add—not the mineral rights." With introversion and shyness, the two personality traits or dimensions do overlap significantly. A major difference is that shy people exhibit an interest in but a strong hesitancy to be social at times. In contrast, non-shy introverts often simply prefer less social interaction.

Practice Opportunity
Introversion and Extroversion Features
Now that we've looked at various important aspects of introversion and extroversion, you can self-assess whether you tend to be one or the other, which is more inwardly or outwardly directed in terms of your preference. Of course, many individuals have an almost equal number of introversive and extroversive traits. It will increase your self-awareness and personal insight to see where you fall. There will be more ways in which to assess introversion and extroversion along with other broad personality features as they relate to shyness after this initial screening opportunity.

The following points present several major introversive and extroversive features that you can check off as they apply to your personality style:

Introversive Features
_____Your energy is directed inward; an example is thinking and reflecting about things.
_____You enjoy some degree of solitude along with contemplation.
_____People may describe you as more reserved.
_____You prefer more low-key environments compared to ones with high external stimulation.
_____Close relationships with a few friends versus many bring your deep trust and loyalty.
_____You've been described by others as being highly sensitive.

Extroversive Features
_____Your energy is directed outward; an example includes enjoying many social activities.
_____You enjoy meeting people and engaging in interpersonal interactions and relationships.
_____People may describe you as an action-oriented person.
_____Stimulating environments help you gain motivation, as does being around other people.
_____You could have a large social network and feel comfortable with team-oriented activities.
_____You've been described by others as being enthusiastic and positive.

Of course, you may identify with both introversive and extroversive traits, and many people can best be described as ambiverts. That is, ambiverts are in the middle,
This common mixed style can demonstrate a type of balanced behavior that reflects both inward (introversive) and outward (extroversive) types of responding. Basically, you don't need to be at war with either of these two major aspects of personality operating in concert. Relative comfort with your main introversive or extroverted propensity is a positive goal. This may take some doing. For example, in a culture such as America that seems to favor extroversion (the saying "Just Do It" comes to mind), feeling comfortable as an introvert will require self-acceptance. The same is true for shyness. You may not always feel at ease in certain social situations, but as you work on lowering your discomfort, it remains okay to allow yourself some shyness latitude.

Many shy individuals may try to practice forced extroversion. This in and of itself is not a bad idea because new social behaviors can be learned. A shy person may push themselves into social interaction in a way they feel approximates how their more outgoing peers proceed. This may not always go well because the shy person is working against type. For example, it would help if a shy individual adopted more of a self-compelled outgoingness that still allows for their being somewhat quiet or reflective. In this regard, more genuine and thereby successful social interactions will result. As mentioned already, a type of liquid extroversion can occur when a shy person uses alcohol or another drug that they feel relaxes them and quells their social anxiety, albeit temporarily. The Practice Opportunities in the treatment section of *Successful Shyness* are designed to be helpful whether you're more introverted, extroverted, or a blend of these two major personality traits.

Assessing Broad Personality Features

In this section, introverted or extroverted personality features are reviewed with six other important personality feature choices or options included. I've used this total of seven personality *pivot points* in my clinical practice for years. Individuals appreciate the opportunity to arrive at a more comprehensive personality picture via self-assessment and selecting the personality style features they can relate to and fit best. After you've reviewed each personality style feature that seems to fit best, you can simply circle it. For example, we start with introversion or extroversion.

The major personality dimensions or style features list is provided below, followed by a detailed description for each of the seven main personality choice points. After reading about each broad area of personality functioning there is a practice opportunity at the end of this section where you can choose which personality dimension or trait fits you best at this time.

Seven Major Personality Feature Choices

1. Introverted or extroverted
2. Compliant or noncompliant (defiant) responding
3. Reserved or outgoing stance
4. Routine (cautious) or spontaneous (action) preference
5. High motivation or low motivation
6. Internalizing (blames self) or externalizing (blames others)
7. Moving toward, away, or against others interpersonally

Here are the detailed descriptions of all seven personality style features:

1. Introverted or Extroverted

The introverted or extroverted trait and style of relating are complex, with many implications for how shy individuals respond; thus, they are first on the list and important to describe in detail.

Introverted individuals are often described as being more to themselves, with extroverts tending to be more socially engaged. Shy individuals can be either introverted or extroverted.

Importantly, introverts often appear to others as shy because they may be quieter socially, yet they do not necessarily experience anxiety or tension in their dealings with others. Extroverts appear to others as more engaged socially, yet if shy, they may feel anxious or tense in different interpersonal situations. For myself, I think that over the years I've become an introverted extrovert. I appreciate quiet contemplation at times, yet I have learned how to develop social skills, especially during my clinical psychology training years. If you're shy, be aware that pulling back to a previously more inhibited stance can occur even though you've developed good social skills. I recall a curious mountain road trip one time with my friend Eric. He was very nonchalant about handling curves, even way up beyond some of the lower clouds appearing outside the passenger window. Eric used a one-handed steering technique around the bending roadway. He would hold his other hand outside the driver's window while smoking a cigarette. I was tense and anxious during these rides. Further, I was initially too hesitant and perhaps a little shy to speak up. This only lasted a while. I found my voice and told my daring friend, repeatedly, to "watch the road."

Many people ask, "What is a personality trait?" According to psychologist Dr. Wiebke Bleidorn and his research team, a broad answer is that a personality trait is a relatively enduring pattern of thoughts, feelings, and behaviors that distinguishes individuals from each other. Introversion and extroversion are examples of major personality traits. By the way, you may have noticed that in this book, I've referred to personality traits, dimensions, styles, or features interchangeably. The different terms share the stability of a personality aspect, and, as such, they are all accurate descriptors, depending on the context in which they are used. As mentioned earlier, you can be either a shy introvert or a shy extrovert, and both are examples of stable combined personality traits. But let's not get ahead of ourselves at this juncture. Providing a description of introversion and extroversion will help flesh out these two distinct traits, and many people have features or characteristics of both. With introversion, you can expect the individual to prefer sensitivity and thinking deeply rather than social stimulation. At the same time, close friendships with family and several others are the norm. If shy, the introvert will likely experience anxiety or tension around many different social interactions. In contrast, most extroverts will display a penchant or active engagement tendency to be with and interact with people in a variety of social settings. Stimulation is sought out, and an extrovert may have many acquaintances, but perhaps fewer very deep friendships. A shy extrovert is likely to feel trapped in the sense that they want very much to socialize with others yet are held back over concerns about how they will perform or what others may think.

Introversion and Extroversion and Shyness   Expression

Introversion	Extroversion
Shyness can be present	Shyness can be present
Reserved	Outgoing
Preference for quiet environment	Preference for many social interactions
Focus on ideas, impressions, and feelings	Focus on people, places, and activities

Prefer depth in their interactions	Prefer breadth in their interactions
Thoughtful, strategic, and focused	Action-oriented, social, and friendly
Tend to observe an activity before joining	Tend to join an activity quickly
May spend less time with others	Spends considerable time with others
Planful	Spontaneous

Oftentimes, people assume introversion means preferring to be alone. It may not be that stark in that introverts simply gravitate toward a quieter environment that suits their more reserved stance. Extroverts, on the other hand, tend to experience more positive emotions socially than introverts. Shyness comes into play with the introvert in that some measure of shyness may simply be developed due to less contact with a variety of social situations. Shyness in an extrovert may not be too visible while participating in social situations, mainly because their occasional discomfort is more hidden. Put another way, interpersonal skills can get rusty, which may cause a shy introvert to become anxious or tense and pull back. On the other hand, the extrovert is more likely to engage readily in many different social interactions, and there is often a bid on their part to gain attention. If positive social attention does not occur, any underlying shyness present is likely to emerge.

In society, we most certainly need both introverts and extroverts. The introvert is more of a detailed planner, for example, and the extrovert is ready to get out there and do things. One of my psychology professors put it succinctly, "The introvert designs the bridge in relative isolation, while the extrovert gets all of his coworkers together to build it." Can people change from being introverted to being extroverted? The answer is, behaviorally, yes. Recall that many individuals have a mixed style of the two traits wherein they exhibit both introverted and extroverted observable features. A comparison can be made to the physical dimension of being both left-handed in some activities and right-handed in others, namely ambidextrous.

Referencing shyness, a shy introvert can learn to practice social skills, which is a type of extroversion exercise, and the extrovert can work on slowing their social pace down and thinking about how to further deepen their relationships. For an interesting example, take a look at why a shy introvert may want to perk up and respond more quickly socially. According to research published by Drs. Ziano and Wang in the *Journal of Personality and Social Psychology*, people judge slower responses as less sincere than quicker replies. Thus, if a shy introvert tends to think too much before saying anything out of concern over how it will be received, they might be thought of as being less truthful. I doubt this line of inquiry holds valid in most social circumstances, though—think of how many people are respected for weighing a question and taking their time to respond accurately.

Come to think of it, shy individuals in general, whether introverted or extroverted, may do well with online forums, such as in dating, meeting people, and talking online. They can think of what to say, there is less pressure than face-to-face, and so-called online matching can take place over time and more leisurely. Sometimes the online route seems preferable to going out there again in the dating world when former relationships haven't worked out.

Case Vignette
Shy and Introverted

Take Dave, for instance, a twenty-three-year-old musician who self-describes as shy. In counseling, he discussed feeling remorseful, having sifted through the wreckage of his previous close relationship. It was a long-term, intimate one, with loads of emotion. He felt abandoned when his girlfriend found another man. Dave said, "The shock of finding that you aren't loved is the deepest cut." Clearly, even though Dave wanted to "get out there" as it were, the sting of rejection increased his shyness. Slow and steady became the therapeutic goal, with helpful support from family and friends along the way. In time, Dave even developed a high degree of awareness and insight into relationships. He said, "You've got to pay attention to the strength and passion of a relationship because they can generate too much positive and negative high-octane energy at times. I'm introverted and not always comfortable talking about my feelings." Dave also commented that when he dedicated too much time to his solo musical pursuits, he would lose rest and sleep. In turn, he seemed harsher with others, particularly those whom he cared about. Balancing the demands of career, relationships, and working through shyness, which was exacerbated by loss, helped Dave regain his forward traction in daily life.

One repeated theme in *Successful Shyness* is finding a balance in whatever endeavors you pursue, including how to become more social. I would like to include the caution, so often accurately expressed in the news, that the internet and its associated online activities need to be used with care. As many information technology experts have exclaimed, "It's still like the Wild West." It's dangerous, at times, to be sure; online activities can have detrimental effects in terms of privacy and unintended consequences. At present, the Wild West analogy remains accurate. I recall watching the old westerns with my brother at a young age, with toy guns at our sides. Looking back, I don't think good things ever did come from the combination of cowboys with guns walking into salons, drinking whiskey, then arguing with each other while outside the sun was scorching down at around a hundred degrees. Indeed, caution is warranted in this new online frontier of ours, wherein words are often used as guns.

To manage shyness effectively, it is constructive to embrace your quieter, more introspective qualities, regardless of your personality style or traits. Beware though, in this society, we are often given the impression or expectation that we need to keep up with a more outgoing "just do it" lifestyle. Perhaps we can all benefit from Mahatma Gandhi, who once wisely said, "There is more to life than increasing its speed." To which I would add "and loudness." Introverts, including those who are shy, generally possess good listening skills. Once they learn strategies to reach out, the shy often do well in small group or one-to-one social situations. Thus, being shy does not necessarily mean being socially inept in any way, and practice can do wonders for increasing interpersonal skills. The treatment sections of this book will focus on specific practice opportunities in which to learn effective social skills and have the benefit of being self-paced. That is, you can work on any practice opportunity that you want, particularly one that appeals to you when you feel it will be helpful for a particular situation or circumstance.

Case Vignette
Shy and Extroverted
Jenny was a bright, attractive young adult who had recently graduated from college. She found a job working at a small business and quickly learned that she would be expected to do some presentations. She became anxious and described her shyness as getting in the way. When she confided to her friends that she was hesitant to talk in front of others, they were surprised. Indeed, Jenny was extroverted, with an outgoing and gregarious side, at least when with her family and friends. In contrast, when she encountered unfamiliar people or situations, she would pull back and become quiet, sometimes shy and inhibited.

Jenny wanted to reach out to others and speak up, but something slowed her responses in various public situations. In working with Jenny, the therapeutic thrust was for her to recognize that being extroverted or outgoing can indeed be combined with shyness. This is true, even though it certainly did not seem that way to those close to her. She could relate to several instances when she would be talkative and spontaneous only to "clam up" if someone she didn't know would enter the conversation. Jenny learned that being outgoing doesn't mean you can't be shy, but extroverted people sometimes do seem perplexed about their own shy side. Conversely, introverted individuals are generally reserved and can be quite self-contained; thus, they can appear to be shy but aren't as often as others might think. Many introverts choose to spend more time alone or in solitary pursuits, yet they do not necessarily feel uncomfortable in social situations. Jenny learned that one main reason she felt anxious in social situations was simply because she didn't know how others might respond to her. Not knowing how she was coming across bothered her. She would become concerned, which in turn increased her social anxiety.

Meanwhile, it became clear that Jenny had high expectations of herself and others. She was, in fact, somewhat of a perfectionist. These personality features make it more understandable why she would become concerned that others might judge her performance in social situations, including work presentations. As she began more serious dating relationships after college, she also recognized that she was capable of critically evaluating others. Probably a good thing, as she once commented that she agreed with her dad, who had instructed her,

"You don't want to fly around the entire garden, then settle for the manure pile." A colorful analogy, to be sure, yet it points out the capacity of those who look with discernment toward others may be ahead of the game. Shyness includes the personal discomfort felt when one anticipates or expects to be socially criticized, judged, or, worse, rejected.

To summarize, you can be introverted and shy, with a tendency to be more anxious in social situations. You can be extroverted and shy and want to be social, but at times, you feel inhibited. A major emphasis on introversion, extroversion, and shyness is well placed, yet there are other prominent personality dimensions for you to also consider.

2. Compliant or Noncompliant (Defiant) Responding

Compliant people tend to be cooperative and agreeable. Noncompliant people are likely to express independence or opposition to some rules.

Compliant individuals have a propensity to go-along-to-get-along and don't like making waves. They are described by others as cooperative and friendly. I think most shy individuals can fit this personality feature, but not all. Take a teenager or young adult who is going through a rebellious phase and is, in fact, noncompliant, even defiant at times, while also being shy. Sometimes defiance in a young person can be seen as asserting independence (with an edge).

3. Reserved or Outgoing Stance

*Those who are reserved are likely to be quieter and contemplative.
*Outgoing individuals are more social and direct with others.

Individuals who are reserved tend to be quiet and even peaceful at times in their approach to the world. Those who are outgoing like to socialize and mix it up with others; they generally take an active stance in life. This personality dimension, or feature, can be situational. That is, someone might be reserved in certain settings and display an outgoing set of behaviors under another set of circumstances. In time, the reserved or outgoing style becomes more characteristic of an individual.

4. Routine (Cautious) or Spontaneous (Action) Preference

*Routine individuals prefer a schedule and predictability in their daily lives and tend to be more alert in new situations.
*Those who are spontaneous demonstrate more of a willingness to take things as they come and are primed for action.

Shy people are often routine because of their cautious stance in life, particularly when it comes to social interactions and new and unfamiliar situations. Spontaneous, action-oriented behavior is oftentimes seen in those who feel comfortable in the world and charge ahead.

5. High Motivation or Low Motivation

*Highly motivated individuals move toward their goals with a strong focus. They are often-times achievement-oriented and, by and large, follow through on projects.

*Those who are low in motivation need to first create some drive before they can act on goals. Speaking of goals, it has been said that "a goal without steps is a wish." Breaking down a large goal into smaller pieces can help increase motivation.

High or low motivation can apply to anyone, anytime. This personality feature is highly situational and subject to many different conditions. There are also many interesting twists and turns in direction. For example, an individual may be highly motivated not to work, which others may judge as low motivation. Along the same lines, a shy fourth grader may be motivated to go last in an oral presentation that has been assigned to all students in their class. In general, though, most of us display a trend of high or low motivation, depending on the situation. It can be helpful to check in with yourself as to when you may be in either mode throughout the day.

6. Internalizing (Blames Self) or Externalizing (Blames Others)

*Internalizers tend to find fault as stemming from something they may have done wrong and blames themselves. They are described as self-critical and inhibited.

*Externalizers will often see problems as outside of themselves and blames others. They are described as impulsive and outgoing.

Internalizing or externalizing problems are terms that are clinically technical, and yet the concrete "blames self or others" captures a lot. These are basically two different preferred ways of dealing with conflict. Nonetheless, I'll describe internalizing and externalizing in more detail because I think it will be helpful in our pursuit of self-awareness and problem-solving.

In general, people who tend to blame themselves or find fault with their own actions in an interaction tend to be internalizers. Shy individuals, sometimes due to low self-esteem and a self-critical stance, tend to internalize their problems. Those who externalize their problems tend to blame others as their preferred way of handling interpersonal conflict. As a result, these individuals tend to be less self-critical because they view others as the responsible party.

Here are some further details regarding internalizing and externalizing the predominant problem-solving styles:

A) Internalizing: The key features can include anxiousness, a fear component, and de-pression. Shy individuals tend to internalize their difficulties more, in part because they may feel embarrassed if they express their problems or if others notice they are uncomfortable. Strategies that promote insight and awareness can help those who tend to internalize problems.

An example of moderate internalizing includes the clinical picture of a young adult woman who came to therapy to work on anxiety due to frustration with her boss. She describes her boss as someone who would have her stay late to do extra work, showing no sensitivity to her needs. Instead of confronting him, she acknowledges "stuffing it," and ends up becoming increasingly anxious and withdrawn. Learning assertion can help with using constructive confrontation when needed, which has the added benefit of keeping our physical functioning optimal versus stressed out.

B) Externalizing: The key features can include a high potential for substance use at times and nonconformist or antisocial actions. Those who externalize their problems and have substance use issues seem less concerned about what others may think of their drinking or drug use. Regarding antisocial behavior, externalizers may not take responsibility, but tend to blame others for their problems. Interestingly, when it comes to children, those who externalize problems and become behaviorally disruptive get referred to psychological treatment more often than shy or quiet internalizing problem kids. Strategies that directly modify behavior in the direction of being more prosocial help those who externalize problems. Please note that we all may externalize a problem here or there, and it doesn't reflect anything broader than a situational action.

A funny but true example of externalizing involves a couple I was seeing in counseling. The wife, who was incredibly angry, told her husband, "You don't take blame for anything." His response was, "Whose fault is that?" Another example of externalizing a problem would be an eighteen-year-old teenager who has been at odds with his father. The teen decides to drink a few beers with his friends and come home later than he agreed to. When his father confronts him, he takes no responsibility. "Hey, Dad, tell me you didn't break a few rules when you were young."

Just as an individual can have both introverted and extroverted personality features, they can also have both internalizing and externalizing aspects to their orientation and general coping efforts. Now you can review the material and assess yourself along these important dimensions. The important consideration to make as you assess your own introversion and extroversion features, as well as internalizing or externalizing problem solving, is what seems most characteristic of how you operate day-to-day. Personality self-assessment along these seven predominant dimensions will give you a level of self-awareness and insight that many might envy. In time, you will be able to proceed in your relationships with family and friends while maintaining increased confidence and effective social responses. The case vignette below, along with the practice opportunity dealing with all seven personality dimensions, will help guide you in your effort.

The following personality dimension is the last of the seven and perhaps the most important for understanding shyness responding in that it deals with important interpersonal styles or ways to interact.

7. Moving Toward, Away, or Against Others Interpersonally

*Moves toward others describes a person who is compliant and respectful.

*Moves away from others is characteristic of people who are detached and sometimes isolative.

*Moves against others occurs when someone is aggressive and challenging.

In the moving toward interpersonal style, the individual is willing to be cooperative and friendly with others. With interpersonally moving away, as is often characteristic of the shy, there is a tendency to avoid others and keep communication to a minimum out of internal discomfort and concern about a social activity. Sometimes the interpersonal situation may simply be too stimulating or overwhelming, making behavioral withdrawal understandable. In moving against others, the interactional set of behaviors an individual takes are usually associated with a very forward, even pushy stance in social situations. For example, a person may insist on always being right in a conversation and get louder and louder until their point of view dominates all other input from being heard.

Case Vignette
Illustrating the Use of Broad Personality Features

Carolyn was a young adult female who held a job as an office manager for a medical practice. She came to counseling because of concerns that her introversion and shyness were being viewed negatively by her office peers and health care professionals. Specifically, she was given feedback during a performance review that she was "standoffish" and simply not approachable at times. Carolyn had many difficult nights at home, ruminating about how being reserved and shy in social situations her whole life was being misconstrued as a type of aloofness. She had read extensively about introversion and extroversion and decided that "being *introverted*" in her words "rang true." Her shyness stemmed from a very young age, and she reported remaining very close to her mother at all times. "I was a 'cling-on' and was hesitant to interact with others."

By her own admission, she always wanted to be *compliant* and took in the message from her parents that "If you don't have anything nice to say, don't say anything." In general, shy people often conform, with the shy child getting the message "to be seen but not heard." Further, shy adults rarely publicly complain. As mentioned, Carolyn was *reserved* and simply preferred to remain this way versus becoming more outgoing. Several sessions were held to work on being more friendly and social as appropriate, both in and outside of work social situations. While *introverted*, Carolyn came to learn that this major personality trait does not necessarily equate with shyness, but if she stayed out of social circulation too long, her interpersonal skills could suffer.

Carolyn talked about being very *routine*, and she would feel uncomfortable in any social situations that were formed on a spontaneous basis. We concluded that she had the combined features of introversion, including valuing her solitary time, but was also shy when it came to socializing with others. Her social discomfort was essentially a painful emotion that she had endured many times over. Not without humor, Carolyn was able to crack a joke at one point, saying, "I'm a social vegan; I avoid meet." Fortunately, Carolyn demonstrated *high motivation* in general, and in counseling she was willing to take some risks and try out various practice opportunities to learn how to manage her shyness more effectively. For example, her first practice opportunity consisted of observing how others initiated conversations, how they responded physically in terms of eye contact and attentive posture, as well as how they ended their interaction. Carolyn said that she got a lot out of watching others. She reflected that she had never really noticed so many details before in terms of how other people interacted. As a sign of progress, she even offered, "Maybe I don't need to be a member of the 'cautious club' anymore."

Oddly, Carolyn became almost too observant at the office. She mentioned that she would feel bad at times if anyone made a mistake at the office. In fact, she remained hard on herself and would frequently get down as the result of others' mistakes. When asked why she would take responsibility and blame herself for just about any troubles at the medical practice, her response was surprising. Carolyn remarked, "If I don't blame myself, who will?" In time, she came to recognize that *internalizing* is certainly not always the way to go and that responsibilities for any particular problem belong with the person or persons who were at fault.

We used the next sessions to explore Carolyn's interpersonal style. At one point, she opened up about her guilt feelings. With insight, she said, "It's really bad sometimes in that I even feel guilty when I shouldn't." When asked to elaborate, Carolyn related a time when she was driving by a Christmas tree lot, and in the cold, bitter evening, she noticed a man trying to sell some trees, but no one was stopping in to even look. She said, "I felt sad, even guilty, like maybe I should have driven into the empty parking lot, gotten out, and at least bought a small tree." I asked, "A small tree?" she responded, "Yes, I already have a large one in my living room." Clearly, Carolyn had a *moving toward* interpersonal style and took pains to get along with others, but in a very controlled, routine, and careful manner. Clinically, her guilt could be described as inappropriate in that it extended into areas concerning which she obviously had no control. Fortunately, her thoughts also revealed the mental considerations of a very sensitive, empathic individual. Shy individuals across the world often share the positive qualities of being caring while possessing a reserved type of accessibility. Which is to say, if you initiate a talk with a shy person, they might just let their guard down and share of themselves in a genuine way with compassion for others. Returning to those guilt feelings, in time, Carolyn's insight and humor were again present and intact. She agreed and said, "I'm not always responsible if it happens to rain somewhere, anywhere, on someone's parade."

Practice Opportunity
Identifying Your Broad Personality Features
Given the descriptions of the broad personality features or dimensions one through seven detailed above, along with the case vignette example—circle the left or right personality style feature below that best represents your current responding.

1. Introverted or extroverted
2. Compliant or defiant response
3. Reserved or outgoing stance
4. Routine (cautious) or spontaneous (action) preference
5. High motivation or low motivation
6. Internalizing (blames self) or externalizing (blames others)
7. Moving toward, away, or against others interpersonally

By identifying your broad personality features, you can better prepare to learn effective shyness strategies, as you'll feel more grounded in how you tend to respond in general. With a greater self-awareness of how you operate in terms of the different personality styles or features, the more you will be able to pivot from one style to the other as a situation warrants. For example, an individual who identifies with being routine may one day wake up and decide spontaneously to join the circus. Not likely, but you get what I mean. Another example is that a father who is generally compliant may become understandably noncompliant at his job. That is, when faced with being told to work overtime, which would involve missing his daughter's dance recital, he puts his foot down and says no, however respectfully.

The BASIC-ID Model: Assessing Day-to-Day Psychological Dimensions
The theoretical orientation for working with the assessment and treatment of shyness in this book includes what is known as a systems approach with cognitive-behavioral, interpersonal, and humanistic strategies employed. Another helpful multimodal therapeutic approach that will be used throughout this book is termed BASIC-ID and was developed by psychologist Dr. Arnold Lazarus. The BASIC-ID acronym stands for B-Behavior, A-Affect, S-Sensation, I-Imagery, C-Cognitive, followed by I-Interpersonal, and finally, D-Drug and physiological areas. This model, along with many other assessment and treatment strategies, provides straightforward ways in which to target specific areas for self-improvement, leading to effective shyness management. The BASIC-ID dimensions provide a way to identify other very

important personality features that can help you self-assess how you tend to deal with daily situations and circumstances.

Clinical psychologists Dr. Arnold Lazarus and Dr. Clifford Lazarus have written extensively on helping people by first gaining a comprehensive understanding of their background using a multimodal method. For our purposes in working with shyness, it is useful to look at yourself through the lens of their BASIC-ID model, which focuses on important, broad psychological dimensions. In this part of Successful Shyness, the focus of the BASIC-ID is on assessment. In the treatment section (Part 2), the BASIC-ID is used to facilitate positive change in our efforts to build confidence and effective social skills.

Practice Opportunity
Identifying your BASIC-ID Dimension Choices

You can circle either the left or right entries for each BASIC-ID dimension or modality listed below, based on which fits best after you review the descriptions. Most people are likely to fall somewhere in between or somewhere in the middle of these two contrasting choices, but just go with which one is more characteristic of how you generally respond.

B is for behavior. Many people are doers in that they like to use action to get things done. Others tend to reflect more before entering into more direct behavior. Shy people may tend to hang back more than others. Consider where you are on the dimension of action or reflection.

Action before reflection   Reflection before action

A is for affect or feelings. People are emotional at times, yet feelings may not be expressed openly by many. The shy are likely to suppress emotions if they feel they will be critically judged for expressing certain feelings but not always. Shy people may be quite direct with those they know well and from whom they do not fear harsh evaluation. Consider whether you openly express emotions or tend to control their expression.

Suppressing feelings   Expressing feelings

S stands for sensations. Many people seek out sensory experiences, such as food, music, art, and other adventures in the world. The shy may like all of these "sensory delights" while not always being in tune with how withdrawing and isolating from social contact can dampen sensory stimulation.

Low Sensory seeking   High Sensory seeking

I for imagery. Mental imaging is a type of daydreaming or fantasy, apart from thinking or planning. Visualizing real or imagined experiences can be a common activity for shy individuals that often involves creativity. In general, people vary widely on their daily use of mental pictures.

Low Imagery   High Imagery

C is for cognition or thinking. Many people, including the shy, like to think about things analytically, to problem solve by thinking things through. Cognition, or thinking, is also the engine we use to plan things. Some people are simply not as analytical in their approach.

Low Cognitive focus   High Cognitive focus

I is for interpersonal relationships. How social are you? For the shy, this is not a trick question. It so happens that shy individuals would like to be more social, but for reasons described in this book, tend to hang back. For example, too much avoidance or withdrawal will necessarily result in being less social. Of course, you can be "low social" in general but still have close family and friendships, as well as emotional intimacy.

Low Interpersonal   High Interpersonal

D stands for drugs and biological factors. Bad habits do occur. For the shy, drinking or other drug use can be used to provide a "social lubricant," yet this can result in not working through some anxiety to get to the other, more relaxing side. In other words, alcohol or drugs can only temporarily block discomfort and tension, but they may well bounce back. It's better to learn how to manage situational stress so that it won't negatively affect your daily performance. Other biological factors that can be enhanced come from getting enough sleep, eating well, and exercising.

Low health awareness   High health awareness

Case Vignette
Illustrating the use of the BASIC-ID

Jeremy was a senior in high school with few friends and a penchant for staying in his room. When he did venture out and socialize, he tended to spend time with younger peers. His *behavior* (B) was appropriate enough, but his father criticized him. For example, he was deeply embarrassed after his dad pronounced, "You should be friends with kids your age." Jeremy's feelings ran from sad to depressed (A for *affect* or feelings). While I was meeting with Jeremy for individual counseling, I asked him to invite his dad, Tim, to come in for a joint counseling session so that the three of us could interact together. I explained that the main purpose would be to talk about their relationship and how things were going. At first, Tim was indeed critical and even sarcastic, stating, "My son is too detached. He's apparently trying to find a way to repeal the laws of gravity, what with all his reading physics and isolating, not to mention his non-stop internet use."

In terms of the clinical picture, it looked like Jeremy was indeed taking care of his need for sensation (S) by reading, going online, relaxing, and likely deriving some vicarious satisfaction by seeing his father get so irritated at times.

In terms of imagery (I) Jeremy acknowledged that he often fantasized about becoming an online gamer because he enjoyed playing so often on the computer. Unfortunately, his visualization of his gaming engagement gets dashed when he thinks about how his dad would react. "He sees me as a slacker, but my mom doesn't seem to mind what I do in my own room." A shy teen can oftentimes feel guilty if parental expectations are not met. They may not verbalize negative emotions, but they sense that they have somehow disappointed a parent. The father in this case may have been anxious that his son wasn't maturing fast enough. Tim benefited from learning that with a shy teen, their efforts to socialize with a variety of people, no matter what age, can be a good thing.

In a subsequent individual session with Jeremy, I asked him if his dad had a point in asking him to hang out with kids around his own age. Jeremy thought about it for a while (C for cognition or thinking) and announced, "No, my dad just likes to dig. He can be a jerk at times." In fact, interpersonal (I) relationships during the adolescent years are often brittle in general. For example, one day a friend is well-liked, and the next, a teen may not want anything to do with that particular individual. Worse, parent-teen relationships can become strained due to nothing more than adolescents asserting their independence, sometimes recklessly. Fortunately, whereas Jeremy freely offers that he is shy, especially around girls, he does not use any alcohol or drugs (D) to calm his tension or interpersonal discomfort.

In this case, once father and son began to view each other's expectations as expressions of personal preference and not necessarily "my way or the highway" type of responses, they got along better. It was my impression that Tim was more extroverted than his son and, as such, needed some guidance on how to deal with a quieter, and at times quite shy, teenager.

Important Areas of General Level of Functioning

In addition to broad personality features, it can also be helpful to address important areas related to your general level of functioning before going further in our assessment of shyness. Listed below are the general level of functioning categories that you can rate. Identifying areas of strength and weakness in the various categories will help point the way for needed improvement as needed. Recognizing areas of strength in certain categories will allow you to take stock of your current accomplishments. At the same time, consider that problems with shyness can be compounded by difficulties with physical or mental health, as well as having few recreation outlets. The practice opportunity below provides a quick and easy means to assess where you currently stand on eight important areas of functioning that affect our daily lives.

Case Vignette

Assessing Eight Areas of General Functioning

For example, Joaquin, a thirty-year-old real estate broker (*occupational attainment*), felt as though his shyness was holding him back from some business opportunities because he was self-conscious when first meeting clients. In time, he learned to take advantage of his *social support* system, which was extensive at work. "They all wanted me to do well because they knew I cared about people and could get them a place they could afford." In other important areas of functioning, Joaquin reported that he was making "okay money" (*financial health*) and enjoyed his weekly tennis matches with several coworkers. He prided himself on keeping in good shape (*physical health*). In fact, the only time he had to visit the doctor was when he thought he had mononucleosis as a teen. Even then, it turned out to be funnier than not. Joaquin said, "The doctor did some tests because I was so tired. When he came back, I asked him if I had mono, and he said I didn't and that it must be that I was just really bored."

Educationally, Joaquin was able to earn a bachelor's degree in business but said he would like to go on for his MBA, probably in an online format "somewhere" as he put it. In terms of his mental health, Joaquin discussed some measure of anxiety (*mental health*) in counseling, which occasionally held him back from reaching out to others. At the time he came in, Joaquin had a steady girlfriend (*intimate relationships*). He was motivated to incorporate more positive statements on a daily basis to increase his, at times, low confidence. Meanwhile, at work, he remained adamant that he didn't want to hear any more of this real estate "mind-numbing" business banter, which was sloganized as simply "You can do it." *Recreationally,* Joaquin's social activities further increased. He was able to reach out to some friends he and his girlfriend shared to go bowling and play some darts. He mentioned that he did better at darts when he had "a few beers." I told him that this is actually common because, with a small amount of alcohol, anxiety and tension that can interfere with performance will go down. However, too much alcohol and the predictable effect are usually worsening task ability.

Practice Opportunity
Assessing Eight Areas of General Functioning
Assess your current level of functioning in each of the categories listed below along the left side (A through H) by using the rating scale along the top, which goes from a low (1) to a high (6).

Listed below are Joaquin's self-ratings (really estimates) of his current level of functioning:

Rating:	Low	1	2	3	4	5	6	High

Category:								
A) Physical health						X		
B) Mental health						X		
C) Financial health						X		
D) Recreation activity						X		
E) Social support						X		
F) Intimate relationships						X		
G) Education level						X		
H) Occupational attainment						X		

To gain more insight into your current level of functioning in the important areas listed below, simply rate any or all of the eight categories:

Rating:	Low	1	2	3	4	5	6	High

Category:
A) Physical health
B) Mental health
C) Financial health
D) Recreation activity
E) Social support
F) Intimate relationships
G) Education level
H) Occupational attainment

If you are shy, it is not realistic to get over your shyness, especially given that it is simply a personality trait. Instead, you can learn to manage it. In fact, to be successfully shy, the first part is managing shyness, and then there is a second part—acknowledging the advantages you have by being shy. For example, shy individuals are often good listeners, sensitive, and loyal in their relationships, as well as known to be humorous (at times).

Other advantages of being shy include a quieter voice during conversations and an ability to exercise psychological flexibility. Considering such flexibility, when Pope Francis was once asked if he had any fears, he surprisingly responded that he feared nothing. There was, however, one thing that bothered him, which, as he put it, involves those with rigid "straitjacket opinions on things." Psychological flexibility, including the cognitive or thinking asset that enables a shy, quiet, deliberate individual to entertain and weigh different views on a topic, is indeed an asset.

Shy individuals do not have a mental health disorder in any way, shape, or form. At the same time, the shy can become unhappy, particularly if they have avoided meaningful relationships, largely due to a lack of social engagement. Shy people may, of course, desire intimate relationships, yet their own avoidance maneuvers or backing away from social interaction interrupt the process. Most of us have felt like we are on the sidelines of everyday life from time to time. Social interaction is a necessary component to build the interpersonal connections we desire. In time, a shy person can lose self-esteem, yet this can improve. As has been described elsewhere in *Successful Shyness*, one grippingly simple, self-paced treatment strategy is to avoid avoidance. The rationale and strategies for reaching out and engaging with others will be detailed in the treatment section of this book.

Case Vignette
Shyness and Socializing

As a young child, David liked to watch birds. His grandmother bought him a plastic bird model labeled Birds of the World—Paint by Number, which he spent hours snapping together and painting. As David related this background piece of information in counseling, I wondered if there was a connection between his interest in birds and our work on effectively managing shyness. David's explanation was interesting. He talked about how many birds loudly sing in the trees, oftentimes high up and usually solo, or independent, of other nearby birds. Then, if a person gets too close or is noisy, the birds will generally run for cover. In fact, he commented, "The birds are able to go deep onto a tree or bush limb close to the trunk so that you couldn't even see them any longer." Then David offered what turned out to be a classic example of avoidance. He said, "A bird would recognize its singing attracted other birds and even people to its realm. Then it seems like it can escape all the close viewing and attention by simply flying into its leafy tree sanctuary."

Birds are cautious by nature. Flying away from any real or perceived threat is an adaptive response. Regrettably, flying away, or avoidance of contact, can be an overused response. In other words, most of the time, birdwatchers just want to view birds (not incidentally, there are an estimated ten to fifteen million self-reported birdwatching participants in the U.S.), and these curious naturalists mean no harm. If only the birds could know that. Like the shy, their avoidance maneuvers are oftentimes unnecessary. The treatment sections of *Successful*

> *Shyness* will offer practice opportunities to learn ways to constructively reach out when it's preferable to avoiding social contact. David began to feel more comfortable in his own skin when he recognized that he could be more social on occasion while avoiding situations when he felt he needed to recharge his energy alone or in a solitary activity.

Fortunately, by first assessing the level of your own shyness and then deciding how to become more effective in socializing with others, relative happiness will follow. I use the term relative because pure happiness is not a realistic goal. I'm reminded of comedian George Carlin commenting on a person who said they were "more than happy." He concluded that anyone who is "more than happy" should probably be in some type of institution. A major component of successful shyness will be your ability to negotiate and compromise with others, a communication skill that can be learned. There is no need to seek out the perfect social activity or interaction. I believe that happiness visits those who function at an average to above-average level, based on the expectations they've set for themselves. This can occur while having the courage to be less than perfect in the process. Put another way, the "courage to be imperfect" while working toward a goal is the way to go, setbacks and all. As Sheryl Sandberg wisely advised, "Done is better than perfect." A similarly formidable quote is from Mark Twain who offered, "Continuous improvement is better than delayed perfection."

Shyness, Social Rejection, and Loneliness

Shy individuals can be sensitive to social rejection. Or it could be that people who are sensitive to rejection turn shier. Either way, especially with developing children and adolescents, relational aggression, which includes rumor spreading and social exclusion, is painful. If, in your self-assessment of shyness, you conclude that you are vulnerable to the effects of relational aggression (and who wouldn't be, shy or not), successfully managing shyness includes learning to buffer, or inoculate. yourself against such social or interpersonal harm.

In the functional family therapy (FFT) model formulated by psychologists Dr. James Alexander and Dr. Bruce Parsons, there is a major focus on whether an individual is merging or separating from others. Merging involves moving toward others, communicating openly, and experiencing the benefits of close relationships. Shy people are likely to engage in more separating behavior. Such pulling away from others can be evidenced by a communication style that is indirect, not initiating much, and at times withdrawing rather than making social connections. For an adolescent, for example, online gaming may look like the teen is fully engaged or merging, but it's with the computer, not another individual. Thus, the teen may be in separation mode, possibly shy, and uncomfortable talking with others. The issue is that shy young people may use online activities as a way to separate from others and thereby insulate themselves from social rejection. The price paid for the shy can be high, as in increased disconnection and loneliness.

Of course, with the internet and, in particular, social media sites, all of us have the capacity to be separated from one another, ironically while using the computer to try and stay connected. A clinical psychologist, Dr. Steven Hickman, has studied so-called Zoom exhaustion and has aptly labeled this as "connected but disconnected." On the positive side of the equation, the young person in the above online gaming example, and perhaps most people who are shy, often demonstrate a reserved accessibility. This type of accessibility simply refers to being willing to talk and relate to others only if the other person initiates the interaction. Thus, at times, a passive or reserved way in which to connect is better than no connection at all. The topic of being a loner comes up often in the same discussions of what shyness is or isn't. There are many people who tend to stick to themselves but are not shy. On the other hand, there are those who are very shy and lead a life of isolation from others. Shy people often long for social connection but must fight through their own high level of discomfort to proceed. Rejection sensitivity can get in the way of reaching out. Finally, a person can be shy and a loner but continue to remain emotionally close to a few others, just being less generally social. As mentioned, a shy person's loyalty is a strong asset, and close relationships among family members and friends really count.

One way to tell if someone is more on the shy side, as opposed to just valuing alone time, is to look for social aversion or avoiding behaviors. That is, a truly shy person may actively find ways to avert eye contact, avoid a gathering, or feel quite anxious if they can't leave the situation quickly. An isolated, non-shy individual, one who is a self-described loner, will tend to remain calm and not avert or avoid social situations. Interestingly, in terms of coping, these individuals usually and comfortably stay away in the first place. It is the shy person who may well want more social contact, but their pulled-back behavior and self-consciousness stop them in their tracks. George Harrison, sometimes termed "the sensitive Beatle," sang an interesting song when he was in the Traveling Wilburys about being tired of being lonely. Most everyone can relate at one or another time in their life to loneliness; the shy sometimes feel trapped in it.

For your own self-assessment, it is important to recognize that everyone feels lonely or left out of things from time to time. In fact, one universal human dilemma involves how to move in and out of closeness and separateness in our interpersonal relationships. For example, a long-term couple might be quite close and emotionally intimate, yet each may feel a unique sense of loneliness from time to time. It is important to make a distinction between loneliness and alienation. A couple of brief definitions will help to clarify the difference. Loneliness can be defined as discomfort from being alone. Alienation is more of a feeling at odds with other groups. One practical solution for loneliness and even alienation can be to regularly engage in personal hobbies and interests.

I have had many clients learn to self-assess their current state of loneliness as either low, moderate, or high. If their self-rating goes into the high range of loneliness, they know to channel their efforts (and energy) into being more social via hobbies and interests. For example, Malcom, an ex-fighter pilot, liked to hang out with his aviation colleagues and friends, yet he began to think that he was becoming too isolated, lonely, and alienated from others outside of his familiar group. In counseling, he lamented that because not everyone knew how to fly a plane, he was limited in who he could pal around with after his workday. Malcom said this made him moderately lonely at times. Upon reflection, we agreed that his birds of a feather flock together logic had limitations. I suggested that if everyone adopted his "narrow affiliation attitude," it would mean that a trapeze artist would have a very limited circle of social contacts. On to problem solving. Malcom was able to develop hobbies and interests outside of his immediate aviation interests. Interestingly, he discovered golf and called up a few friends, suggesting a driving range that was adjacent to an airstrip so he could watch the planes.

Practice Opportunity
Current Loneliness Range and Action Plan
Assess and rate your own current level of loneliness, then develop a simple action plan to engage in hobbies and interests that will likely bring more social contact. We can use Malcom's strategy for widening his social contacts as an example.

Here are Malcom's responses:

Current Loneliness Range	Action Plan
Low Moderate High	(Circle which one)
1. Moderate	Engaging a few friends to head out to the golf driving range

Assess your own current level of loneliness, then create a simple or brief action plan to engage in hobbies and interests below (1, 2, 3, or 4 different points in time). The main goal is to develop more social contact. Rate your current loneliness range on the left, followed by your action plan on the right.

Current Loneliness Range	Action Plan
Low Moderate High	(Circle which one)
1. _____	_____ _____
2. _____	_____ _____
3. _____	_____ _____
4. _____	_____ _____

Assessing Three Major Types of Conflict

There are three major types of conflict that we all engage in from time to time, and one of the best ways to describe them is to list them, provide a short definition, and then give an example. The three types of conflict are named approach-approach, approach-avoidance, and avoidance-avoidance. The next Practice Opportunity will provide a convenient way to describe each conflict, provide examples for each conflict type, and explain how they might be resolved. After the examples, you'll be able to input your own situations and describe what you did or could have done to resolve your own approach-approach, approach-avoidance, and avoidance-avoidance conflict.

Practice Opportunity

Encountering and Resolving Three Major Types of Conflicts

Each major type of conflict is briefly defined below, with an example given, followed by blank lines for you to complete. The focus is on identifying one or more of the three conflicts below (approach-approach; approach-avoidance; avoidance-avoidance) that you've encountered. Next, indicate how you may have resolved or are resolving the conflict. It sounds complex, but it really isn't in that we all deal with these common conflicts on a near daily basis, and the examples will help guide you.

A. Approach-approach conflict occurs when you are deciding to choose between two things that are both desirable.

An example of an approach-approach conflict involves Blaine, a seventeen-year-old high school student, being asked by a friend to come over and listen to an album by a band named The Shys that was recorded in 2008. Minutes later, he was told by his parents to stick around to visit with his aunt, who had just come back from Mexico and was bringing gifts. Blaine judged both alternative activities as desirable. He knew that he had to choose one over the other. Blaine decided that seeing his aunt was the better of the two choices because he hadn't seen her in a long time. He reasoned he could listen to the album at a friend's house another time.

As an example, here are Blaine's responses to approach-approach conflict.

Write down one or two situations when you encountered an approach-approach conflict:
  1. Asked by a friend to hear an album or wait for an aunt coming a long way to visit.
Next, describe what you did or could have done to resolve the conflict:
  2. "I decided to see my aunt because it's been a long time."

Write down one or two situations when you encountered an approach-approach conflict:
  1._____
  2._____

Next, describe what you did or could have done to resolve the conflict:

1._____

2._____

B. Approach-avoidance conflict involves deciding to choose between two things, one of which is considered desirable and another that appears more undesirable. This type of conflict is quite common with shy individuals, particularly in the social sphere of everyday life. For example, it is typical for shy individuals to want to be more social, which can be described as a desire to approach others. At the same time, there is often a reaction by the shy to hold themselves back, oftentimes over concern about being critically evaluated or judged.

Muhammad was a young adult male who lived with his parents and described himself as shy. We worked on his social skills in counseling. During one session, he remarked that he was pleased that he had gotten up enough fortitude to join a boxing class at the local YMCA. His coach, whom he greatly respected, would sometimes comment to him that he had the same first name as Muhammad Ali, a champion boxer, who could serve as a role model. The coach would then usually go on to teach the lesson at hand. Muhammad wanted to approach him to discuss technique but was concerned that his coach would simply say something like, "Try harder." Thus, he avoided initiating conversation. In time, Muhammad found that by approaching his coach, even though anxiety remained, his avoidance behavior decreased. At one point in counseling, he described being overly excited after he asked how he was doing when his coach offered, "You are trying harder. Good." Muhammad was incredibly happy with his social reaching out. We can appreciate that sometimes even small doses of verbal reinforcement can go a long way.

As an example, here are Muhammad's responses to approach-avoidance conflict.

Write down one or two situations when you encountered an approach-avoidance conflict:
1   Avoided initiating a conversation with the coach
Next, describe what you did or could have done to resolve the conflict:
1. I asked his coach how I was doing and received praise.

Write down one or two situations when you encountered an approach-avoidance conflict:

1._____

2._____

Next, describe what you did or could have done to resolve the conflict:

1._____

2._____

C) Avoidance-avoidance conflict is the opposite of approach-approach conflict. It occurs when you have to choose between two undesirable options.

For shy parents, an atypical example involves a well-respected mom on the block, Lynette, who is the safety consultant at her company. She has been asked to give a presentation to the local elementary school on stranger danger. Or, as the principal of the school offered, Lynette might instead want to have her son's classroom come over to the nuclear plant where she worked to see how it runs. It turns out this shy parent didn't want to present the talk or have her son's class run around her potentially radioactive workplace. The presentation won out, and Lynette proceeded, feeling as though this was the less "dangerous" of the two options, given her experience with safety issues.

As an example, here are Lynette's responses:

Avoidance-avoidance conflict:
Write down one or two situations when you encountered an avoidance-avoidance conflict:
1. Give a safety-oriented class presentation, or tour of my workplace. Next, describe what you did or could have done to resolve the conflict:
2. I delivered a presentation at the school on stranger danger.

Write down one or two situations when you encountered an avoidance-avoidance conflict:
1._____
2._____
Next, describe what you did or could have done to resolve the conflict:
1._____
2._____

Situational Shyness with Four Common Social Anxiety Reactions

When shyness arises in a conversation or other social situation, you may find yourself becoming anxious. Common reactions or symptoms generally associated with social anxiety can occur in one or more of the following four major domains:

A) Physical: increased heart rate (racing heart) and blood pressure. Blushing, sweating.
B) Cognitive: negative thoughts and images.
C) Emotional: anxiety, multiple fears, and discomfort.
D) Behavioral: avoidance of social situations.

It can be helpful to identify social situations and the physical, cognitive, emotional, and behavioral reactions you may have to them that are related to your own shy response. Self-assessment in these areas will increase your ability to recognize these common social anxiety reactions when they occur.

Case Vignette
Situational Shyness and Anxiety Responding

Kailani, a forty-year-old community college instructor in southern California, came in for individual counseling to "deal with being too uptight" as she put it. She said, "I'm generally calm and get along well with others." Kailani worked full-time at the college, teaching four classes per semester. She clearly had a busy load with many students in each of her classes. Kailani described feeling her heart rate rise at the beginning of each instruction period because she had negative thoughts about students thinking she was too strict. She ended up avoiding interactions with her students after class, fearful that they would confront her "hard grading habits." While working with Kailani, it became apparent that she was judging herself in an overly harsh manner. Regarding her work, she commented, "Maybe I'm not cut out for this," which in turn was responsible for her significant anxiety and discomfort. She did discuss being thorough, even exacting, with her subject matter. Kailani offered the rationale that she only wanted her students to learn the most they could. When asked if anyone had approached her about being too strict, she remarked that it was only one student that gave her that impression. We embarked upon a course of treatment that included relaxation strategies to lower her physical symptoms of increased heart rate while also addressing her avoidance of social situations and internal discomfort. All relaxation strategies and techniques, as well as many other therapeutic interventions for situational shyness accompanied by anxiety, will be discussed in detail within the treatment section of this book. In this case, we agreed that Kailani's first task was to talk with a few of her students on a one-to-one basis. She followed through, was less reactive overall, and had fewer symptoms as a result of learning to be more direct with others.

Practice Opportunity
Managing Situational Shyness and Anxiety

List an experience or two that you can link to either physical, cognitive, emotional, or behavioral reactions that have occurred in social situations. Oftentimes, you can have a combination of these symptoms:

As an example, here are Kailani's responses:

A) Physical: For example, many shy individuals say their body reacts with tightness.
   1) Kailani self-reported that she was "too uptight" at the outset of counseling.
B) Cognitive: For example, a common response in thinking is "I'm not ready for this."
   1) Kailani had stated at one point "Maybe I'm not cutout for this" in reference to her teaching approach.
C) Emotional: For example, a shy individual may report feeling discomfort or upset.

1) Internal discomfort occurred due to Kailiani's overly harsh self-judgment.
D) Behavioral: For example, many people shy or not state, "I felt like I should walk out," in reference to becoming uptight about joining a certain social situation.
1) Kailani avoided interactions with her students after class.

In the four domains below, list an experience or two of your own that you can link to either physical, cognitive, emotional, or behavioral reactions that have occurred in social situations. A combination of one or more of these symptoms is common:

A) Physical: For example, many shy individuals say their bodies reacts with tightness.
1. _____
2. _____
B) Cognitive: For example, negative thoughts and images are common.
1. _____
2. _____
C) Emotional: For example, anxiety, multiple fears, and discomfort.
1. _____
2. _____
D) Behavioral: For example, avoidance of social situations often occurs.
1. _____
2. _____

Developing Interdependence

One concept that is helpful to assess is to what extent you foster interdependence. The term is an interesting one. Interdependent means that you are not dependent on someone as much as you are relying on each other. For example, when family members and friends form close, intimate personal relationships, they become interdependent to the extent that they can care for and support one another. When you are shy, the tendency to pull back or be hesitant in close relationships may make it harder to generate the two-way close interactions, which is defined by interdependence. In terms of problem solving, awareness is key. If you're aware that you haven't yet formed many close relationships, then that becomes the goal. In the treatment section of this book, you will be able to go through several different practice opportunities that help you reach out to others to form meaningful relationships.

When you have positive experiences with family and friends, you'll find that many negative feelings you have will diminish. At times, social encounters will seem awkward or go awry, thus self-compassion and self-support are what you want to foster when things don't go just right. Considering that things definitely don't go just right at times, it is important for those who are shy and perfectionistic to watch out for *just right experiences*. That is, many shy individuals won't even enter a conversation if they feel they will come across as less than skilled or even perfect. Why is imperfection not tolerated and just right experiences the expectation?

This approach by the shy seems to be yet another defense against being socially criticized or judged. "If I'm perfect, then I can't be faulted" may be a true sentiment, but it is not realistic.

As will be discussed in the treatment section of this book, learning to relax one's stance and essentially practicing the courage to be imperfect can really help. If a shy person doesn't come across perfectly in conversation or even misspeaks a time or two, what happens? They learn that whereas their social interaction was imperfect, their message was still well received. Equipped with reasonable observational skills, we will usually note that the other person wasn't flawless in their communication efforts either. It becomes the natural, and yes, imperfect, way in which all people communicate. There is time to relax about it, and you can learn how in the pages that follow. Once you're able to go forth and relate to others more while allowing for less than perfect social interaction, loneliness will decrease. In time, mutual relating or interdependence with others will increase, not to mention be rewarding in the process.

Urge Intensity

There is yet another component a shy person can assess themselves with, one that might drive some of this high standard and perfect performance expectation. The term that applies is "urge intensity." If a shy person feels compelled to respond to almost any upcoming conversation or social interaction with the thought that it should be a "just right experience," then the urge intensity to simply avoid the social activity could be quite high. One way to lower urge intensity is to consider what could go right in a particular social interaction and practice a few conversation openers to relax the urge intensity. For example, having even brief conversations with friends, family members, teachers, and employers can reinforce that you're indeed able to relate to others. Longer interactions can come later when you're ready.

Relaxation methods to decrease urge intensity can be helpful as well and will be described in the treatment section (Part 2) of *Successful Shyness*. For example, and by way of introduction, an effective method to calm yourself before an upcoming social activity or situation is to learn Progressive Muscle Relaxation (PMR). In this straightforward procedure, you can go through several major muscle groups, tensing and relaxing those muscles, resulting in a calmer feeling. The rationale for this extensively researched method is that relaxation is incompatible with muscle tension. In other words, when you're more relaxed, tension will decrease automatically.

Social Cost Bias

Another area of concern for shy individuals is self-pressure. Because we are concerned about what others think of our actions, especially when we're shy, there can be a tendency to push for just right experiences as discussed. For example, a shy person may feel courageous enough to join in with friends they don't know very well—but then they expect themselves to operate in a series of perfect interactions with these near strangers. This response style can also lead to what has been termed "social cost bias." Social cost bias refers to a socially anxious individual contemplating or having perceived the high cost of a future social situation ending poorly.

Faced with things which might not go exactly right, the person ends up avoiding the social situation all together.

Shy people often seem to have a remarkably high "social cost bias" at times. As mentioned, this type of bias occurs when we anticipate that a particular social situation will somehow turn negative. Because social cost bias is in fact a true bias, it means that social situations may not turn out nearly as problematic as anticipated, thus there is hope. Through assessing or evaluating your own thoughts prior to entering a social situation, it can be helpful to challenge any negativity you may have before a given conversation. Research has shown that when we feel like we might have a chance of doing well in a social situation, and focus on what we want to say, the likelihood of completing the interaction successfully goes up.

As will be discussed throughout this book, exposure to social situations, or taking Direct-Action as I've termed it, by following through in an interaction will increase your self-efficacy. Self-efficacy refers to feeling or believing that you're more effective in social situations because of having more encounters. Practice makes perfect, or as I like to say practice makes for improvement, really does work. Also, the often used phrase "fake it until you make it" while sounding negative, can be a positive at times. That is, if the phrase means yes, you could be awkward at times socially, but then are willing to act more confident and convincing, it might just work. Improving your interactions and thereby increasing your confidence takes time; it's a process. Interestingly, some people self-identify as being "socially awkward" and don't seem to mind the label. Or, like most of us, aspire to be more "socially skilled," yet recognize that awkward comes before skilled. Therefore, self-compassion is in order.

Chapter 4

Problematic Aspects of Shyness

This chapter includes several aspects of shyness that are considered to be particularly problematic at times in terms of the direct psychological effects they have on the shy person and often those around them. The topics of shyness, Rejection-Sensitivity, depressive responding, isolation, avoidance and withdrawal, cynical shyness, shyness and anger, worry as thinking on overdrive, and shyness and loneliness are all covered.

Shyness, Rejection-Sensitivity, and Depressive Responding

Shy individuals, largely due to a high degree of self-consciousness and wanting to fit in, are often rejection sensitive. In general, depressed individuals are more sensitive to rejection than non-depressed individuals. In depressive responding accompanied by rejection-sensitivity, individuals do experience an uptick in mood when something good happens but are more susceptible to feeling down in response to any negative social event. These individuals tend to bounce back more slowly. People high in rejection-sensitivity, whether shy or not, are more likely than others to become depressed in the aftermath of a romantic breakup. Those who are shy and pulled back, especially as developing adolescents, may be particularly vulnerable to this atypical type of depression. Common rejection-sensitivity, which most everyone has experienced and can relate to, seems different from the more hurtful rejection reactions many shy individuals self-report.

What specifically is the difference between a normal response to rebuffs and an oversensitive one? Simply put, rumination. High rejection-sensitive individuals tend to be overthinkers who ruminate excessively about everyday experiences. Overthinking, then, may become the engine of hypersensitivity to rejection. When individuals dwell on their negative thoughts, anxiety and even hostility may increase. Particularly with rejection-sensitive shy individuals, there may be a leap to a false conclusion that someone has rejected them when, in fact, they have not.

At times, other people may not respond well to a person who is rejection-sensitive (and distressed). In fact, reactions by others can include irritability and negativity, so they sometimes detach or withdraw from the overly sensitive depressed individual. Thus, the self-fulfilling prophecy of rejection-sensitivity could be at work again. In other words, the shy individual clams up out of concern over being rejected, gets depressed, and then others keep their distance, sometimes viewing the shy detachment as aloofness.

Main points regarding rejection-sensitivity:
1. Rejection-sensitivity is common. Can rejection-sensitivity lead to oversensitivity to rejection? Yes. The drive to bond lies deep in our DNA.
2. Self-esteem reflects our internal appraisal. It involves how we view ourselves. But self-esteem can also be a barometer of our standing with others. Dr. Mark Leary, a Duke University psychologist, found that social self-esteem (an interesting term) increases with acceptance from others. For example, when we are friendly at a social gathering, people are pleased and friendly back. Social self-esteem can fall when feedback toward us turns critical, which, for example, could happen if we don't say a word at a group meeting.
3. Remaining vigilant through social self-esteem scanning, such as looking for any acceptance or rejection signals, has had an evolutionary advantage. This is because, for much of our early human history, we depended on small groups for survival. It has been speculated that obsessive interest in celebrities and world leaders may be due to an unconscious concern to stay abreast of things so as not to be excluded from the collective group. Of course, there is a limitation with this type of connection, and there is even a name for it: "para-social interaction." This implies that when we develop emotional ties to well-known performers and personalities, the relationships are one-sided. Millions of people may express affection for a president Tor the Pope, but they will never receive any type of reciprocity or response from them in return.
4. Sadly, if an individual has a penchant for detecting rejection anywhere and everywhere, they may end up enduring significant anxiety and unfounded jealousy. A shy person may find that their own overly anxious response, out of fear of rejection, could set up a self-fulfilling prophecy. The main reason this could happen to the shy is that their tense, overly cautious stance could cause others to turn away.

   Prominent psychologist Dr. Robert Leahy explains in more detail the self-fulfilling prophecy effect of rejection-sensitivity. "They (those who are highly rejection-sensitive) live life in panic mode, which not only brings them relentless emotional turmoil but also sets off the most frustrating feature of rejection-sensitivity: it becomes a self-fulfilling prophecy. Magnifying oversights and seeing slipups as proof of catastrophe, they unleash hostility, anger, despondency, or jealousy. Their emotional storms often drive away the very people they hoped to hook." Interestingly, Dr. Leahy, in his work on rejection-sensitivity, has discussed how individuals sensitive to rejection can be less willing to have friends different from themselves. Bonding with a narrower group of peers may afford a lower chance of being rejected. Also, in romance, the rejection-sensitive individual is at particular risk because they may frequently "trust test" the relationship. Trust testing could include checking up on the consistency of the partner's statements, their where-abouts, and generally being overly questioning. They tend to seek frequent reassurance from their partners. Also, these misdirected queries seem to be an effort by the individual to be sure the partner remains committed to the relationship.

Rejection does have an emotional pain pathway associated with it such that, like physical pain, it hurts. As it turns out, the experience of rejection activates the same brain area that generates the negative reaction to physical pain, causing an increase in activity within the anterior cingulate. Dr. Leahy once commented, "Being left behind by your friends on a particular occasion can be as threatening to your well-being as touching a hot stove." Dramatic perhaps, but we get the point. An increased sense of uncertainty makes us more vulnerable to rejection in general. Still, over reading signs of rejection may be preferable to underreading, in that much disappointment can be avoided by putting energy into those who do reciprocate with us as opposed to those who are distancing.

5. There are negative results for society at large due to rejection-sensitivity. People may pull back, particularly the shy and inhibited, out of concern over their public behavior or interpersonal reactions. Public life could become less public, with people retreating to social media online or simply isolating in their homes and at work. Dr. Leahy makes the case that this can weaken a culture due to the relative lack of input from an incredibly talented and diverse quiet and/or shy segment of society. The reason that America is becoming more rejection-sensitive is due to how fragmented and mobile our society has become. There has been a drop in the number of social activities we can arrange. Families are spread out further than before geographically, and society is now amazingly fast paced.

6. Shy adolescents may become more withdrawn in the face of rejection and end up avoiding others as a result. The social media acronym FOMO, or "fear of missing out," conveys the specter of emotional pain, such as pulling back. I have observed that many shy clients with continuing detachment versus connection may set up a pattern of withdrawal that can lead to loneliness and depression. Importantly, studies have shown that young adults are affected by loneliness as often or as much as the elderly.

One potentially positive aspect of social networking sites is that research points out that many people are willing to talk about themselves on these sites when they are stressed. Thus, by reaching out during troubled times, an individual may gain social support from peers. Such interpersonal caring, online or offline (and of course, be careful to use only trusted sites online), can provide a means to buffer people against loneliness and depression, thus increasing happiness.

To improve social interactions and connections, it is helpful to decrease negative thoughts that drive loneliness. As F. Scott Fitzgerald once wrote, "In a real dark night of the soul, it is always three o'clock in the morning, day after day." Loneliness is painful, but with efforts "to get out there," it is usually never permanent. High social anxiety, as well as significant shyness, can be followed by some measure of loneliness. At the same time, and what is sometimes characteristic of shy responses, it is important to make the distinction that loneliness is different from aloneness, which is a desire for solitude.

General efforts to decrease loneliness, especially for the shy, involve that which is sensible. Try to be with people, at least part of the time, and more often. Slowly increasing quality social relationships does help. For the shy, quality social media, including chat and discussion groups, may be less anxiety arousing than face-to-face initial interpersonal contact. When interacting with others face-to-face, caution is in order. Perhaps meant humorously or not, to avoid conflict, it is a good idea to steer away from talking about religion or politics, as they can inflame an otherwise nice conversation.

7. Interestingly, one advantage of shy individuals carefully reading their environment for signs of rejection is that it makes it easier for them to maintain relationships with those who are accepting and supportive.

How to break the rejection-sensitivity cycle will be discussed in detail within the treatment sections of *Successful Shyness*.

Isolation, Avoidance, and Withdrawal

Isolation is another prominent symptom of shyness in that the shy individual who experiences discomfort in social situations will oftentimes pull back, avoid, or withdraw from interpersonal contact. The withdrawal from being social is usually due to behavioral inhibition. This type of inhibition is simply a way to engage in the safety behavior of keeping to oneself as a habitual self-imposed strategy to manage any social discomfort. Psychological research points to an underlying feature of behavioral inhibition as being due to intolerance of uncertainty. That is, if a shy person cannot reasonably tell that their upcoming social encounter is going to go well, they may not be able to deal with the uncertainty and withdraw. Of course, most social situations are somewhat fluid and don't always go according to script; thus, they can be uncertain in nature for all of us to some degree. The point is that even though behavioral inhibition and withdrawal are not always problems, seeking refuge comes at a cost. Therefore, we can all benefit from venturing out at times, and by using the techniques and strategies in *Successful Shyness* as described, your efforts in this regard will become easier.

Fortunately, as the shy learn to decrease their anxiety by participating socially on their own terms, they develop a greater tolerance of uncertainty. One helpful method in this regard is to learn that you don't need to have just right experiences. That is, you can allow for some imperfection when socially interacting and learn to be self-accepting. Psychologist Dr. Nathaniel Branden goes so far as to say that we really don't do anything "wrong;" we've just tried something, and it didn't work. Back to the drawing board we go is the only natural consequence, or "try, try, again." As has long been informally advised in clinical psychology, the "courage to be imperfect," or just letting things flow, flaws and all, can help eliminate the need for exactly right or perfectionistic responding. It was Woody Allen who said, "80 percent of success is showing up." In other words, just get involved, make that call, introduce yourself to someone, and meet someone new. It may well go better than you think, not necessarily flawless, but imperfectly good.

Shyness research also indicates that shy people often exhibit "hypervigilance for negative social cues and problematic self-focused attention." In clearer language, a shy person can quickly become aware of how others may be reacting to them, even in the slightest of ways. In turn, the shy person will strongly focus on their own concern about how they think they are coming across to others. Not surprisingly, public speaking is listed by the largest number of people in surveys that assess for types of social anxiety and avoidant behavior. Public speaking involves direct and instant evaluation by others, which can be concerning for many, if not most, people, including the shy and non-shy alike. It is common to hear, "What if my talk doesn't go well?" or "What if those people are critical of what I have to say?" Instead of engaging in unproductive worry, such as often asking "What if" type questions, simply suspending the self-reflection for a time can help. Shy individuals can use productive worry as an antidote by asking themselves, "What can I do to solve this problem or proceed with optimism?" Another way to view thoughts is that they do not necessarily turn out to be reality. We may worry about possible misfortune, but we can remind ourselves that this type of thought is merely a passing consideration. Anticipatory concern doesn't need to stop us from proceeding with what we like to do. Oftentimes, by just going ahead, many find that their tension decreases. This book will show you ways to relax yourself right before proceeding.

One way to determine whether shyness is a problem for you is if it interferes with what you would like to do. Common examples include dating, socializing with friends and family, giving a presentation, or advancing one's career. The contemporary question is, can the cyberworld help? In general, social media sites on the internet may promote social interaction, including support, which can result in shy participants feeling more comfortable. Currently, popular social media platforms include instant messaging, chatting, and social networking sites. These sites include podcasts, blogging, microblogging (e.g., Twitter), and video sharing sites. On the downside, internet social media platforms can also contribute to FOMO, when individuals aren't able to participate as often as they would like.

Of course, one appropriate reason for avoidance is cyberbullying. In the case of shy and sensitive individuals who are exposed to cyberbullying, one way to combat it, interestingly enough, is with other social media. That is, the shy (or non-shy) can access online sites that provide acceptance and support. Also, social media activities give a little more time for contemplation before responding compared to off-line or face-to-face interactions.

Research on social media has pointed toward extroverts as more likely to use social networking sites, instant messaging, and video chats. By contrast, introversion has been associated with more passive social media involvement. More specifically, internet studies have shown that extroverts tend to use interacting social media sites more, while shy individuals have less webcam usage. Further, introverts may like social media platforms that provide anonymity. Some social psychological research has pointed toward individuals with greater emotional stability (including those who are less anxious) apparently relying less on these sites. However, constructive use of social media sites can induce higher arousal and elevate mood for an individual, resulting in positive emotional experiences. In general, social media has provided mechanisms to connect, communicate, and interact. With the rapidly advancing use of social media, individuals are becoming more aware of their own self-identity and social identity. The downside involved in online social media is the FOMO and cyberbullying potential mentioned above. And of course, there is a downside for the shy when its use provides a way to frequently avoid face-to-face interactions.

Many individuals socially isolate by choice, but shy people may pull back more out of a concern that interactions will turn negative for them. Of course, dealing with other people in various social situations can be challenging for everyone, yet more so for the shy, quiet, or reserved individual. On the satirically humorous side, as Linus stated in one of Charles Schulz's *Peanuts* comic strips, "I love mankind…It's people I can't stand." Indeed, to ward off negative emotions such as depression, shy individuals can be gently guided into some easy, positive social situations. By engaging socially online or in everyday life, you can learn that people can, in fact, be quite tolerable, even enjoyable. Importantly, when face-to-face time increases through connection and involvement, self-esteem generally improves.

Cynical Shyness

Dr. Bernard Carducci, a psychology expert on the concept of cynical shyness, describes a subset of shy teens who can become shy, withdrawn, and basically incredibly angry at others for having been rejected or ignored. This can be considered the dark side of shyness and withdrawal, with negative social media posts and school threats as powerful examples. It is certainly not shyness alone that causes the problem, but the teen's unwillingness, or in some cases, incapability, to express their frustration and anger appropriately. Tension builds in the cynically shy and can be acted out in negative and sometimes violent ways. Adolescents with this behavioral pattern, again to emphasize, are not simply shy but are also usually angry, anxious, depressed, and have significant antisocial tendencies.

Shyness and anger, combined with acting out behavior, can be a problematic mixture if not processed and expressed constructively. In fact, profound cynical shyness can sometimes lead to impulsive, out-of-nowhere rage responses. Of course, we must be mindful, at least with adolescents, that, as has been accurately said, "Teens have better accelerators than brakes." With cynical shyness, immediate treatment in the form of individual and group counseling or psychotherapy is indicated. The process can start with a thorough evaluation with a qualified mental health professional. Once rapport and trust are established, cynical shyness can be turned around by focusing on positive ways in which to communicate frustration and anger. Meanwhile, if there are indicators of more enduring negative personality traits developing, such as a tendency to be antisocial, more intensive psychological treatment is needed.

Shyness and Anger

At times, anger is a natural, even appropriate, response to threats. When we need to defend ourselves, anger can be viewed as necessary for survival. Important for the shy person to know is that there are basically two approaches to handling anger—expression or suppression. Expression of anger, or angry feelings, in an assertive manner is healthy. If shy, there can be a priority on blending in with others or not standing out. Taking such a backseat approach can lead to suppressing anger—essentially holding it all in, which can be problematic. One other barrier to the expression of anger can be the shy person's concern over any social disapproval. On the one hand, the suppression of anger could prevent a difficult interpersonal situation from escalating. One major risk is that anger not expressed can turn inward, which may result in physical symptoms such as high blood pressure and overall tension. Also, holding on to anger might ultimately be expressed in disguised form. This is why psychology came up with the term "passive-aggressive" behavior to explain the roundabout way some individuals deal with their anger. Examples of passive-aggressive responses include the use of indirect, hostile humor (sarcasm), or through silence and withdrawn behavior. Some psychology experts insist that people who show up late for important on-time events are being passive-aggressive. I'm not so sure. My mom always said that those who arrive late were just being "slightly rude."

Case Vignette
When Anger is Situational
It is important to consider that anger can be highly situational. For example, an ordinarily calm, self-described shy person, thirty-four-year-old Asad, found himself getting angry on an infrequent basis in his role as a finance manager at a large office. He became surprised at his own uncharacteristic tirade about the office coffee maker not working on one occasion. Asad self-reported that he usually "stuffed it" when it came to negative feelings and only rarely openly expressed problems. That is, until his anger got the best of him. He offered an explanation in counseling that included a cascade of negative events. On the day of his coffee maker problem, it turns out that earlier in the morning he had just gotten a speeding ticket as he was hightailing it to work. This caused him to be late, and he was habitually concerned about any criticism he might receive from his superiors. He said, "I'm too anxious to speak up at times because I don't want to be criticized." Asad then followed with, "My angry outburst was embarrassing to me." Further, the reason he was delayed going out the door

in the first place was because he had an extended argument with his wife the night before and was sleepy in the morning. Situations and circumstances like this can wreak havoc with our equanimity, or, simply put, our ability to remain calm under stress.

In working with Asad, I likened his situational anger response that came on so strongly to a ball of string that is bound up and needs to be unraveled. Shy individuals often report not wanting to communicate negative actions or reactions to others possibly because they could be criticized or judged. There are alternatives. For example, as will be discussed in detail within the treatment section of *Successful Shyness*, acknowledging frustration and anger to others can bring understanding. Asad was willing and motivated to work on some simple phrases to use when anger might override his ordinarily calm manner. We rehearsed several assertive responses, including, "Wow, I just overreacted, which I don't do too often, but the last twenty-four hours have been kind of rough for me." Or, if others in the office were taken aback, Asad came up with his own verbal reaction, "Geez, sorry—my annoyance with this damn coffee maker got the best of me." Finally, it is important to use self-compassion when we generate an unanticipated meltdown. When accurate, positive statements such as "I'm glad that I normally handle these kinds of situations relatively well enough" will be helpful.

In general, if you are shy but also find yourself angry at times, look for positive ways to respond. For example, asserting yourself can work in many different situations. When we are assertive, we are representing our feelings and communicating them effectively with others. Whether it be frustration or anger, you can convey your displeasure without being aggressive or, on the contrary, too passive. Learning assertive responding will be discussed in the main treatment section as a helpful way to clearly communicate with others. Many other tools and strategies for developing successful shyness will be detailed throughout this book.

Worry as Thinking on Overdrive

Worrying can be painful. Have you heard of the term worrywart? A worrywart is someone who dwells or ruminates too much on difficulty or troubles. As Descartes famously stated, "I think, therefore I am." Enter modern psychology to remind us, "Just don't overthink." Dr. Michael Yapko, a prominent psychologist, has also offered an important observation on thoughts and rumination. Initially, Dr. Yapko quoted Socrates, the great philosopher who offered the famous dictum: "The unexamined life is not worth living." Next, he went on to offer a counterpoint: "But a life overexamined may not be worth living either." Of course, a healthy dose of worry can help us move away from potentially threatening situations and operate with safety in mind. This is true whether we decide to drive around a storm rather than right into it or decide not to ask for a raise from the boss immediately after he fell down some stairs at work. Unfortunately, those who are tense, including the shy and anxious, tend to worry more and are likely to view their worry as "forecasting" potentially dangerous or uncontrollable situations. Also, in the context of those who are shy and socially anxious, their worry is likely to focus on not performing well in interactions with others.

Fortunately, learning to decrease any negative self-talk can rapidly help those who are concerned about how worry has impeded their ability to socialize. A simple example would be a shy, socially anxious young adult worrying about whether they came across well when talking with friends about politics. Worry may come in the form of negative self-talk when this shy person thinks, "I keep going over and over what I said yesterday, and I think I upset my friends. I shouldn't talk about politics in the first place. It's my fault." However, many shy individuals have learned to turn down or decrease their high reactivity level and thought preoccupations. Healthy social adjustment may depend, to some extent, on not worrying too often about how family and friends may react. In fact, overt or visible worry can backfire as others may notice and keep their distance so as not to cause the shy person more discomfort. Learning relaxation procedures along with focused breathing (both of which are detailed in the treatment section) can go a long way in terms of being able to respond to others in a calmer way.

Shyness and Loneliness

There is a distinction to be made between being alone, social isolation, and loneliness. Regarding being alone, it is often seen as a choice. In social isolation, an individual simply has few connections. In loneliness, there is a sense of discomfort about being alone or socially isolated. Thus, a shy person may be socially isolated and not particularly concerned about having only a few connections, or lonely and feel emotional pain from not being with as many other people as they would like. Because being apart from others can be a risk factor for depression, it is important to find opportunities to be engaged. We can appreciate that for a shy person, even though they may want to reach out, it is often hard to accomplish, at least initially. This is an oblique reference, but the following Japanese proverb seems to apply: "The nail that sticks out gets pounded down." In the case of the shy, the internal thought process seems to run in the direction of "not sticking out" thus "I won't get shot down or rejected." The chapters on effectively managing shyness offered in this book will include various Practice Opportunities to help with engagement. These social interaction guides, so to speak, will help you gain skills to increase face-to-face time with others as appropriate or desired and come to enjoy it as you follow through.

As we have seen, social media has positive and negative implications for loneliness. For example, in the case of cyberbullying, social media has been used to harass people. Should this happen to an already shy, sensitive individual, near-total isolation may occur. Loneliness can then take hold after isolation keeps someone from virtually any social contact. In general, limiting social media, not eliminating it, will help to lower loneliness and depression—mostly by getting out there and spending time with those you know can be supportive. An important research statistic is that loneliness can occur in young adults as often as in the elderly.

Interestingly, millions of people now engage in what's called "parasocial interaction." In this type of interaction, the internet makes it easy to form emotional ties with performers and personalities or follow them as "friends" on social media. This might help with loneliness, but not completely because socializing is one-sided, thus parasocial. This is true because celebrities and others do not usually respond. There is more reason to increase social skills while young and keep those face-to-face interactions going.

Chapter 5

Further Assessment Aspects of Shyness

In this final assessment chapter, before heading into the treatment section (Part 2), several different approaches to assessing shyness will be discussed, including: attributional style and locus of control, a simple method to assess and structure a shyness problem, the three main interpersonal styles model, and finally, the BASIC-ID Model: assessing day-to-day psychological dimensions.

Attributional Style and Locus of Control
Attributional Style
Basically, all of us attribute events to different types of causes and produce reasons for why they occurred. Psychologist Dr. Bernard Weiner has conducted research in this area wherein attributions for success (versus failure) can be assessed. Listed below are the three main types of attributes and their relationship to how we interpret events.

1. Internal or external. With an internal attribution, an individual can conclude that something happened that they were responsible for (e.g., "I wasn't communicating with her clearly; that's why she walked away."). Or with an external attribution, something outside of their actions was responsible (e.g., "She walked away, but I noticed her friend was calling her over.").
2. Stable or unstable. The cause or attribution is something that is stable or permanent (e.g., "I can never speak up in public."). An unstable cause or attribution would sound quite different (e.g., "I don't think I speak up very well when the room is too loud to hear feedback from others.").
3. Specific or global. A specific attribution is one in which there is a certain set of circumstances (e.g., "I have a hard time reading technical journals but can really get the meaning out of most other types of materials."). The more global cause or attribution is one that occurs in every situation, (e.g., "I don't know what it is, but when I pick up anything to read these days, I get distracted and put the material down."). Shy individuals can be hard on themselves and therefore are more likely to make negative internal, stable, and global attributions if not careful. Let's look at a clinical example in the form of a case vignette.

Case Vignette
Making a Negative Internal, Stable, and Global Attribution

Raul was an engaging middle-aged man who worked for a beverage distributor. He not only had a stable job, was married with children, and had several hobbies as well. He attended counseling sessions to work on what he considered to be his "dour outlook." His wife wholeheartedly agreed that dour was an apt description for him. Further, he self-reported being shy and saying that it had affected his work with colleagues at times. They viewed him as being "distant," as he put it. Looking at Raul's explanations for his social behavior, it was clear that he was on the more troubling side of the three main attributional styles. First, in response to his increasingly negative outlook on life, he said, "I just am always down, I guess. It's me; I can't help it." Clearly, this was a pessimistic *internal* attribution that not only affected him but also his family. When exploring whether his attributions also ran in the direction of stable or unstable, sure enough, they were *stable*. Raul would comment that he is always down, and when he recognizes that it affects his family, he stated that he feels even worse. Further, he attributed the cause of his problems to being *global* in the sense that they had a permanent quality. "My father said he was depressed, and I think I've been too—probably for the longest time off and on when I think about it."

Raul's set of circumstances sound difficult and were, but changing one's attributions is not always that hard—it just requires some thought combined with attitude adjustment. Dr. Paul Watzlawick, a prominent psychologist, wrote a book with the interesting title *The Situation is Hopeless: But Not Serious*. In other words, if we just examine how we are looking at things and don't let our shyness or depression do all the talking, things can change for the better. In Raul's case, he was able to come up with examples wherein he wasn't dour or down. When he looked at happy times, he became less internally responsible, so to speak. That is, his attribution turned more *external* to himself. Also, once he took stock in his self-assessment of not always being down, he could consider that even though his father was depressed, it didn't necessarily mean he would be to the same degree or as often (*unstable*). Importantly, when working on his attributions, as is true for any shy person, the shyness tended to recede to a more comfortable level over time. That is, when Raul came up with more realistic, *specific* attributional causes for his behavior, he became more hopeful and, as a result, began to speak up more at work and with his family.

Indeed, things seemed hopeless, but they weren't that serious in that Raul could change his outlook, which resulted in more social relating while feeling fairly positive. This is basically the premise of CBT: we look at our own thoughts, do some fine tuning in the direction of being more accurate and realistic, and good things begin to happen more often. Interestingly enough, it turns out Abraham Lincoln may have been one of the original cognitive theorists. At one point in his long political career, after having interacted with thousands, he stated, "Most people are about as happy as they make up their minds to be." In our psychological treatment, it is rewarding to see people find the positive when it is there rather than overly focusing on the negative, which can be a distortion of reality. Basically, the goal is to move from an external locus of control to an internal one (note that an external locus of control is not the same as an external attribution in this context). There are those who can be stubborn though, not to mention humorous. I recall one instance wherein I finally had to agree with a client concerning his pessimistic stance. I essentially had to acknowledge, "You do still seem cognitively poised to interpret many situations negatively." His reply was, "Yes, but recently I've been feeling more positive about my negative views."

Practice Opportunity
Working with Your Attributional Style and Locus of Control
As an informal way to assess your own attributional style in a specific social situation, use the lines below to write down what causes you came up with. Ones that represented internal or external, stable or unstable, specific or global attributions, or explanations for what you thought and how you responded.

Identify a social situation (e.g., asking a friend to go to the movies and they decline).

_____

_____

Did I make an internal or external attribution (e.g., I forgot he doesn't like doomsday themes anyway [external])?

_____

_____

Was it a stable or unstable attribution (e.g., I have a problem remembering my friends' preferences [stable]?

_____

_____

Did it have a specific or global attribution aspect (e.g., it seems that I can't recall only those movies my friends dislike [specific])?

_____

_____

Locus of Control

Attributional style includes the internal-external dimensions of locus of control as two alternative causes but deserves special attention. That is, if we are in a specific set of circumstances during a busy social activity, we might not be able to actively think about how we are coming across. We can think about what types of attributions we made afterward. However, if we concentrate on the related concept of just locus of control, we can think on our feet quickly. We can decide whether we believe our actions are our own (internal locus of control) or somehow controlled by outside influences beyond ourselves (external locus of control) during the conversation.

Case Vignette
Internal or External Locus of Control

For example, take Avril, a young adult waitress who demonstrated her internal locus of control in one conversation. She believed that when she was talking with her friend Stan and he said he had to go, it was not because of anything she said. In fact, she inferred that Stan tended to keep his conversations under one minute for fear that otherwise he would be viewed as elaborating too much. Later the same day, Avril had a discussion with her restaurant manager, who tended to have an *external* locus of control causation. She said, "Whenever my manager talks with me, I really don't get the sense he's listening to my issues. It seems like a one-way conversation and out of my hands." In counseling, Avril learned to use more assertions when talking with her manager as well as with others. She learned to mention her issues at the beginning of conversations and remind the person she was talking to what those issues were toward the end of any talk. Avril said, "I used my 'issue reminders' at the end of talks, and people did seem to acknowledge them more. I felt like my take on things was actually being heard." Good progress was made in combining an assertive stance with a strong internal locus of control.

Regarding the *internal or external attribution style* concept and the *internal or external locus of control* theory, there is a twist as the terms seem to overlap. By accurately making an external attribution as the cause of a particular problem rather than an internal one, such as self-blame, we are on solid ground. However, with an external locus of control, a person is likely to see things happen in one's life that may be beyond their personal efforts. There is a conclusion drawn about a particular event: external circumstances will determine what happens. We generally want to develop an internal locus of control, meaning that we are determining our own actions and taking credit for what we've accomplished. People with an internal locus of control seem to have a more productive time in social and other situations. Thus, we can strive to make an accurate internal or external attribution to any situation, but in general, we want to build an internal locus of control rather than an external locus of control. Referencing an internal locus of control, we perceive our actions as due to our own effort and abilities. With an external locus of control, we feel that forces outside of our direct control are responsible for many of our actions.

In summary, we can all work on developing a relatively optimistic attributional style appropriate to the situation. Making accurate attributions for our actions can help us effectively manage our daily behavior and outlook. In assessing your attributional style and locus of control, take stock in the fact that these important ways of assessing our own actions will be helpful in managing social situations effectively.

A Simple Method to Assess and Structure a Shyness Problem

One way to assess and structure a problem you're having with shyness during a social situation or activity is to follow the FIDO acronym as outlined below:

F is for frequency
I is for intensity
D is for duration
O is for outcome

Case Vignette

Frequency, Intensity, Duration, and Outcome Assessment

For example, Isaac, an elderly man, complained of not hearing well, such that when he met with people for a social event, he became frustrated when more than one person talked at a time. In counseling, we reviewed the FIDO method as something he could use and remember when involved in conversation with others. Isaac estimated that the *frequency* of having discussions with multiple people was only about once or twice a month. He said, "Usually I'm at home and reading or going online. I like studying history." Regarding *intensity*, Isaac recalled how he could get quite flustered when trying to hear people all at once, as when there is a crossover of voices. He commented, "I think they notice my facial expressions. It's crazy because my thought at these times is that my friends must think I'm constipated. Geez, it's just that I'm 'straining' to hear each one." Fortunately, the *duration* of these difficult encounters is not that long because Isaac has learned to be assertive enough to ask others, "One at a time, please. I'd like to hear what everyone has to say." The *outcome* for this individual has been good because he hasn't let his occasional shyness and retiring style get the best of him. Instead, Isaac finds himself stepping into conversations rather than avoiding them to go and read. He was pleased with his progress in this area and commented, "I just think of FIDO like the dog; not that I have a dog named Fido, but you know what I mean."

Practice Opportunity

Using the Four FIDO Assessment Elements

You can use the FIDO method to assess a shyness problem by detailing its four elements on the left side. Then, on the right side, write down your responses as they pertain to a shyness problem you had in a social situation or activity.

As an example, here are Isaac's responses:

	FIDO	Response
Frequency:	Only once or twice a month	"I might socialize more if I can update my hearing aids."
Intensity:	Moderate, gets flustered	Crosstalk makes hearing each person difficult.
Duration:	Brief, due to ability to assert	"One at a time please. I'd like to hear everyone."
Outcome:	Good	Increased motivation to converse with others

Try the FIDO method yourself by detailing its four elements on the left and then writing down your responses to a recent problematic social activity or situation on the right.

	FIDO	Response
Frequency:	_____	_____
Intensity:	_____	_____
Duration:	_____	_____
Outcome:	_____	_____

Three Main Interpersonal Styles Model

One useful way to assess your own interpersonal style, as first listed in chapter 3 in the **Assessing Broad Personality Features section** above, is to consider Dr. Karen Horney's straightforward model. In the works of psychiatrist Dr. Horney, she succinctly discusses three different main interpersonal response styles:

A. Moving toward people
B. Moving away from people
C. Moving against people

Dr. Horney's theory is that we use one of the above main interpersonal styles predominantly. In doing so, the style predominantly used may work as much as 80 percent of the time. Regarding the other 20 percent of your dealings with others, you may need to switch to one of the other three styles. For example, if a shy individual uses the "moving away" style most of the time, then it is likely to work yet does not foster social interaction. When another, let's say, bolder individual approaches and begins to annoy a shy individual, then they need to switch styles. In this instance, a brief change to the "moving against" style could work, with the shy person telling the bully firmly to "back off."

Similar to the introversion/ambivert/extroversion continuum, many people may have a hybrid style wherein they use a combination of the moving away and moving toward styles depending on the circumstances. The main point is that there is usually one of the three interpersonal styles that is used predominantly by an individual. If you can identify and become aware of which of the three styles you mainly use, there is a good chance you can learn to relate to others, taking advantage of the positive characteristics associated with your main interpersonal style. For example, it is likely that the shy use a moving away interpersonal style for the most part. In this style, many shy individuals can relate because it is essentially avoidance. By moving away from others, they have not only fewer social interactions but also perceived safety for the shy in not feeling scrutinized or judged. The moving toward style may also be a predominant one for shy people to use. In this style, moving toward others is akin to "going along to get along." With this style, people generally see the shy person as cooperative and friendly; indeed, positive behaviors cultivate mutual support. The third interpersonal style, that of moving against, is probably the lowest frequency found in the shy, because it is essentially an aggressive style, seen more in those who are socially dominant, and at times even pushy.

Case Vignette

Rafael, a fifty-year-old father of two teenage children, supported his family as a retail salesperson for a high-end home remodeling firm. His wife worked as a registered nurse in the home healthcare sector. When Rafael entered counseling, it became clear that he seemed always eager to please. And please he did to everyone who met him. His wife said, "Everyone loves Rafael; he's so approachable and friendly." Rafael himself agreed that he had the moving toward style when the three main interpersonal ways of being in our social world were discussed. He also said that he was more introverted than not and had adopted an outgoing way of expressing himself only as the result of extensive sales training. A recent problem arose when "upper management," as Rafael put it, cut salaries for the entire workforce. His wife and close friends, in whom he often confided, told him that he should use his "gift of gab" to sway management to keep his salary right where it had been. This approach did not meet with Rafael's approval. He explained that "my immediate boss will see right through it because he went to the same sales seminars that I did." We discussed a simple strategy to tryout. Basically, I suggested that he try the moving against style, but not in a mean way. Rafael was a quick study, and he agreed that if he was just more direct and assertive but not overly nice, management might get the point. He said that they well know that "we are all just trying to support our families." The next time I saw Rafael, he excitedly exclaimed, "I did it. I talked with my immediate boss very directly, and he listened to me." I congratulated him and asked if he had heard anything back from management. Rafael commented that, regrettably, they told the whole salesforce, "We are taking your concerns under advisement." He and I thought about it and agreed that when rendering such a "corporate response," it is usually company code for "We'll think about it." Nevertheless, Rafael felt confident about his new ability to switch interpersonal styles as the situation called for it. Further, he said that he wanted to teach the three different interpersonal styles to his wife and children.

Practice Opportunity

As an example, here are Rafael's responses:
- A) Moving toward (e.g., "I went out with a friend and offered to pay for our coffee drinks at BucksStar.")
    1) Rafael demonstrated a consistently friendly approach to others.
- B) Moving away (e.g., "I became even more detached and withdrawn when my mother-in law wanted to discuss why I've been so quiet.")
    1) This individual only became temporarily detached when he heard "no raises" and withdrew from contact with his managers only briefly.
- C) Moving against (e.g., If Evan tells me to comb my hair again, I'm going to let him know he should knock it off.")
    1) "I did it. I talked with my immediate boss very directly, and he listened to me." (Note: Rafael was being appropriately assertive here).

In the lines below, write down one or two examples of when you used each of the three interpersonal styles.
- A) Moving toward (e.g., "I went out with a friend and offered to pay for our coffee drinks at BucksStar.")
    1. _____
    2. _____

- B) Moving away (e.g., "I became even more detached and withdrawn when my mother- in-law wanted to discuss why I've been so quiet.")
    1. _____
    2. _____

C) Moving against (e.g., If Evan tells me to comb my hair again, I'm going to let him know he should knock it off.")

    1. _____

    2. _____

Summary Points in Shyness Assessment

In Part 1 of this book, you've had the opportunity to learn more about the characteristics and dimensions of shyness as well as its counterpart, social anxiety. Regarding anxiety, specifically social anxiety, it is not a good idea to try to suppress it. The practice opportunities in both Part 1 and the next section, Part 2, offer various techniques and strategies to instead acknowledge "social interaction distress" and manage it constructively. Studies have shown that trying to suppress anxiety by attempting to stop your anxious thoughts seems to have the paradoxical effect of increasing such thinking. It may not surprise anyone that simply letting anxious thoughts float by can be difficult. In fact, individuals with shyness problems, oftentimes accompanied by social anxiety, have a lot with which to contend. For example, one research effort found that patients with significant social anxiety showed greater concern over mistakes, doubted their own actions, and were high in self-consciousness. Such internal distress will certainly cause one to have anxious thoughts, as in wondering what is going wrong, in an attempt to stop the emotional pain. Fortunately, as this will be explained in Part 2, the treatment section of *Successful Shyness*, you can work on modifying your thoughts to be more positive and realistic.

Social skills in most individuals may be at least adequate, but for a shy person, it is their self-confidence in these skills that is low. One main reason that we want to effectively manage shyness is that even though it's a trait and not abnormal in any way, it can involve emotional pain or suffering. For example, when we feel as though a social activity didn't go well because we weren't able to reach out or interact much, we take a hit to our self-confidence. As we've learned in the assessment of shyness, when we are concerned about how we're coming across to others, practicing social interactions can help us improve. Experiencing emotional pain can be reduced as social skills effectiveness improves. Implications for treatment will be discussed in Part 2 with CBT-type intervention strategies focusing on challenging any unrealistic, negative appraisals the shy person may have regarding their social skills. With more accurate attributions made for our social actions, an increase in self-confidence can be expected. In addition to the above CBT interventions mentioned, paying attention to the emotional expressions of those around us can shift the focus from ourselves and allow us to be more attuned to others. Thus, the interpersonal and relational strategies in Part 2 will provide concrete problem-solving avenues to explore through relevant Practice Opportunities.

As a shy person recognizes they are becoming anxious, they may misinterpret the sensations as causing harmful physical consequences. Thus, the shy may then back away from social interactions further as anxiety rises. Mindfulness and relaxation training methods can bring down the anxiety and reactivity level of a shy individual, which can then facilitate meaningful social involvement. As Part I has shown, once you've assessed your own level of shyness and social anxiety, you can learn how to deal with built-up tension and avoidance by getting out there and engaging in interpersonal activities. But how? The treatment section of this book (Part 2) will detail several ways to engage others. Practice opportunities provide the vehicle to learn how to cope in easy to more challenging situations. Apart from effectively interacting with others, much of becoming successfully shy involves improving your own awareness and insight. There are practice opportunities in both Part 1 and Part 2 of *Successful Shyness* that will help you learn more about your own personality style and characteristics, as well as positive coping behaviors, with increasing confidence toward the goal.

Social distress is often described by individuals as causing sadness, pain, or hurt. In fact, studies done with functional magnetic resonance imaging (fMRI) have shown that social distress and physical pain appear to be mediated by the same neural substrates. This finding points toward social and physical pain sharing the same neuroanatomical basis. Another interesting finding deals with social embarrassment. In a study on blood pressure, it was found that the longer one tries to hide one's feelings, the more demanding it becomes physically on an individual. This blood pressure dimension of higher arousal could explain why shy people avoid long social interactions. In essence, prolonged social engagement may be taxing for them due to embarrassment, or more likely, simply the fear of being embarrassed.

In general, when people experience a potentially embarrassing event, research has shown that they expect to be judged more harshly than they are. Interestingly, it is conjectured that shy, anxious individuals can relax somewhat for one main reason. It is that other people are seldom as judgmental as one would think, and they aren't all that attentive anyway. I suppose this could be the result of a presently individualistic and sometimes narcissistic cultural trend where "I" matters most in terms of self vs. other focus.

The reason I've included the above research in this summary, before we move on to treatment in Part 2, is that it demonstrates that you can learn to relax, people are less preoccupied with your actions than you might think, and you can unwind the worry about being embarrassed somewhat as a result. If you want to prove this to yourself, try the simple strategy of watching other people with a high level of attention and concentration. You will no doubt find that it is hard to maintain interest for very long. Indeed, the average human attention span has been decreasing over the years, likely due to an overall increase in the daily complexities of modern life. One important goal for becoming less preoccupied is to prioritize perceived self-efficacy. That is, developing the accurate belief that you can be effective in social situations through practice will go a long way in decreasing painful preoccupation. The treatment section of this book will explore several different strategies to increase self-efficacy. Techniques will also be detailed to better manage anxious thoughts and lead one to successful shyness responses.

Interestingly, one problem that shy and socially anxious individuals have actually stems from an asset. That is, because the shy and socially anxious are sensitive to how they interact in public, they have developed a highly tuned error activating system. Noticing potential errors before you make them in interactions with others has the advantage of, for example, not saying something insensitive or inappropriate. The problem aspect stems from being so quick to react to incoming information that it can be difficult to filter out irrelevant information. Apparently, calmer or less reactive adults are able to accomplish this filtering process more easily. These less sensitive, non-shy individuals simply don't have their "social radar" up. I even had one friend who once commented, "I talk so much that I've learned to tune myself out!" A unique, if odd, skill or talent indeed. If shy and socially anxious people happen to misread a social cue as negative when in fact nothing was meant by it, say a neutral hand gesture from another, the misinterpretations can leave them feeling the social exchange went poorly. Of course, we don't want misinterpretation of neutral gestures to interfere, so what to do? Like so many other shyness problems that can be effectively managed better, we now turn to the treatment section (Part 2) of *Successful Shyness*. As it follows the assessment chapters, the following broad treatment portion of the book will provide detailed strategies and techniques to build confidence and effective social skills.

Part 2

Developing and Maintaining
Successful Shyness

The chapters in Part 1 of *Successful Shyness* covered the assessment of various important aspects and dimensions of shyness. Assessment practice opportunities were designed to help you identify how you experience your own shy behavior. It's now time to cover the many ways to deal with the complex psychological trait of shyness. Part 2 includes many more practice opportunities, with their focus being on helping you learn ways to effectively manage shyness.

The main treatment for shyness is straightforward. Basically, get out more, do more things, and communicate with others throughout. The catch is that to be successfully shy, it is a good idea to socialize largely on your own terms to begin with and when you are ready. This will help you gain the confidence needed to initiate social interactions without becoming unnecessarily discouraged. One relevant saying is "small shoes for small feet;" and then you can try larger social roles in time with more confidence. In other words, as your confidence grows, and it will with increased social interactions, your inhibition will decrease.

A lot of becoming successfully shy involves what I would term "repeated engagement," which simply refers to spending time with friends and other important relationship opportunities over and over again. People like to associate with others who have earned their trust. By continuing to shoot at the target of frequent encounters, you will gain more familiarity with being social, which lowers anxiety and tension. Rejection may occur from time to time, but this is a fact of life. Strategies for dealing with rejection effectively are offered in the following chapters.

Let's not get ahead of ourselves, though. We first want to learn how to relax when anxious, particularly in social situations, so that we can approach interacting with others more calmly. The next chapter provides well-researched relaxation methods, including progressive muscle relaxation (PMR) which includes focused breathing and mindfulness.

Chapter 6

Ways to Relax When Anxious or Tense

Stress management, including relaxation methods, initially involves learning about the common warning signs of stress. You can apply the many general and specific coping strategies offered to deal with the effects of any stressful reactions you may be experiencing.

Warning Signs of Stress

Recognize common warning signs of stress, which can vary widely from one individual to another. Several of the most common warning signs are listed below.

1. Emotional and physical tension
2. Fatigue or lethargy
3. Accident proneness
4. Neck and back pain or strain
5. Headaches
6. Appetite and sleep changes
7. Alcohol or drug abuse

General Coping Strategies for Stress

A certain amount of stress in life is inevitable, and some stress is actually good for you if it helps to keep you alert and motivated. However, too much stress can elevate cortisol and other mobilizing biochemicals in your body, which can result in mood difficulties and undue wear and tear. Fortunately, there are specific ways to reduce tension and engage in constructive activities to counterbalance the stress in your life. Many of these helpful activities are listed below.

1. Be physically active: walking, sports, yoga, aerobic exercise
2. Set realistic goals and expectations; know your limitations
3. Be positive: and practice self-compliments
4. Learn relaxation skills:
    a. Progressive muscle relaxation (PMR)
    b. Focused breathing

    c. Mindfulness or present focus
5. Utilize good nutrition:
    a. Balanced diet
    b. Regular meals
    c. Decrease or eliminate alcohol and drugs.
6. Make lifestyle changes: realistic expectations, delegate responsibilities
7. Manage crises constructively: danger and opportunity both exist
8. Increase support system: Be active and direct in seeking connection
9. Decrease workload: take some time off, staycations or vacations
10. Develop hobbies and recreation: solo or participatory activities
11. Get organized
12. Use quiet time to relax
13. Listen to calming music
14. Try to get seven to nine hours of sleep each night
15. Enjoy meals with family or friends
16. Spiritual activities
17. Learn time-management skills; allow for breaks in your schedule
18. Engage in social activities of your choice

Active and Passive Relaxation Strategies

Physical exercise, including low-intensity walking and higher-intensity sports like jogging, can be very helpful in producing the relaxation response and reducing stress. Cardiovascular activities also help to reduce anxiety and anxiety-related physical discomfort. Some individuals like to relax in more passive ways, including playing board games, doing crossword puzzles, reading a book, browsing the internet, or watching TV. Both active and passive methods of relaxing are effective. Shy individuals may assess their own level of active versus passive ways in which to relax. This is one way to make sure that if you are engaged in many passive activities, you can balance them out with some active exercise and relaxation efforts, which can easily involve one or two other people.

As a result of engaging in active and passive relaxation strategies, you will become more aware of your physical reactions in general. For example, you can pay attention to how you're feeling in a social interaction. You can also actively attend to the facial expressions and body language of others, which can be instructive. However, paying too close attention can have the effect of causing others to experience negative feelings about the social exchange. In short, I suppose it is a matter of not looking too vigilant or uptight, which can make the other person feel uneasy. As will be discussed in detail in the chapters that follow, using relaxation techniques, mindfulness, or present focus, combined with breathing exercises, can help us achieve a desirable level of calmness. Relaxing and centering yourself before, during, and after a social encounter will help you maintain emotional and physical equilibrium.

Another characteristic of shyness and social anxiety that you may want to consider is how sensitive you are to common "social blunders." A social blunder can be as minor as forgetting to say goodbye. What happens with socially anxious individuals is that they view social blunders as having a large cost, such as people judging them as being socially incompetent. This is, of course, not true; everyone commits social blunders from time to time, knowingly or unknowingly. Most of us are able to view such blunders as temporarily embarrassing, but certainly not dire.

Interestingly, many performers have made looking socially inept an art form—truly comical. Take for example *The Three Stooges* sitcoms, which some have described as hilarious for their "stupid-funny" content. In the various episodes, it isn't hard to identify a social blunder, which happens nearly every thirty seconds. Of course, it could be that the audience is laughing at them, but it also seems clear that humanity is laughing with them—we recognize ourselves in such awkward social situations that occur in everyday life.

Anxiety has been broadly viewed by healthcare professionals as a fear of the unknown. When we don't know what is about to happen in certain situations, anxiety can rise rapidly. A corollary that could easily apply to shy and socially anxious individuals is the so-called intolerance of uncertainty. It means that by not tolerating a certain amount of uncertainty, negative cognitive, behavioral, and emotional reactions to events can occur. An example would be when someone who is socially anxious is invited to a party, but they aren't sure who will be attending, and their tension builds. Intolerance of uncertainty is a stark phrase as opposed to being uncomfortable with uncertainty, which everyone is from time to time. The problem comes when we are so intolerant of a naturally uncertain set of circumstances that worry and depression can follow. I suppose this is where a healthy denial comes into play; we can't constructively be worried about every uncertainty all the time. For example, living in California would be much more difficult if people had to think about earthquake potential every living moment. Of course, there is that Cal Tech scientist who offered the scary opinion regarding the large earth movement: "We are all here by geological consent, subject to change without notice." It would be interesting to survey all those who live in California, some forty million. I suspect most of us have not developed a complete intolerance of uncertainty, given the potential "Big One" remains a vague yet very real threat.

One main point in assessing your level of shyness and social anxiety is to be aware of how it might impact your worry and depressive responding. For example, if you notice that by avoiding situations and unfamiliar circumstances, your mood lowers and you're overthinking things, your anxiety is probably too high. Strategies to lower anxiety will be discussed in detail in the following treatment chapters of this book. Help will come in the form of learning how to regulate your emotions, increase your perceived control over situations, and use positive coping techniques to deal with social interactions. Another factor to consider, especially if you would like to see a mental health professional to help with managing your shyness or social anxiety, is a concept known as psychological mindedness. Those who develop high psychological mindedness are able to gain insight into their own actions, reflect on changing negative habits by bringing them into recognition, and then act positively. Individuals with lower psychological mindedness tend to benefit more by first learning about their shyness, social anxiety, and interpersonal behavior before attempting to change it. Not to worry, there are several important ways to establish psychological mindedness. First, simply pay attention to how you are coming across to others. Second, ask for feedback from a trusted peer so that you can check for any social interaction blind spots. Third, practice being aware of your emotions throughout the day.

Progressive Muscle Relaxation (PMR)

There is a method of relaxing the mind and body that is both active and yet calming. The procedure is called progressive muscle relaxation (PMR). This stress reduction procedure is an effective tool for decreasing anxiety and tension. PMR has been used for many years in clinical settings to facilitate the relaxation response. The procedure is easily learned in steps and can be routinely practiced at home. PMR can help boost confidence and calmer responses heading into any number of social situations or unfamiliar circumstances. Having this relaxation skill can also help in preparing for a meditation or mindfulness stance when under stress.

For those who are shy, learning the procedure, which includes focused breathing, can facilitate engagement in social interactions while experiencing less internal distress. Specifically, PMR can help you lower that uncomfortable feeling that comes from the muscles being activated and tense when anxious rather than relaxed. I have taught hundreds of clients how to systematically tense and then relax a series of major muscle groups to feel calmer and more relaxed in social situations. It works well, and because PMR is a skill-based procedure, regular practice will enable you to get better and better at unwinding tension. I initially used the original procedure from the popular manual *Progressive Relaxation Training* by psychologists Dr. Doug Bernstein and Dr. Tom Borkovec. Over the years, I've modified the PMR to include focused breathing. I also shortened some of the steps so that the entire muscle tension/relaxation cycle or sequence can be done in about twenty minutes.

Introduction to PMR

When we get anxious, our body's reaction is to tense muscles in preparation for action. This, of course, has its place, as we may need to react quickly to a threat. Because shy individuals tend to be on the high reactive side of the equation when it comes to social situations, learning a procedure that lowers muscle tension in the body can really help. By going through the muscle tension-relaxation exercises prior to a social interaction or situation, you can bring your physiological or body tension down significantly. When the body is less tense, our brains interpret this to mean that less threat exists, thus making it easier to calm down emotionally.

One PMR question that comes up from the get-go is: How does tensing muscles help to relax them? It is paradoxical, but a given muscle group cannot be tense and relaxed at the same time. Thus, first tensing a muscle group and then letting it relax tends to unwind any tightness that has built up in that area. One good analogy is a rubber band that is coiled or twisted up;

once you let go, it unwinds completely. In PMR, the goal is to become calmer from the muscle relaxation exercises, which involve first tensing up various muscle groups, then relaxing them. Practicing the procedure two to three times a week or more can help the body and mind learn how to relax fairly quickly.

Preparing for PMR

1. Find a comfortable place where you can go through the relaxation procedure with minimal distractions. Some people use a darkened room. When I use the procedure, it doesn't seem to matter how light or dark the room is; I just don't want to fall asleep.
2. Comfort is key. Wear loose-fitting clothes. Although even this simple guideline can be relaxed (no pun intended) in that no matter what you're wearing, it will still take only a matter of minutes to go through the entire procedure. I mention this because someone may want to do a select few of the total muscle tension-relaxation cycles before an event, for example in their car before giving a speech. This reminds me of when I went to physical therapy for my knee and was instructed to wear loose, gym-type clothing. The next thing I knew, I was being put through grueling exercises (not to be dramatic) to improve my condition. There is nothing grueling about PMR.
3. Importantly, if you have any physical complaint, condition, or injury that might cause muscular pain, always consult your physician before starting PMR. In fact, it is probably a good idea to go ahead and get a medical checkup first. One measure of success in this procedure is to witness your blood pressure go down from its baseline from the beginning of your practice sessions to the present.

As you go through the PMR procedure, don't worry if you go out of sequence or forget a particular muscle tension-relaxation group. I've done it many times. I just try to remember not to overlook that section of muscles the next time I practice. You'll get what I mean when you try PMR a few times. Speaking of remembering, it reminds me of a conversation I had with my dad one time as he was getting older. I asked him, "Are you having any memory difficulties?" and he said, "Not that I recall."

The General PMR procedure

1. Find a place where you can relax for about twenty to thirty minutes. When you begin, it's okay to look at each of the muscle tension and relaxation cycles listed and described here. In time, you may not even need to refer to the list, as the muscle groups have a logical order that is fairly easy to remember.
2. Following the PMR sequence, simply tense the muscle group described and hold for approximately five seconds. The timeframe does not need to be exact, and when tensing, there is no need to push it to the point of pain; stop before any discomfort.

3. The next step for each muscle group is to relax those muscles for about ten seconds. I recommend doing each muscle group twice. Basically, once doesn't seem to get the progressive relaxation effect, and more than twice doesn't add that much more relaxation. The scientific background to the progressive nature of the procedure refers to the physiological fact that as you tense and relax muscle groups, progression to adjacent muscle groups occurs. In this way, we become less tense and more relaxed across our entire body.

One physical analogy of this propagation effect would be a game of pool. Notice that when you rack up the balls and then hit them at the center point with the cue ball, the energy seems to go through or transfer from one ball to the next. Once all the major muscle groups of the body are more settled, the brain seems to automatically register or read this relaxation as "there must not be a threat, so let's calm down." The muscles relax just as dominos fall in a line.

The PMR Relaxation Sequence

1. Settle back in a chair. Lying down is also okay. Close your eyes if you want to concentrate on the muscle tension-relaxation cycle, but some people like to keep their eyes open. Make a fist with both hands and tense for five seconds. Next, relax the hands for about ten seconds.
2. Next, bend both hands back at the wrist, which will tense the muscles in the back of the hands and the forearms. Hold the tension for five seconds, then relax your hands back to a resting position for around ten seconds. If you type a lot, you may find yourself doing this simple tension-relaxation cycle almost automatically to prevent cramping during sustained activity. A good habit in and of itself.
3. Now clench both your hands into fists and bring them up toward your shoulders. This movement will help tighten the large muscles in the upper part of your arms, mainly the biceps. After holding the arms up on each side for five seconds, relax by slowly letting your arms down to your sides. Note the relaxation as the muscles in the arms are no longer tensed. As with all the muscle tension-relaxation cycles in the sequence, do each twice.

   My experience is that by doing both sides of the body at the same time, instead of the left and then the right (regarding the arms and legs), things move along at a quicker pace, yet the desired relaxation response still occurs.
4. The muscles in the face are next, and because they are smaller than other areas of the body, it may take a few practice sessions to notice changes. That is, in time, you will be able to tell how all your facial muscles will become more relaxed as the progression from the top of the face to the bottom facilitates a loosening of those muscles.

   First, wrinkle up your forehead and brow, somewhat like making a surprised stare, as you hold the tension for five seconds, then relax for ten seconds. As with the other muscle-tension cycles, repeat one more time. Notice how relaxing it can feel when your forehead smooths back out. Many researchers have hypothesized that tension headaches can involve the many forehead muscles that become constricted, almost like an unwanted headband.

5. Moving downward on the face, we come to the eyes, which you can close very tightly for five seconds. This muscle exercise is often seen spontaneously in those whom I would consider natural relaxers. These people know how to step away from reading or writing briefly to shut their eyelids, tense, and then release. Remember, the muscle tension-relaxation timeframes are all the same: tense for five seconds, then relax for ten seconds.

   As mentioned earlier, the number of seconds is approximate. The use of a stopwatch, while comical, is way over the top for simply trying to comply with the procedure. In other words, getting more uptight in the process of trying to relax is not the objective. Relax.

6. Here's a good one. Our jaws are powerful, and if we tense them up in response to stressful situations, our ancestral makeup tells us it may well be fight or flight time. This muscle tension-relaxation cycle is easy and effective. Tighten your jaw muscles by clenching your teeth together (carefully) and holding for five seconds, then relax for ten seconds. Regarding any areas of the body where you may have had a previous injury or even just mild pain, skip this or that part as you work through the PMR procedure.

   As a reminder, get clearance from your physician before you engage in PMR in the first place. Most people find that one or another area of their body is more tense as they go through this relaxation procedure. This is to be expected. But please recognize that tension is normal; pain is not. Common areas of more tension versus less are the jaw, neck, and back areas.

7. Now purse your lips, as in, press your lips together. Tension should build immediately all around the mouth area. Hold for five seconds, then relax for ten seconds. Repeat a second time. With only a few practice sessions with PMR, you will be able to notice how your hands, forearms, upper arms, facial muscles, neck muscles, and shoulders tend to relax together. Again, this spread effect is the progressive nature of how one muscle group is connected to another, which lets the tension fall like a row of dominoes.

   As American researcher Robert Sapolsky, PhD, explains in his book *Why Zebras Don't Get Ulcers*, these animals will tense up without thinking when they notice a lion's presence but otherwise leisurely forage around. In essence, they have, without giving it a single thought or practice, let the magic of progressive muscle relaxation return them to a state of calm. Our effort, particularly when shy, is not to overestimate any threat from social contact. If we do overrespond, we can go through our PMR procedure to help us turn down any high reactivity. Who knows? Over the long run, an ulcer or two may be spared, or at least there will be far less muscle tension.

8. Next, we turn our attention to below the face, basically the neck area and its major muscles. First, press your head backward against the chair you're seated in, or the bed if you're lying down. Tilting your head backward against a surface allows for instant tension. And as usual, tense for five seconds, then relax for ten seconds. As an aside, I've had good enough tension build simply by pulling my head back without anything to press against. The neck muscles always seem to respond quickly by tightening in the direction of the head movement. Have you ever watched an owl? I still can't figure out anatomically how they can move their head almost completely around. It seems like the owl's neck muscles would snap it back forward from all the torque-like exertion.

   Onward we go, with the next neck muscle tension-relaxation cycle achieved by now bringing your head forward. You can try to touch your chin to your chest, but you really don't have to bend your head down that far. Hold the tension for about five seconds, and then relax for around ten seconds. Allow yourself to relax further and further at this point, as it is what the body is designed to do, thus allowing nature to take its intended course. What's that physics law? A body at rest tends to stay at rest, and a body in motion tends to stay in motion. Through PMR, we are trying to get our body to temporarily rest or calm down so that we can then get it moving again for what will be an upcoming (and now more relaxing) social interaction or situation.

9. Now you can move on to the shoulder area. Shrug your shoulders and bring both up toward your ears (it sounds much harder than it is). Hold this position in tension for five seconds, and now relax by lowering your shoulders back to a resting position. As you take a ten-second relaxation, pause before you raise your shoulders for a second time and notice the contrast between how it is to tense the muscle groups done so far and the relaxation that comes upon the release of that tension.

10. This next area is the back, which is a common source for stress-related tension. To tense and relax this important part of the body, simply arch your back, which will cause your chest and stomach area to stick out slightly. Feel the tension in the upper body, then relax using the same five-second tension, ten-second relaxation cycle. Some people like to hold the tension and relaxation cycles longer, but it isn't necessary to get the full benefit of PMR.

11. It is at this juncture in PMR that I like to help clients with their breathing to relax even more. Because the back was just arched and the chest then expanded, it seems like a good point to interpolate or bring in the focused breathing technique. First, take a deep breath, filling your lungs, then hold it for five seconds, followed by ten seconds of relaxation, and repeat once. While now relaxing, breathe in through your nose, take a deeper breath if you are able, and exhale out through your mouth.

I'd say on average, people need to do this for only a minute or two, and their breathing "gets the idea" and tends to slow more naturally without prompting.

The main reason for a slower, deeper breathing pattern while you're doing PMR is that it accomplishes a couple of important physical goals. One is that it allows circulation to improve, which again lets the brain know that whatever threat is present, such as a complex social interaction, it can't be that demanding. The second is that it allows oxygen to be delivered more effectively throughout the body. Finally, we are then able to automatically receive the twin benefit of improved circulation and oxygen flow, which the brain interprets as…wait for it…we must be relaxing, no worries.

As a self-test, once you feel comfortable practicing the PMR procedure, notice how your hands may warm up a bit. This warming pattern is physiological proof that your body is indeed relaxing, with the blood circulating better and improved oxygenation coming alongside. The main result is a more aware, yet relaxed self. You are now equipped to face social situations with less hesitation and more openness. Continue through the last few tension-relaxation cycles in the PMR sequence.

12. Tighten up the stomach muscles next. This is a little easier said than done because the stomach muscles aren't that strong in the first place. When people complain of stomach tension, they are generally referring to the stomach itself, not the overlying muscles. I've found over the years that simply bearing down builds enough tension. We had one postdoctoral psychology intern at a psychiatric hospital where I practiced suggesting mental imagery for this area. I asked what he had in mind, and he said, "Just picture yourself getting punched in the stomach and the wind knocked out of you." Upon reflection, he agreed that such an image was ridiculously negative and overblown, just the opposite of relaxation's intent. Thus, let's just go with bear down, tensing the stomach area for five seconds, then relax for ten seconds while noticing the contrast between how the area feels when it is tense versus the now relaxed state.

13. We are almost done, with the next two exercises covering the waist down, basically the legs. The first tension cycle involves stretching the legs. Just stretch both legs out with your toes pointed straight or down for five seconds, then relax while taking a ten-second pause. As with the other muscle groups, repeat a second time. To get to the underside of the legs, below the knee area, or, in other words, the calf muscles, there is a second tension cycle. In this last one, stretch your legs out again, but this time point your toes up toward the ceiling, and you will feel the tension in your calves build immediately. Hold for five seconds, followed by ten seconds of relaxation, then repeat.

Throughout the tension-relaxation cycles, note how much more relaxed the muscle groups feel after you've done each muscle group twice. Some people report feeling warmer throughout their body, which is a direct result of increased blood circulation, which is a good thing. In general, people seem to fall into two groups—those who feel lighter because of their body relaxing, and others who feel a comfortable heaviness as their body relaxes into a chair, for example. Either lightness or heaviness is a physiological sign that you are relaxing, and you can count it as a successful overall response to the PMR procedure.

Finally, without having to tense or relax any muscles further, you can now mentally calm your entire body. Paying attention to how the arms feel more relaxed, the entire face, the neck and shoulder areas, and the back, you'll be able to unwind further. Check in once more with your breathing and slow it down again if there is any residual tension. Let your legs remain relaxed while you put it together with several simple self-statements, such as, "I just reviewed the major muscle groups in my body; I'm now calmer than when I started." You can also add, "I'll remember to breathe in through my nose and exhale out my mouth if I get tense again." If that sounds too long and wordy, try, "I'm now more relaxed." Accurate brevity has its benefits.

Once you've practiced the PMR procedure several times a week and feel comfortable, try using it prior to different social situations. You can employ any number of abbreviated PMR techniques, particularly if you're pressed for time. For example, many people lift their shoulders, then let them back down a few times and go into focused breathing. Sometimes this combination alone provides a cue for your entire body to relax somewhat. By the way, I've done this many times, and no one seems to notice. Do not, however, keep your shoulders in the lifted position as that would be akin to a Frankenstein posture. Come to think of it, don't let your shoulders droop either, as that might make you appear sad or tired. But I digress. The case vignette below reflects how one individual used this abbreviated PMR procedure to her advantage at work.

Case Vignette
Using an Abbreviated PMR Procedure
This brief case vignette explains how abbreviating the PMR procedure can work well on the fly or in stressful everyday situations. I had a business executive as a client. Mia, a young mother of two, would often need to go to an important meeting on a moment's notice. Mia would first raise and lower her shoulder muscles a couple of times. Next, she would pause to use focused breathing and include a brief mantra by saying to herself, "Breathe in confidence, exhale doubt," a phrase that she liked. Mia would then loosen her entire body by recalling the now familiar relaxing feeling she often achieved. She had essentially earned the calm response after having gone through the PMR procedure so many times. Mia reported that using these straightforward, abbreviated PMR steps helped her relax right before walking into a given meeting. She would practice the entire procedure when she was home and had the time, with her average number of relaxation sessions averaging two to three times a week.

To summarize, PMR puts the physiological phenomenon of muscle memory to work. When you do the entire PMR procedure enough times, as soon as you start with the hands, you might find your breathing automatically slowing down and relaxation increasing. Try PRM routinely to find out for yourself. By the way, I recommend practicing the PRM procedure about two to three times a week (or more if you like), consistent with a permissive approach. Many workbooks proclaim the benefits of going through PRM daily. This approach may work well for some, but I think it can add stress instead of reducing tension if you feel guilty for missing one day. Our new clinical mantra is to "strive for imperfection" as appropriate, which insulates us from preoccupation with having just right experiences.

The following points identify positive responses to PMR and how to manage problems with the procedure if any occur.

Benefits of Positive Responses to PMR
1. Stopped or decreased anxiety. Good work; give yourself some praise or reward.
2. Improved sleep. This indicates solid progress with PMR.
3. Decreased muscle aches. A good result is that with continued PMR is likely to help further.

Management of Problems with PMR
1. Falling asleep. Schedule your PMR at other times than after meals or right before bedtime.
2. Mind wanders. This tends to lessen with practice in PMR. Alternatively, let your mind wander some. That's okay; no harm, no foul.
3. It gets better, then worse. Recognize that learning takes place in increments with some setbacks and plateaus from time to time to be expected.

Once you've benefited from PMR's calming effects, you can use it before going through any of the Practice Opportunities offered in this book. Of course, you may still feel anxious when trying out new social interactions and situations, but you'll probably be less tense if you use PMR. Over the long run, PMR is a skill set that you can beneficially use for the rest of your life. As I recall from my graduate training in psychology, we were invited to "learn one, do one, teach one." This mantra works well for PMR wherein you can first learn the procedure, then do it (and practice during the week). Finally, you can help family and friends by teaching it.

I would encourage you to view any other PMR procedures that have been published in various books and clinical research offerings on stress management. Each one will offer a unique approach that may best fit your personal style. Recognize that in whatever form or shape it takes, the main goal for PMR is the same—to relax our muscles from built-up tension. The result of PMR is a calmer you.. As many of us are aware, or have come to learn, shyness can bring on internal discomfort when we are faced with a wide variety of social situations and new or unfamiliar circumstances. By using the PMR procedure before entering a given social interaction, you will be equipped with a calmer, more relaxed stance.

Case Vignette
Using a Complete PMR Procedure

Maria came to counseling with a concern about speaking to others at work. She felt as though her every move was being monitored. At thirty-five years old, she felt being shy and inhibited was "unreasonable." "I've gone to high school and college with several friends and had a good time interacting. Why do I hesitate with others now?" We discussed the fact that the various performance demands of a workplace can get many people anxious and tense at times.

Maria was receptive to counseling for her anxiety once it was explained as a natural response to her perception that she was being critically examined by others at work. Also, her work as a financial analyst at a large company was objectively stressful. She had high-stakes meetings on a regular basis and said that informal discussions with coworkers were also important. Maria had some insight into how her self-consciousness, mainly in terms of her sensitivity to how she was coming across to others, contributed to her being hesitant to speak to coworkers. We briefly reviewed the research on how it has been shown that many shy people worry about social criticism or judgment from others. The response by the shy is oftentimes clamming up, as in, it is better to not say anything and keep interactions to a minimum, thus avoiding possible ridicule.

In time, it will be helpful for Maria to speak up more and feel better about herself, yet we agreed that before more frequent interactions occur, learning to relax and decrease tension is the way to go. Progressive Muscle Relaxation (PMR) was taught to Maria, and she was willing to practice the procedure several times a week. In our first session after she had tried PMR at home, she reported that it didn't really work very well. When asked what happened, she said that she drifted off to sleep. The sleep issue is not uncommon and is fairly easy to remedy. A few relevant questions later, Maria said that when she tried the procedure at home, she had turned the heat way up in the room where she practiced PMR. The reason she had increased the temperature was because it was late and cold in the house. Comfort is good, but in Maria's set of circumstances, the urge to sleep was then too strong. Her experience reminded me of being at my grandparents' home in Michigan, with frigid weather outside. My grandmother would always crank the heat way up. and, while only a child, I recognized that even midday one could nod off relatively quickly. Of course, the large meals and the constant sound of a nearby black-and-white TV, as well as cigarette smoke wafting through, didn't help.

Maria changed her PMR routine to earlier in the day and made good progress. Her communication efforts were improving now that her PMR procedure resulted in calmer responses. When it came time to talk with her coworkers on a regular basis, she would first slow down her breathing, thus allowing for slightly deeper breaths, and tell herself she could get through an interaction more easily. She did well over time and was able to use the PMR the evening before her next workday to ensure that her anxiety would be more manageable. I let Maria know that we could go on an "as needed" basis for further sessions, but mentioned that progress is often followed by setbacks, which are to be expected.

Mindfulness

Mindfulness has become an immensely popular method for lowering stress, including stress related to social situations. It is also the age-old practice of learning to relax and become more present focused. Basically, we can learn to be nonjudgmental observers while paying full attention. Another way of looking at mindfulness is that it involves paying attention to present moment experiences with openness and a willingness to be with what is, as in just experiencing it. For shy individuals, mindfulness meditation can provide a way to relax while being attentive and oriented to others with clarity and compassion. It is relatively straightforward to learn and can help those who are shy focus more on others instead of becoming too preoccupied with their own social performance concerns. Psychologist Dr. Michael Yapko uses the apt phrase, "What we focus on, we amplify." Thus, a shy person can focus on being confident in the moment and paying attention to others rather than being too highly self-focused. It works with practice.

Key Mindfulness Points:

1. Mindfulness benefits both physical and mental health.
2. Mindfulness can lower stress by fostering focus, clarity, and calm.
3. Mindfulness meditation can help improve anxiety and depression.
4. Mindfulness can help you pay attention in the present moment.
5. You can learn to calm your thoughts and build self-compassion.
6. You can learn to be more present in general by using mindfulness.
7. Mindfulness has sometimes been referred to as promoting "mind fitness."
8. When you use a mindfulness approach, you can look at yourself in an objective and clear way.
9. With mindfulness, you can step away from your preoccupations and stay centered and focused while interacting with others.

Specific Methods to Decrease Anxiety

1. Progressive Muscle Relaxation (PMR) as described above.
2. Mindfulness. You can employ mindfulness almost anytime to help you focus on the here and now. This way, you won't become as easily lost in your own negative thoughts about an upcoming social interaction. Reflect on what your values are, for example, building relationships or being genuine with others. By reminding

yourself of positive values before a conversation, you can focus more on the purpose of what you're saying rather than become preoccupied with the specific content.

3. Meditation. This form of relaxation can contribute to the release of endorphins, akin to a runner's high. Feeling calmer and relaxed can contribute to more pleasant and meaningful social interactions.

4. Yoga. Balancing poses in yoga can help boost a sense of stability and confidence. When used in conjunction with other relaxation procedures, the ability to pay attention and focus on others are likely to improve.

5. Biofeedback. When it comes to subtle changes in the body that are initially undetectable, biofeedback can be a great aid. For example, when we get stressed, our blood tends to concentrate at our core in preparation for the "freeze, fight, or flight" response. When this happens, our hands and feet often become cooler because of the decrease in blood flow to the periphery of our bodies. When I conducted biofeedback sessions in a hospital setting, it was always rewarding to observe anxious individuals become more relaxed during the procedure. One type of biofeedback for producing calmer responses involves a sensor positioned on the outside of a finger. The individual then can watch their temperature increase as measured by the sensor on their fingertip, indicating that the blood flow to their limbs is increasing. This becomes visible evidence of the body providing biological feedback, now perceptible, to the individual engaging in a relaxation procedure. It was always rewarding to watch the surprised look on an individual's face as they were able to increase their peripheral temperature   (and therefore blood and oxygen flow) to their arm and hand, sometimes upward of five to ten degrees.

The Power of Encouragement to Decrease Anxiety

One major component of anxiety is our sense that we don't have control over our ability to respond effectively. When things get tense in a hurry, we sometimes need support from others in the form of encouragement to help us proceed.

Case Vignette
Finding Encouragement

Carmelita, a young elementary school student, was anxious about an upcoming ceremony after she was selected to recite the Pledge of Allegiance. The pledge was held each day at the beginning of her class. In counseling, it was suggested that she pay attention to how her peers were performing and go on the internet with her parents to watch how others run through the pledge at meetings. Her father, in a failed attempt to humor her, offered, "Saying the Pledge of Allegiance isn't so bad. And if you don't say it, your teacher might think you're a communist." Of course, young as she was, Carmelita asked, "What's a communist?" With her one parent momentarily tone deaf to the nature of her anxiety, her mother offered reassurance by saying, "I think you can handle this. Let's practice." With external encouragement, we can oftentimes increase our perceived ability a notch or two, knowing that others can make an accurate assessment of our true abilities. This type of feedback is especially valuable when we are too anxious or concerned about the immediate future. Carmelita was a little anxious when she recited the pledge and yet went through what could have been her first public presentation well enough, with praise from her teacher being the cherry on top.

Using Safety Behaviors—The Pros and Cons

When we are trying to engage in situations that increase our anxiety, using a safety behavior, such as avoidance or escape to opt out, is not usually in our best interest. By staying in a social interaction that initially makes you tense or anxious, you will likely notice that the discomfort subsides somewhat if you stick it out. Whether you "stay or go" doesn't need to be an all-or-none proposition. Some shy individuals do well by taking a few minutes to calm down, then returning to a social interaction or activity. The bottom line is that, equipped with relaxation techniques, our ability to stay or go is enhanced.

Case Vignette
Learning to Relax Instead of Using a Safety Behavior

Spencer, a fifteen-year-old sophomore in high school, was shy and didn't like to go to the "Parent-Student Drug Awareness" classes offered in the evening on campus. He stated to his counselor more than once that the group meeting format wasn't helpful and that some of the parents asked "stupid" questions. At the same time, it was clear that it was Spencer's shyness that held him back from interacting. His pressure to leave the group, usually only five minutes into a given meeting, was intense. Seeking safety by opting out of the meeting and not having to interact resulted in a short-term gain for Spencer. Dealing with the "stay or go" alternative, his counselor worked out a less all-or-none problem-solving compromise. Spencer could announce that he needed some air, leave the meeting for a few minutes, then return after he practiced his focused breathing to relax. He liked this approach, and it worked well—that is, until one time when a parent saw him outside the meeting smoking a cigarette. Spencer divulged that he smoked because he was intimidated by some of the group members, and it helped him not "stress-out" as much. Upon supportive confrontation from his counselor, he agreed that smoking a cigarette was not an example of focused breathing and that he would return to his healthier ways.

Basically, safety behaviors are called that for a reason. If you leave a social event out of concern, you will be overly scrutinized, removing yourself will provide you with some measure of "emotional safety" or relief. Importantly, safety behaviors can be used without feeling guilty. With old behavior better established than new behavior, leaving a tense situation (the old behavior) versus staying in it until anxiety decreases (the new behavior) will take some time to establish. Over the long term, if you want to be more comfortable in social situations, you will want to engage by taking direct action in several different types of interactions. Trying to stay longer in social situations is a good goal. Give yourself some flexibility as to when you want to take direct action or engage in a particular social activity, as in when you are ready. It's somewhat of a tired phrase, but venturing out of your "comfort zone" can and does work. This is especially true as you learn to stick with and stay in social situations and circumstances for longer periods of time.

General Stress Management Treatment Points

1. Working on emotion regulation strategies to decrease high interpersonal sensitivity or reactivity can be very helpful. For example, mindfulness, or being presently focused, is a method by which we can better regulate our emotions. Mindfulness can be summarized by the phrase "being present." Meditation can also be helpful and is often summarized by the comment "just breathe." Thus, if you're getting worked up about a particular social situation, a productive focus can be on simply focusing on the present moment while quieting the mind and body by using slower, deeper breathing. Other active relaxation methods can include walking, running, yoga, and just about any sports activity (while trying not to be too competitive).

2. Use preventive health strategies: sleep, nutrition, exercise, religious or spiritual practice, and the art of just hanging out. One marker of sound sleep that is worth noting is the common clinical observation that "good" sleepers tend to think about next to nothing as they head into slumber. On the other hand, "bad," or, should we less judgmentally say, problematic sleepers, tend to think about everything—their preoccupations continue into the night. The solution for difficulty sleeping, especially sleep onset or trying to fall asleep, is to develop a mind-clearing strategy. For example, one effective self-talk or prompt that can work well is "I'll think about my concerns at around 10:00 a.m. tomorrow, when I have some time. Now I want to sleep."

3. Relaxation strategies to deal with shyness as well as quietness (if an individual would like to be more verbal) are also important when thoughts turn in the direction of "what-ifs." That is, social anxiety rises when those who are shy engage in the what-ifs, such as "What if I stumble in my conversation with others, or worse—start to stutter?" When we become anxious, particularly socially anxious, there is a tendency to view any associated physical tension as negative or bad. However, such tension is not necessarily undesirable; it is oftentimes just putting us on alert status. Thus, one way

to reframe anxiety is to recognize the apt saying, "Anxiety is sometimes the price we pay for planning and organizing our actions."

Using relaxation techniques, including focused breathing, helps to keep anxiety within an acceptable range. One caveat that is important to consider involves any significant ongoing anxiety and tension. Be aware that if significant anxiety persists for too long and calmer methods of responding aren't in place, depression can follow. Basically, we can get emotionally worn out under the continual pressure a high degree of shyness and social anxiety can produce. Once feeling depleted, some depressed individuals will express their lack of motivation as "Why bother?" So, keep that relaxation going, especially the focused breathing, before you enter any socially stressful situation. The good news is that when we use relaxation techniques on a regular basis, we tend to develop a degree of emotional and even physical calm. One main result is that you will not get as tense or depressed about participating in social activities.

4. For parents or other individuals interested in helping someone with shyness, identify several social media strategies that create connection for a shy person versus isolation. In general, shy and socially anxious individuals may tend to be more passive than others as users of social media. They'll observe rather than post content while, unfortunately, still entertaining the fear of missing out (FOMO). It's as if a teen using social media sites (e.g., Facebook, X (formerly Twitter), Instagram) may feel socially incompetent if they don't participate. You can encourage a shy individual to engage online when they want, but they should also feel it's okay to sit back and observe how others are relating to one another on social media sites.

To complicate the picture somewhat—spending time online may be a way for the shy and socially anxious to avoid interactions where they might otherwise engage face-to-face. That is, connecting online with others does serve to engage interpersonally, at least on a physically remote basis. However, such "distance relating" may not help much overall with the goal of face-to-face social skills development. One effective strategy to balance social media with other interests is to strive to reconnect with both people and nature, basically the world outside ourselves. At the same time, recognize that socializing generally does have some bumps or awkward moments, whether online or face-to-face. In fact, everyone experiences these slight missteps in dealing with others. Thus, in your effort to move forward socially, consider that many community resources can provide immediate opportunities to reach out and connect with others. These small to large socially based facilities include peer groups, schools, faith organizations, part-time jobs, or volunteer work.

5. Take a look at the introversion-extroversion personality dimension and its relevance to shy responding. The assessment chapters of this book offer an opportunity to explore your own main personality dimensions. Synonyms for introversion include quiet and for extroversion, outgoing. Importantly, some introverts feel as though

they want to be (or should be) more extroverted or outgoing. At times, introverts, including shy introverts, will benefit from taking the initiative to find ways to reach out to others more. At the same time, introverts tend to do well by mostly spending time alone or by themselves. That is, they can be comfortable with their own company or with a few others and feel good about it. Extroverts, on the other hand, will sometimes do well by considering a pullback from a high level of social interaction. Such individuals, who are very people oriented, may enjoy the benefits of a solitary hobby or short periods of personal deliberation and reflection. The main point for shy individuals, whether they are primarily introverted or extroverted, is to seek balance by alternating between their less preferred ways of responding when it better meets their goals.

Chapter 7

Helping Shy Children and Teens Succeed

This chapter will focus on parenting tips for children as well as developmental issues in shy children transitioning to the teen years. Working with shy and withdrawn teens will be discussed in detail. Individual and interpersonal goals for young people are offered along with specific strategies to constructively deal with anger management and bullying.

This area, detailed in *Successful Shyness*, is essentially a parent guide meant to be helpful for understanding and working with shy and withdrawn children and teens. My view is that this section can also be helpful for teens to read and benefit from in that you can know what your parents are trying to encourage you to do, and you can learn some techniques to follow that will help you manage your shyness and any withdrawn behavior more effectively. As has been discussed, shyness and behavioral withdrawal often occur together. At any given time, roughly 20 percent of children and teens are likely to experience significant emotional difficulty.

Parenting Tips for Younger and Older Children
1. Give choices.
2. Let them make decisions.
3. Give them greater responsibilities.
4. Give them more opportunities to socialize.
5. Apologize when you are wrong or make a mistake.
6. Let them experience the process of getting frustrated, struggling, making mistakes, and then succeeding.
7. Teach your children to be kind to others and to avoid teasing or harassing others.
8. As an alternative to labeling a child "shy," you can use the descriptor cautious, quiet, or reserved. Of course, you can also simply say, "You've got some shy behavior going on. I see you pulling back. Being cautious is okay." As a child becomes more socialized in the school setting, it is important to look at their interpersonal world while also paying attention to developmental issues. For example, some children may want to reach out to others but find themselves less mature than their same age peers. Thus, they may simply need more support, encouragement, and patience.

9. Shyness in a child can be a contributor to loneliness, which in turn can have negative implications for adjustment. Thus, it is helpful as a parent to see that your child
gets out there and has at least some social exchanges during the week, even if they
are short-type interactions.

Developmental Issues in the Shy Child Transitioning to the Teen Years

The capacity for developing healthy interpersonal relationships is a marker for true maturity
in children and adolescents. Thus, working with shy children and teens to reach out to others becomes especially important to facilitate productive social interactions and friendships.
Social skills begin at home. Parents and their children benefit from a stable relationship with
each other. Conflict can occur and is even expected, yet when communication is constructive
and direct, teenagers learn the value of interpersonal relationships. Positive interactions with
parents can broaden or generalize to include mutually rewarding interpersonal relationships
with peers. Similarly, positive communication between siblings can influence the development of effective social skills. Finally, helpful peer relationships can enhance self-confidence
and negotiation-type skills in the context of meaningful social activities.

From childhood to the adolescent years, teens have been described as "adrenaline-acti-
vated organisms." As we age into mature adulthood, emotion-regulating brain mechanisms
are able to catch up and engage. The following is an apt tongue-in-cheek characterization of
children and teens. "They have great accelerators, but not very good brakes." When children
and teens have problems, including difficulties with shyness or social anxiety, it is important to
recognize that they occur in a context. The context for young people includes family (parents
and siblings), peers, school, and often the neighborhood or community. In general, themes
to work on with a child or teen include self-control or self-regulation, which will ultimately
help in their social relationships. Importantly, when working with children and adolescents,
it is helpful to be engaged and use active listening skills to effectively reach their shy or quiet
stance.

Also, helping young people to think critically—or, in a different way, improve their decision-making—is a valuable skill to teach. For parents, prompting their teen with the phrase
"remember to practice" is a good one. Another helpful phrase that can be applied and may
resonate because it's true, is "You can practice your way out of problems with shyness and
achieve improved social skills." Adolescents who are shy and inhibited may need reminders
that it takes practice in socializing to improve their relationships with others. By internalizing
stress, the inhibited teen will, at times, tend to hold things in. Thus, practice for those who
are inhibited involves talking with others about their stress. In sharing with others, problems
get externalized, and the shy teen then benefits by being open to constructive feedback from
others. In fact, studies have shown that adolescents who interact frequently with friends or
are in a positive dating relationship are less likely to experience feelings of social anxiety.
Importantly, socially reinforcing one another can provide individuals with a protective barrier from their own tension and distress. Overall, support from family and friends can help

insulate us from the negative effects of stress. Seeking out a positive support network is a major plus in becoming successfully shy.

Understanding and Working with Shy and Withdrawn Teens

A large number of adolescents are oftentimes shy and withdrawn. I've coupled the term withdrawn with shyness in teens because it has been observed so often, or, as we say clinically—it's prevalent. Shy adults drop some of the withdrawn behavior as it becomes somewhat easier to socialize in a variety of settings, including the workplace and around living situations.

The shy and withdrawn adolescent may have major conflicts and issues, but others are sometimes the last to know. In fact, parents are not always able to detect the internal storm or struggle in the shy teen, largely because the teen may reflect external calm to others. A unique warning alert for parents of a shy and withdrawn teen could easily be "It's 9:00 p.m. on Saturday night: How come you know where your shy and withdrawn teen is?" At the same time, shy teens can oftentimes be extremely sensitive to their immediate environment. Thus, trust becomes an important issue. Parents do well by fostering trust through consistent actions of their own and being available to their teens when needed. Many adolescents lack an internal structure for control. Due to the many biochemical and behavioral changes teens are going through, it can be difficult for them to focus on a consistent, constructive, problem-solving plan. Also, shy teens may not have the self-awareness to recognize that their own detachment and withdrawal from adults can stimulate frustration and even anger in parents. Parental patience is important here, because teens need the benefit of a strong relationship with a trusting adult. With guidance, children, teens, and even adults in many cases, can learn to speak up and are then able to better navigate conflicts. By learning more about how shy and withdrawn behavior in teens occurs, parents can learn how to treat its problematic aspects. In time, shy teens with strong support from parents and peers can begin to succeed, even thrive.

In working with any adolescent—parents, teachers, and mental health professionals need to remember one word: flexibility. Most teens tend to deflect from important, sensitive issues and have learned to see problems they have as being external or not of their own creation. That is, teens often see others as somehow thwarting their lifestyle or creating difficulty for them. Conversely, adults can learn to accurately assess whether the teen is trying to cause trouble, or if it is their immaturity and, at times, questionable judgment that results in conflict. One way to head power struggles off at the pass is to recognize that most adolescents respond better to requests than commands. An example would be a parent stating a request such as, "I would like you to broaden your interests and hobbies over the next four weeks," versus, "You need to play tennis every weekend this month; the couch potato behavior has got to go."

In general, teens who are not assuming more independence, as well as wider involvement with others and the world around them, can be concerning. Further, shy teens who are holding back or not expressing interest (and ease) with others socially may be at heightened risk. It's safe to say that for the shy and outgoing alike, all teens can be expected to display drama. For example, "I'm starving" instead of "I'm hungry" is a typical refrain. Also, demanding behavior along with strong self-focus are standard adolescent operating themes. For example, a shy teen may say, "I've got to finish my homework, and save time for two more hours of video games tonight. Isn't dinner ready?" Even so, when teens are not in full rebellion or limit testing, there remain other signs of concern. For example, a shy teen exhibiting moodiness and anger, along with a withdrawn stance and unpredictable behavior, may well need help from others. However, it is not time to catastrophize. The distinction between non-serious and serious rebellion in adolescents is humorously reflected in the following refrain: "Adolescents are sometimes more disturbing than they are disturbed."

Brain Development and Social Responding

Several interesting research findings have emerged that indicate what neurological changes happen and when the brain continues to develop during adolescence. Specific to social interactions, there is an apparent dip in the ability to decode social cues and recognize emotions. Whereas the condition is likely just a temporary effect of normal growth, it could explain why teenagers may miss important social cues. This would, of course, include the shy teen who already may have pulled back from many social interactions; thus, social cue recognition is still being learned. An example of not recognizing a social cue is when one teen notices another who looks incredibly sad, but instead asks, "Are you as excited as I am about the big game tonight?" Another implication of this neuropsychological research is that rather than simply being rebellious or difficult, teens may go through a period of missing important social cues, which can impair face-to-face conversations. For example, signs of disapproval in facial expressions from parents, teachers, and other adults could go unnoticed and ultimately ignored. Finally, teens may then blindly proceed with insensitive behaviors, at times not fully aware of others' negative reactions.

As teens progress academically through high school, their social-emotional development can be choppy. Significant struggles with becoming more independent and establishing an identity are common. Lack of independence, especially for shy teens, can result in continued high levels of dependency on parents. The main difficulty is that without forming an individual identity pattern, role confusion can result for a teen. For example, one shy teen I saw for individual counseling complained about how he could do well at school, took the courses he wanted, and enjoyed building small furniture pieces in shop class on his own. However, while at home, he reported that, "It's weird. I let my parents tell me what I should wear. They do my laundry, which is nice, yet I don't think they feel I'm mature enough to drive at seventeen. Also, they tell me I need to invite a friend over." In helping shy teens who are no longer children but not yet adults, it is important to recognize three important developmental goals:

1. The establishment of autonomy and independence in one's family.
2. Stabilization of a positive self-concept.
3. In time, the consolidation of an adult identity.

Shy teens sometimes cope by using withdrawn behavior, such as spending all their time away from home and other people, or if home, in their room. In fact, almost all adolescents like to withdraw into their rooms at such a high frequency that this particularly characteristic behavior can be considered normative. Think of the famous Beach Boys song "In My Room." The payoff for this type of withdrawal is isolated comfort and sometimes conflict avoidance, but at the price of resolving interpersonal difficulty. That is, if teens just get out there and mix it up with their friends and peers, good times will happen, but conflicts will also occur. Even the conflicts are desirable because resolving them builds social skills. If shyness and withdrawal are largely the consequences of substance abuse, significant depression or other emotional difficulties may result. In this case, parents need to become involved immediately. Given the proliferation of social media and online news outlets, many teens are influenced positively, but also negatively by a variety of non-face-to-face peer situations and circumstances. If alcohol and drug use are portrayed in favorable or exciting ways, misuse by impressionable teens can follow. Importantly, because adolescents tend to believe in and rely upon peers, healthy peer contact is everyone's best ally.

It is important to recognize that positive withdrawal actions in a teen can also occur and are advantageous. Consider when the detached behavior of a sixteen-year-old follows a period of intense face-to-face contact, such as in close peer relationships at school or in the neighborhood. The teen might be resisting friends regarding their newfound habit of reckless driving. In this situation, there is an adaptive withdrawal from dangerous behavior. Problematic withdrawal occurs when there is a pullback from constructive contact or isolation from helpful, age-appropriate social activities. Family, peers, schools, and community support are all important in guiding child and adolescent development, with successful shyness clearly a team approach.

In assessing your teen's psychological style, look at whether your child is compliant or defiant, reserved or outgoing, routine or spontaneous, and also, whether they move away or against others when in conflict. These personality dimensions are described in detail in the assessment section (Part 1) of *Successful Shyness* and summarized below. Generally, the shy and withdrawn teen will tend toward compliance, be reserved, and prefer routine. They may move away or psychologically avoid others when interpersonal difficulty arises.

Summary Listing of Main Personality Styles
    A. Compliant or defiant responses
    B. Reserved or outgoing stance
    C. Routine (cautious) or spontaneous (action) preference
    D. High motivation or low motivation
    E. Internalizing (blames self) or externalizing (blames others) orientation
    F. Moves toward, away from, or against others

At times, withdrawn behavior can take on the role of a coping style, complete with indirect (sometimes passive-aggressive) anger expression. For example, a shy teen may be mildly confronted in class to speak up, with many other students observing the interaction. The shy teen is embarrassed, then buries their frustration and anger in response to the brief encounter. Over the next several weeks, they come to class late or not at all, which is a roundabout or passive-aggressive anger response. A more assertive response by the shy teen, perhaps after class, could be, "I don't mind you telling me to speak up. I know I'm on the quiet side, but could you please remind me without all the other kids around."

A simple yet effective way to deal with teenagers, particularly those who are shy and withdrawn, is to list two or three current problem behaviors you have identified as an observant parent, teacher, or health care professional. Next, simply write down specific future desired behaviors for each. Accomplishing this task together, both parent and teen, is the most productive approach. While clearly simplistic in design, this parent-to-teen current and future behaviors outline (see below) puts in writing suggestions that might otherwise be given verbally and then promptly forgotten. I suppose one way to look at this outline is that it becomes an informal contract in which both parties, parent and teen, have had input.

Case Vignette
Going from Problem to Desired Behavior
Nate, a fifteen-year-old high school student, had reached the sophomore slump period in his academic trajectory. He had become manipulative with his parents and less so with his peers. In family counseling, his mother said, "Nate, your near continual reference to school ending at 11:30 a.m. each day is simply not being honest." The father, following the parent-to-teen behavior outline, then brought in a positive request, "I would like you to be more truthful and direct in the future. If you are, we will listen to your request for more free time." The problem behavior is not being honest, with the future desired behavior being more truthful. Things went better until one day Nate was caught ditching his PE class toward the end of the school day. He said, "I went skateboarding with my friends. Isn't that as good as PE?" Not amused, his parents set a future goal for his ditching behavior to include 90 percent attendance. Nate had input into the future desired behavior his parents wanted to see and agreed that it was reasonable, but only because there were two months left of his sophomore year.

Practice Opportunity
Parent-to-Teen Current and Future Behaviors Outline
List two or three current "problem" behaviors you have identified on the left side of the outline. Next, simply write down specific future "desired" behaviors for each.

As an example, here are Nate's responses:

Current "Problem" Behaviors	Future "Desired" Behaviors
1. Simply not being honest	1) Be more truthful and direct
2. Ditching his PE class	2) Ninety percent attendance

List two or three current "problem" behaviors you have identified on the left side of the outline. Next, simply write down specific future "desired" behaviors for each.

Current "Problem" Behaviors	Future "Desired" Behaviors
1. _____	1. _____
2. _____	2. _____
3. _____	3. _____

In general, it is important to remember that a shy adolescent may have a harder time breaking out of withdrawn behavior than a shy adult because they haven't yet developed broad, adaptive coping skills. One helpful strategy for parents is to support their teen's effort in mastering a task, then have them share their skill with others. For example, a teen can learn to play chess, practice regularly, and then play the game with others. In addition to helping with task mastery, parents can lead with positive, constructive behaviors of their own. Teens watch and learn from their parents' actions, which is referred to simply as observational learning. What is asked of the shy teen is mutual participation rather than continued detachment. Another useful strategy you can employ often is a cognitive style that finds optimism in life. This stance is important as many teens turn temporarily pessimistic, oftentimes due to internal strife. For example, a parent who wants to pull their teen out of isolating in their room for too long can ask if they would like to go exercise together. During, say, a jog, the parent can share struggles of their own growing up with a positive spin at the end, including thanks for the shy teen they've been able to raise. Teens listen better to genuine parental reflections.

As many parents are aware, shy and withdrawn teenagers can sometimes slip through the cracks due to their sometimes overt comments that "nothing is wrong." Clearly, this makes an accurate assessment of any major problem areas important. For example, in assessing adolescent excessive shyness and/or withdrawal, the following contributors are helpful to review.

Common Reasons for Teen Shyness and Withdrawal
1. Self-consciousness (related to appearance, behavior)
2. Underdeveloped social skills
3. Underlying feelings of insecurity and/or inadequacy
4. Substance abuse
5. Identity confusion or uncertainty

Developmentally, a certain amount of estrangement in parent-teen relationships can be expected. At the same time, if the extent of detachment approaches something akin to permanent status, there is a problem. In older adolescents, some reengagement with parents does occur, yet communication problems will likely persist from time to time. Broadly, in American society, there has been a long-standing can-do collective mentality, which is fine, but only as far as it goes. That is, to mobilize youth, a strong action orientation can be helpful, yet some measure of detachment and withdrawal can be healthy. For example, a shy adolescent's slower, deliberative approach can help curb impulsivity. Such a careful approach is an advantage, largely because occasional poor impulse control is a major concern in teenagers.

One way to conceptualize significant withdrawn behavior is to view the shy teen as often internalizing their difficulties, as in becoming preoccupied and self-conscious. This type of behavior is to be contrasted with the sometimes more obvious externalizing problems of an outgoing, direct teen. These individuals may, at times, be acting out built-up distress by skipping school, drinking, and causing trouble for others. Or as one mother described her two teens: "One asks for permission (then acts); the other acts (then asks) for forgiveness." The teen asking before acting is more likely the internalizing type, and the teen who acts first and apologizes later, more characteristically externalizing. By way of example, I once had a teenage client who asked his parents if he could smash some pumpkins around Halloween. Surprised by his candor, his father said, "Thanks for bringing it up, but no way." He was a shy teen who clearly was asking for permission and tended to internalize his problems and become withdrawn. I saw another teen in individual counseling who was outgoing and would frequently externalize her difficulties. At one point, she complained that her mother had confronted her for low grades. She said, "My mom is checked out. She doesn't know that I've tried to study. Besides, the teachers are really unfair." Not finished in her explanation of how others are at fault for her slipping academic performance, she added, "And my dad, he just ignores me, and instead of helping me with my math homework, he goes golfing seven days a week."

As mentioned, withdrawn behavior can be adaptive and constructive. Oftentimes, an adolescent may need to pull back from the demands of friends, family, school, a part-time job, and other roles. Taking a break can provide a healthy counterbalance to overexposure or high levels of contact. For example, if a child or teen is being harshly treated, they may respond by either escaping or withdrawing. Active strategies may not have worked to avoid the rough parental behavior, largely because an adult can overpower. Thus, the child or teen may engage in a more passive, withdrawn sequence of behaviors to self-sooth. Examples include TV watching, the internet, video games, or even, if shy, calming themselves by reaching out to trusted family members.

Other examples of positive withdrawal actions include periods of detached behavior that follow problematic contact, such as in peer relationships at school or in the neighborhood. For example, a teen might be resisting friends regarding a newfound habit involving tobacco and alcohol use. In this situation, there is a behavioral withdrawal from dangerous behavior. As mentioned, problematic withdrawal occurs when there is self-removal from constructive contact or isolation from fun and helpful activities. Be wary of a teen's slide into significant avoidance, rumination of problems, and corresponding self-consciousness. Parents reaching out to their shy teens and letting them know that they are available to talk is important. Reflecting on times when you may have been avoidant and worrisome can create a connection. Even if the teen is not all that communicative—they are listening. Of course, if they are covering their ears with their hands, it may be a good time to depart with the simple line, "Please think about what I've said."

Problem Signs with Shyness and Withdrawal in Teens

As a parent, how do you know when shyness and withdrawal are problems? How can you tell? The following are troubling signs keyed to specific common issues:

A) Alienation. Withdrawal or isolation in teens today may be accelerated due to the vast array of electronic devices that offer everything from solo music to video time via the internet. With television, streaming, and computer use on the rise, many adolescents who are already somewhat pulled back or inhibited can find quick diversions through technology, which only a persistent friend or parent can hope to penetrate. Solitary electronic entertainment is fine, yet the important question to ask is how the teen is using it. If a young person is using this type of diversion simply to withdraw or avoid, anxiety and depression may not be far behind.

B) Anxiety and depression. Sometimes shyness and withdrawal can include symptoms of significant anxiety and depression. Internalizing reactions such as tension, fearfulness, and withdrawal can be associated with an individual's psychological response to stressors. For those who are shy, stressors are often associated with social interactions or circumstances. Shy teens can be sensitively asked about persistent fears as well as about actual behavioral withdrawal from family members and friends. Major anxiety and depression can sometimes lead to substance abuse. When parents and friends supportively talk with shy teens, there can be significant progress. Professional help is an important option and is often helpful to both teens and parents.

C) Substance use. Alcohol and drugs may decrease inhibition, so that their use can be tempting, particularly for shy teens. The dangers of alcohol and drug abuse, especially for minors, are significant. The price of lessening anxiety might later be increased irritability or poor concentration. At the extreme, many adolescents who commit suicide have been intoxicated or high on alcohol or drugs. In general, adolescents, including shy ones, may resort to alcohol and drug use for social acceptance, self-esteem enhancement, escape, risk-taking, or the opposite—stress reduction. Talk with your teen children.

Careful observation by supervising parents is generally helpful in guiding a shy teen. In general, teens do like to withdraw into their rooms, to a point where such behavior can be considered the norm. However, when the withdrawal significantly decreases social contact and substance use, depression or other emotional difficulties may emerge. In this set of circumstances, parents need to become involved with their teen and provide helpful direction, as well as outside professional mental health intervention if indicated.

Adolescents may resort to alcohol or drug use for several different reasons. Research has shown that peer pressure and risk-taking are the primary reasons for using alcohol or drugs as acknowledged by teens themselves. Regarding quiet, shy, and withdrawn teens, a major reason or contributor to substance use is social acceptance, which can reflect lower self-esteem in some. Teaching adolescents more positive coping skills, including focusing on constructive goals such as academics and developing a support group of friends, can help lower substance use potential. One caution is that if adolescents begin to drink or take drugs habitually, a second underlying problem, such as significant anxiety or depression, may be present. In clinical work, having a substance use disorder along with an anxiety or depression disorder is referred to as a dual diagnosis. Dealing with one problematic issue with a shy teen, such as drinking to become more social, can be further complicated if the same teen is also grappling with significant emotional pain in the form of severe anxiety or depression. As adults, it is especially important for us to be there for our teens, and with shy teens we may need to reach out and initiate sensitive conversations so that they can develop a broader perspective than their peers alone provide.

Of course, when talking with a teen about important or concerning subjects, do not expect immediate acknowledgment of any problems. In time, if your teen senses you care and are supportive, opening up to your feedback will follow. It can be helpful for parents to role model giving and receiving emotional support in their own community among friends, peers, and family.

D) Motivation. Sometimes motivation hums along well enough. I was seeing a shy teen in individual counseling who stated, "I would like to get to know some more people." In this type of situation, positive interactions are likely to occur between the teen and their parents. Basically, the adolescent is highly motivated internally, thus the parents do not need to supply much external motivation in the form of verbal reward or reinforcement. In fact, the parents can simply encourage via a suggestion. For example, "If you want to get to know some people, go to youth night with your friend Jim. You know, the one who occasionally goes to church."

Conversely, motivation can decrease or dip at any time. Consider a shy teen's remark to his parents, "I don't care about friends, leave me alone. It's a free country anyway—I can be on the computer eighteen hours a day if I want. Why not?" In this set of circumstances, difficulty is likely to arise between the teen and parent, largely because little self-motivation is generated. Parents then need to supply external motivation at a higher rate of both intensity and frequency. "Look, I know you like the computer, but if you at least call one of your friends today, we'll get off your back for a while. How does that sound?"

E) School truancy or failure. Many adolescents, shy or not, may do worse in high school for a time, but the drop in grades is not immediately evident in that they remain quiet about their difficulty. Further, resistance to authority may be covert rather than out in the open. Evasiveness in talking about a new group of friends should raise an alert. Whereas some measure of escape or withdrawal from the family is common in almost all teens, continued academic slippage, secretiveness, lying, and chronic dishonesty are not. The following suggestions are offered to help connect with your teen when grades may be an issue. Be a consultant to the academic problem, not antagonistic. Find out what reasons there may be for the dropping grades. Be realistic about your teen's true abilities and achievement level. Focus on abilities, while learning how to address relative academic weaknesses in an organized manner. For example, a teen may excel in English but may need a tutor in math.

Individual and Interpersonal Goals for Teens Leading to Successful Shyness

Once an accurate assessment is made of potentially problematic shy and withdrawn behavior, meaningful interventions can be designed. The next sections on shy teens will focus on effective pathways to successful shyness in the form of specific strategies. Throughout, maintaining an optimistic stance is important for parents to counterbalance the occasional negativity most teens will convey. As discussed in the overview segment on shy and withdrawn teens, trust is a key issue. If an adolescent develops an individual pattern of moving away from or avoiding others, parents can counter. That is, by parents extending trust, a teen can learn from a more direct way of responding. Parents need to follow through on being available and direct in communication such that the trust engendered runs both ways with their teen.

Accept that your teen may not always be communicative, and do not interpret this sign alone as compelling evidence for shyness, avoidance, or even non-compliance. Teenagers do not like interlopers, that is, individuals who pop in and out of their lives from the adult world without due sensitivity. Thus, take some time to assess your own thoughts, feelings, and behaviors in order to help your son or daughter. Note that being sensitive to teenagers does not mean that they are in charge. Parents can run the show while setting reasonable boundaries, limits, and the basic requirements of daily living in a family. Effective parents do engage in broad negotiation and compromise skills with their adolescents, and in general, this give and take works well.

If a shy teenager is overly criticized for pulling back or withdrawing, a miscalculation in constructive parental intervention has occurred. Yet confrontation with what President Abraham Lincoln called "the slows" can be constructive. Here's an example: "Terrell, it's been over a month since you've used the phone to call a friend. We would like you to get on it this week." This can be a delicate parent-teen issue because, in general, a longer period of time needs to be spent waiting for responses from a detached versus more outgoing teen. In general, encouraging family connections, teen social ties, and exercise to reduce internal tension can be greatly beneficial.

Shy and withdrawn behavior can be healthy for adolescents at times. For example, a sensitive and caring teen may need to pull back occasionally from the demands of friends, family, school, part-time jobs, and other roles. Behavioral withdrawal can form a constructive counterbalance to overexposure or high levels of contact. Many shy and withdrawn teens seem to need some alone time, whether introverted or extroverted, as it can help them reflect and process their rapidly changing lifestyle. But be careful, as too much withdrawal can lead to habitual avoidance, which in turn can contribute to further self-consciousness about interacting socially.

To be successfully shy, it is important to learn more effective social skills. As discussed, adolescents who are shy oftentimes tend to hang back or avoid interacting with others due to their inhibitions and self-consciousness. Sadly, this occurs even though many shy teens, as well as shy children and adults, would like to have more contact with others. Internal emotional discomfort, coupled with concern over being evaluated for their performance in social interactions, can stop shy individuals from reaching out. An important corollary issue pertains to the loss to all of society when those who are shy do not interact with others, thereby not sharing their interests and talents. Clearly, focusing on goals that can help you move out of any difficulties you are having with shyness will help not only you but also the world around you as we are beneficiaries as you join us at your own pace.

Below are several specific individual and interpersonal goals that will facilitate effective responding, leading to successful shyness.

Individual goals:

1. Develop self-control. Teenagers who can learn to reasonably control their impulses are more attractive to peers from a social interaction perspective. When others sense calm, they are more likely to approach. I recall working with a family in which the adolescent, with whom the parents were frustrated, was quite impulsive. The tension was particularly high in one session when the parents discovered that their daughter had stolen a book from a local Barnes & Noble bookstore. I felt for her. She was so action-oriented and impulsive, yet she needed a consequence. Trying to think fast and wanting to break the tension, I simply stated, "Maybe the book she swiped was entitled 'How to Control Your Impulses.'" Everyone laughed, and family members were able to enter the problem-solving phase of her actions. The parents ended up simply telling her to return the book to the store. I asked this action-oriented teen if she could do it and recall her confident reply, "Of course. If I could sneak it out, I know I can get it back in with no one knowing the difference."

2. Use compassion. Dealing with others in an empathetic manner involves the use of compassion. Cooperation and mutual respect are corollaries of compassion. Just as you may feel shy in certain situations, so do others. You can observe their quiet

responses and then initiate a conversation with them. This strategy works well to learn together, using empathy. As the saying goes: "Birds of a feather flock together." A shy person is likely to engage at least a little more than usual when another shy person, demonstrating sensitivity, approaches. Mutual empathy and compassion will help you reach your next goal, which is to improve your self-confidence.

3. Improve self-confidence. With self-confidence, you will be able to constructively assert yourself in a variety of social situations. Fortunately, this attribute can be developed over time, and there is no need to worry if your self-confidence isn't high in all situations. Most people report vulnerabilities wherein they continue to work on developing their self-confidence, depending on the situation. Learn how to recognize the underlying vulnerabilities that contribute to your discomfort in social situations; everyone has them.

Case Vignette
Vulnerability in a Social Situation

A client I had seen in outpatient counseling, fourteen-year-old Denzel, always spoke of being corrected by his parents if he misspoke or mispronounced any words as he grew up. Not surprisingly, this young teenager felt vulnerable to possible criticism in most any social situation he encountered, so he earned that withdrawal and avoided any public slipups.

In one session, Denzel was given the suggestion to stay in social situations long enough to test out whether people commented on any of his slipups or had any kind of reaction. After several weeks and a fair amount of conversing with others, Denzel came back in and was smiling. Proud of his progress, he said, "No one commented on any of my slipups, not one odd facial reaction, but I was still trying to be careful in what I said." My response was to the point. "Congratulations, and being careful in what you say and how you say it shows good self-awareness." I then asked, "By the way, how were you able to stick with these social situations and interact?" Denzel mentioned two things: "First, I slowed my breathing, then I made sure to ask the other person questions so I could take the focus off myself." He added, "It was kind of cool, I actually calmed down enough to listen to others and became interested in what they had to say."

Practice Opportunity
Dealing with Specific Vulnerabilities in Social Situations

List a vulnerability you've had related to shyness on the left . On the right, indicate anything that you've done or would like to do in terms of problem solving that decreases that vulnerability.

As an example, here are Denzel's responses:

Vulnerability in Social Situations	Problem-Solving Response
1. "People will criticize any slipups I make in conversations."	Slower breathing; focus on what the other person is saying.

Think about a couple of instances when you felt vulnerable in a social situation. List the vulnerability on the left. On the right, indicate what you've done to decrease that vulnerability or would like to do in the future.

Vulnerability in Social Situations	Problem-Solving Response
1._____	_____
_____	_____
2._____	_____
_____	_____

Interpersonal goals:
1. Conflict resolution skills. The ability to resolve disputes through constructive communication and compromise/negotiation skills can be learned.
2. Developing intimacy. The ability of adolescents and adults to become emotionally close to others and exercise compassion and empathy.
3. Helpful behavior. Teens who are shy can be proactive by expressing their sensitivity to others, which can also foster their own self-worth. Being attentive and caring with those around you is an easily reachable goal and can be carried out daily.

To be realistic, we want to recognize or consider that even extremely helpful individual and interpersonal goals are in competition with all the immediate electronic and social networking sites that are available to teens. Concern has grown that those adolescents, who are already withdrawn, can end up engaging all too often in the detached, non-face-to-face online world. This is not an all-or-nothing matter, with some electronic entertaining and socializing likely helpful, depending on how we use it.

The problem is that if an adolescent is using their screen time too often, they may not realize that it is aiding their avoidance and withdrawal. In turn, they are heading down the path of not reaching out to others in face-to-face interactions. Further, significant withdrawal can lead to depressive symptoms. As discussed, effective social skills grow out of social relating. Thus, one central thrust of this book, especially for those who are very shy, is to get out there, but at your own pace. Improved social relationships with a growing peer base are a realistic goal and will go a long way toward becoming successfully shy.

In the next section, we turn to how positive parenting can facilitate those individual and interpersonal goals their teen has chosen to work on. The following important areas are included: A) social skill and assertiveness training, B) positive coping skills, C) the weekly family meeting, D) reframing issues, E) constructive communication, and F) dealing effectively with anger.

Strategies and Techniques for Parenting the Shy Teen

A) Social skills and assertiveness training. A major focus on improving social interaction skills and direct, assertive communication can be very productive. Think about how sensitive we can all be from time to time regarding the experience of rejection. One main difference between popularity and rejection during adolescence is the ability to use constructive social skills. Shy teens need help in thinking through new social responses (cognitive rehearsal) as well as in trying out new ways of interacting (behavioral rehearsal) with others. An effective bridging method involves having your teen bring in a helpful friend or peer. That is, the shy and withdrawn teen can benefit from a buddy system wherein they can spend time with a more social and outgoing peer to learn the ropes of successful peer interaction. It can be explained to a young individual that "just as people have a 'study' buddy, they can also enjoy the benefits of a 'social' buddy."

One caution with the social buddy intervention is that the friend or peer chosen to help a shy teen learn more communication and interaction skills should be a positive role model. There are some adolescents who are socially skilled but unfortunately tend to act out, are rebellious toward authority, and can be highly manipulative. Individuals with these personality characteristics aren't the best choice, unless, of course, your teen aspires to be a used-car salesman or politician. Just kidding. On a more serious note, a helpful social buddy is a peer who can guide a shy teen toward being more effective in getting along and interacting with others. This is accomplished by social buddy role modeling, which involves effective communication and interaction skills. A mature social buddy will relate to their quieter buddy with compassion and patience, recognizing that the shy teen often needs time to warm up in social interactions. Take Devon, a reserved young adult who described himself as "really shy." He talked about his friend Brett as being outgoing, and he was envious of Brett's smooth, relaxed communication style. Unfortunately, based on Devon's detailed accounting of their friendship, Brett did not seem to be an ideal social buddy choice. Basically, Brett did what he wanted, seemingly unaffected by whether his behavior was appropriate or otherwise. Further, he tended to push people toward adventurous and, at times, antisocial activities—including shoplifting. But he certainly was social, just not the best fit for a social buddy.

Note that an adolescent may have a harder time breaking out of shy and withdrawn behavior than an adult because they haven't yet developed broad, adaptive coping skills. Actively support, even embrace, your teen's awkwardness as a step toward mastery. For example, we all needed to learn how to walk before we could run. One helpful strategy for parents is to support their teen's effort in mastering a task, then have them share their skill with others. For example, a teen can learn to play tennis, practice regularly, and then play the game with others.

As a teenager works on establishing their own identity, there can be role confusion, and independence may falter. Recognizing the upheaval, parents can provide more active support through attention and nurturance. Broadly speaking, some kids simply need a longer runway before their takeoff into adulthood. In any event, it is helpful for parents to encourage independence in their teens because it implicitly conveys trust. If you can help it, don't freak out at adolescent angst; by maintaining faith and hope, parents will someday enjoy the natural benefits developmental maturity can provide their teen.

Questions to ask yourself as a parent to help you focus when your teen is shy or withdrawn and you don't want to overreact:

1. Do I have a sense of the reasons my teen may be shy or withdrawn? Is anyone else in our family shy, quiet, anxious, or withdrawn?
2. What coping skills have I learned when shy or withdrawn that my teen could benefit from trying out?
3. Is there any help outside the family, such as school, peer groups, religious affiliation, or counseling, that my teen might benefit from?

B) Positive coping skills. As mentioned, let your teen know what current problem you would like addressed and what future desired behavior is expected. An all-too-common example would be "You're late for school again." A usually accurate problem depiction, but many parents forget the future desired behavior part. This second step of the equation could be a simple statement, such as, "I would like you to use your alarm to wake up so that you can get to school on time." Consider that many power struggles can be alleviated by learning to parent via requests versus commands. For example, with a shy teen you could say, "After your warm-up period, I'd like you ask your new friends to come over for our barbecue." This would be a request. A command is more authoritarian and directive, which usually invites a negative reaction. Commands are easy to discern as in, "Hey, once you've warmed up, get those new friends over here for our barbecue. You've got to socialize more." Again, requests work better than commands, in fact for just about everyone, not just teens.

Case Vignette
Seeking Feedback for a Job Interview
Dixon, a senior in high school, wanted to get a part-time job to have some extra money. As most would agree, a major social demand situation for many teens is an upcoming job interview. As Dixon was very motivated to find work, his individual counseling sessions could help him find positive coping behaviors that would facilitate the process. For example, when approaching a job interview, it can be helpful to practice with a friend. Dixon said he had several friends who had already found part-time jobs and that they could help him with interview pointers. I suggested in one session that many people like to consider what routine

questions may come up during an interview and how they can best answer them. We practiced a few common questions that might be asked in a job interview and role-played reasonable responses. In the role as employer, I asked a regrettably common (and slightly irritating) question, "Tell me about yourself." Clearly meant as a possibly intimidating type of question, especially for a part-time job, Dixon was able to respond by stating, "I'm a senior in high school and plan on going to college. I'd like a job that can help me learn what it's like to work for someone and to make some extra money." Dixon said he would also talk with his parents about their early job experiences, especially the hiring parts.

Practice Opportunity
Dealing Effectively with Interpersonal Pressures and Demands
List the current interpersonal pressures that you are having on the left side. On the right side, you can indicate what type of positive coping skills you used that were helpful.

As an example, here are Dixon's responses:

Current Interpersonal Pressure	Positive Coping Skill
1. Upcoming part-time job interview	1. Practice with friends, discuss in counseling, talk with parents

Identify one or two interpersonal pressures or demands that you're having and list them on the left side. On the right side, indicate what positive coping skill or skills you've used to decrease the interpersonal pressure.

Current Interpersonal Pressure	Positive Coping Skill
1. _____	_____
	_____
2. _____	_____
	_____

C) The weekly family meeting. Talk openly with your teen regarding sensitive topics, including identity and sexuality. Explain what it was like when you were a teenager exploring difficult feelings and experiences. Refer your teen to age-appropriate materials while recognizing that a shy teen may need more time to process and respond to the information you provide. Keep the communication channels open. Recognize that decreasing any problematic shy and withdrawn behavior is the more appropriate and realistic goal than attempting to eliminate it completely.

During a family talk, encourage your teen to use positive versus negative self-appraisals if they speak disparagingly about how they're doing. For example, if a teen says that they just aren't connecting at school and "no one seems to care about me there," follow up with a few questions. You can ask your teen to come up with one or two positive aspects of their personality, such as "Maybe you're the strong, silent type. What do you think?" or "Have you heard the saying 'still water runs deep'? This means that there could be a lot of depth to your way of thinking." This parental prompting, along with a developing optimistic outlook in a teen because family members believe in them, can do wonders in building a positive identity.

D) Reframing Issues. As discussed above, in utilizing a positive approach, it is important to let a child or adolescent know what you want, rather than focus on problematic behavior, at the outset. For example, better results will be obtained from the parental prompt, "I would like you to be more responsible" than the critical remark "Why are you so irresponsible?" Instead of "Just say no" to drugs, the improved positive comment might well be "Say yes to health." Also, while you're at it, encourage your teen to discuss feelings on at least an occasional basis, positive or negative. All the better if you can role model the expression of feelings yourself. For example, "I was really frustrated yesterday when my friend Jenny didn't even return my call. At least, she apologized to me today for not getting back. She said something about her pet turtle getting the hiccups again."

Yet another example of reframing includes the possibility that an angry teen may be coming across as menacing, but, in fact, may be demonstrating an individual (yet emotionally charged) interest in a topic. "Well, Spencer, by threatening to kick your bedroom door in and hurling insults, I take it you're not happy with our decision to set your curfew around sundown." Note that the use of humor can also be an important tool in curbing adolescent reactivity and belligerence.

E) Constructive communication. In general, focusing on the individual adolescent's personal motives is superior to assuming all behaviors are the result of peer pressure. It is better to have the teen focus on their own role in making independent decisions rather than have them misperceive that their behavior is entirely influenced or controlled by peers. Also, if a shy teen is feeling inhibited due to stressful circumstances, vagueness may set in. As an example of how vague teenagers can be in general, the following parent-teen communication segment is informative, if not all too common:

Parent: How was school today?
Teen: I don't know.
Parent: Well, did you go?
Teen: Yeah.
Parent: What did you do?
Teen: Not much.
Parent: Typical day?
Teen: I guess so.
Parent: It was you who was there, right?
Teen: Yeah.
Parent: I'd like you to provide more detail. That way, I can help with some feedback.
Teen: Oh.

Clearly, and particularly with the shy adolescent, time needs to be spent drawing out dialogue. Thus, parents can role model by talking freely between themselves and then encouraging their children to do so. Focusing on the everyday concerns of adolescents can be a valuable starting point. Parental support and involvement are crucial for raising an emotionally healthy adolescent, even when the teen may not always want to talk. In other words, verbal communication can sometimes take a back seat, but as long as the adult world is there for the teen, they will benefit.

F) Dealing effectively with anger. Negative emotions, including anger, will occur between adolescents and their parents. Fortunately, there is no need to fight a teen (or a friend or a spouse, for that matter) on all issues, all the time. This all-out type of action simply serves to make you predictable and uniformly stimulates the ignore response pattern, especially in teens. For maximal benefit, choose your battles while making sure to point out some positive, nurturing behaviors that you've observed in your shy or non-shy teen. This approach tends to break up the war zone or stilted my-way-or-the-highway type of interaction when parent-teen conflicts occur. For example, if a parent asks, "Why do you always have to hibernate in your room instead of going out with your friends? This seems to be your daily routine." This will be perceived as a demanding parental broken record by most teens. A few changes in the direction of a more positive parental prompt could be "You seem to hang out in your room a lot, and your quiet time is fine. Yet if you get out a little more with your friends, I think you'd enjoy it. Try it and let me know how it goes."

Also, in the context of arguments or conflict, try to avoid the pursuer-distancer dynamic. In this pattern, the more a parent pursues, the more the teenager distances. This pattern is also common between marital partners and in other adult relationships. Promoting occasional positive activities (ones your teen likes) breaks up this problematic dynamic. Active parent-teen collaboration, including negotiation and compromise, is the key.

Helpful Communication Tips and Techniques

1. When communicating with others, watch both your verbal and nonverbal behavior. Being pleasant will encourage others to engage more. For example, smiles, good eye contact, and an open body posture are conducive to positive social interactions.
2. Another helpful communication technique is the *answer-question* method. For example, you may answer, "Yes, I come here often," and then immediately follow up with the question, "How about you?" Also, try to use *what* type of questions rather than *why*. In talking with a friend, you might ask her why they liked a certain movie, with the predictable response being something vague like, "I don't know exactly. It was interesting though." Asking the same question with a what type question can usually yield a clearer response: "What are some things you liked about the movie?" Here's a more detailed response the what type of prompt can stimulate: "I was pleased with the action scenes and was also impressed with the way the characters interacted. Those are a few of the things I liked."

3. Reframing can be immensely helpful. For example, instead of saying to yourself that you failed to meet your goal of speaking up in a particular office meeting, you could consider the broader information that occurred. Deirdre, a fifty-four-year-old DMV worker, used a realistic reframing: "Last week's office meetings were particularly noisy, and no one could get a word in edgewise." "Also, the content wasn't relevant to my job responsibilities, but I did remain on task."

4. Promote your own self-efficacy. If you're having a hard time in a particular social interaction, recognize that you can go to what's been termed your *islands of competence*. We all have them—those are areas of psychological coping that work for us. The term self-efficacy applies because it involves believing in your own ability to reach certain goals. Take Dakota, a young school counselor, who stated in therapy that he felt particularly skilled in being socially sensitive yet quiet. He would typically let the other person expand on their conversation while listening intently, then make insightful comments when appropriate. Dakota believed in his own active listening skills, which others recognized and praised.

5. Positive shyness communication. Advantages of shyness can include a quiet yet attentive response style, along with effective active listening skills as referenced above with Dakota. Also, shy individuals can be very loyal in their relationships, as well as have a finely tuned sense of humor (on occasion). I'm sure you've recognized how positive communication with another can be when it includes a joke, funny story, or comical situation.

   If you find yourself becoming too negatively thought preoccupied, you can cognitively refocus to more adaptive thought content. For example, Fred dreaded going to his high school speech class. He was concerned his prepared talks would be judged harshly, if not outright ridiculed. He became preoccupied with the notion that he was going to choke and get a bad grade in the class. His school counselor taught him how to cognitively refocus on the positive aspects of his presentations. He was able to consider that he performed as well as his classmates, and no one seemed to laugh or snicker at anyone's talks. He did less obsessing, but some anxiety and thought preoccupation did creep back in one time. Fred said, "It would be the worst if, what if, oh, I don't know, I'm not sure, but what if my teacher rolled her eyes during my talk?" Fred calmed himself down by considering that, in general, his teacher was highly supportive of everyone. Thinking more realistically will decrease negativity as your thoughts become more balanced, and hopefully include a dash of optimism versus undue pessimism.

6. Find an interpersonal skill training program or social skills training group that has as its major goal increasing social contacts and maintaining meaningful relationships. Many of these programs are offered in the context of group therapy at community facilities or in private practices run by licensed mental health professionals.

General Treatment Strategies for Shy Teens

Oftentimes, it is the disruptive teen who is seen in counseling, but parents will also want to be attentive to the needs of a shy, sensitive child or teen. An accurate assessment and treatment course with a shy and possibly withdrawn teen can be life changing. It is important to note that whereas adults have a variety of ways in which they seek professional help, teens are usually brought to counseling by their parents. If parents recognize the needs of a shy teen who is simply not interacting with others and beginning to isolate more, they will benefit from early evaluation and intervention.

In fact, many teens with significant shyness and social anxiety have a good prognosis with professional psychological help—meaning they get better over time. It can take a while for a shy teen to learn how to handle social situations more effectively, thus patience is important. Research on adolescent cognitive development has shown that as teens become more self-aware, they also grow more self-conscious socially. It seems to be a matter of frequently contemplating how others may be viewing them.

Another related developmental reality is that when an adolescent's behavior raises social anxiety, avoidance can occur, and they scoot away rather than engage in involvement with others. Wondering about how others may view them, coupled with not wanting to entirely avoid or miss out on things, can be quite a dilemma. Fear of missing out can cause tension and ultimately affect self-esteem. With support and empathy, young people can learn that being overly self-conscious lessens with age, and this can help to redirect their efforts to better focus on others.

In summary, teens benefit from engaging in different types of social interactions to learn how to respond to social cues. Further, when parents and schools include focus and structure in their efforts to draw students out, improved social functioning will result. In particular, shy and withdrawn teens will benefit from learning effective strategies to reduce social anxiety by increasing their relaxation response. Responding in a calmer manner will then facilitate decreasing interpersonal reactivity. Increasing relaxation while decreasing reactivity around others will be discussed in detail in the upcoming chapters.

Specific Strategies and Techniques for Anger Management

Because anger can be such a dominant emotion in teens from time to time, whether it gets suppressed or expressed and how parents respond deserves close attention. The following specific strategies and techniques have helped many parents avoid, as they say, "going ballistic" themselves.

1. In shy and withdrawn teens, anger may come out indirectly. In that case, listening becomes especially important. Try to identify the central issue and discuss it directly with your teen. If your teen is shy and they don't want to talk about it, there is a good parental response to take. Saying something like, "I get that you don't want to talk about it right now, so just think about what the issue may be" gives the teen decision power. You can always then add, "We can talk about it when you're ready, or maybe I'll just approach you on it later."

2. Try to resist retaliation with anger of your own. If your teen senses you care and are supportive, appreciation will follow (sometimes not immediately). There will be plenty of time to get your point of view or opinion across a little later and in detail so that your son or daughter will listen better and understand your position.

3. Explain to your son or daughter how you cope with strong, negative emotions. Anger is one predominant feeling state, but there are others, such as disappointment or frustration. It can be helpful to let a teen know of a situation or two in which you had difficulty controlling a particularly strong emotion and what you did to cope more constructively in the future.

4. Because everyone makes mistakes (including both adults and teens), role models learn to forgive. Remember, adolescents work primarily on the pleasure principle rather than finding pleasure in the work ethic. Given that teens are not fully mature adults yet, parents sometimes need to hold their frustration in check. Parental attempts to relate to their teen with statements like "I was afraid to even make a mistake because my parents were strict. Oh, and it wasn't easy while trying to maintain As in school and working two part-time jobs." These aren't that helpful.

Ideally, parents and teenagers can give and receive emotional support in their own family and community, as well as among friends and peers. In discussing a problem with your teen, particularly when strong emotions such as anger rise, try to work toward cooperation. A final step in this process productively involves brainstorming ideas to avoid that same problem in the future. For parents to better understand their teen, an appreciation of the economic, social, and cultural context surrounding the family's day-to-day world is important.

Seeking Professional Help for a Shy Teen

The basic operations of counseling or psychotherapy when working with teens and their families are generally straightforward. The below outline, followed by an individual and family case vignette, should take much of the mystery out of the process.

1. Counseling or psychotherapy. There are three main areas of clinical focus:
    a. Symptom reduction: If a teen is anxious, especially around other people, learning how to relax and use self-calming techniques can reduce symptoms associated with anxiety and tension.
    b. Conflict resolution: In many families, the parents want their teen to go to school and enjoy some measure of a social life. Meanwhile, the teen may want to simply hang out in their room. This is a typical conflict that can be resolved through compromise and negotiation between parent and teen.
    c. Skill building: Perhaps the teen hasn't learned effective communication and assertion yet. Learning these broad skills can help tremendously with social interaction.

2. Counseling or psychotherapy. There are four main therapeutic goals:
   a. Insight into the nature of the problems addressed. Help your teen learn that shyness is a personality feature or trait that can be modified based on specific situations. Also, shyness is not a disorder as in "something is wrong with me." Once this is understood by the entire family, problem solving can move along quickly.
   b. Decreased distress (addresses symptom reduction). When parents and teens learn to communicate more and have empathy for each other, distress will decrease.
   c. Modifying irrational cognitions, beliefs, and dysfunctional habits. Identifying irrational cognitions or thoughts and working on beliefs and dysfunctional habits (such as attempting to avoid anything social) can be a productive goal. This type of therapeutic work will help a shy adolescent constructively change their thoughts, feelings, and actions.
   d. Environmental restructuring to change behavior. Things may go better for most teens if their social world includes supportive friends and peers, as well as family members who now understand how to create a calming, nurturing household.

Case Vignette
Individual Adolescent Counseling Session
This case vignette includes a description of the main areas of clinical focus and therapeutic goals in working with a shy, adolescent client one-on-one. Modalities from the BASIC-ID offered in the assessment section will be in bold print for easy identification.

Individual counseling with an adolescent client includes a more relaxed and open stance by the mental health professional to earn the trust of someone who is not yet an adult. Greta is a fifteen-year-old sophomore at her local public high school. She currently lives with her parents, who have been alarmed by her shy and withdrawing stance (behavior, **B**). It turns out she has been skipping some school days and hanging out at the town's library instead, without telling her parents. In talking with Greta during the first counseling session, she self-reported feeling hopeless at times and expressed anger (affect, **A**) at her parents because they "don't understand what I'm going through."

When asked to describe her feelings of hopelessness and anger, she said, "It feels like a heaviness, and I get headaches" (sensations, **S**). When asked what she pictures in her mind about how she feels, Greta remarked, "I see myself in a dark room, kind of shut off, and the whole world is going by outside" (imagery, **I**). When asked what thoughts (cognition, **C**) she has had about her situation, she said, "I'm a loner; no one really misses me." In terms of Greta's relationships (interpersonal, **I**), she has had a strained relationship with her parents and has distanced herself from her peers. Given Greta's moderate struggles both at home and school, I was concerned about any physical stress (drug or biological, D). Greta denied any alcohol or drug use but did acknowledge that she has reduced her physical activity and doesn't eat as much.

As we began to think about treatment strategies, it was clear that Greta had insight into the nature of her problems and was amenable to working with her family together in several joint counseling sessions. At the same time, she complained that it had been her shyness that had caused the behavioral withdrawal and skipping school. The initial goal in this realm was to go to school each day, and if she felt overwhelmed, it was okay to remain quiet and "look studious." When ready, she agreed to at least talk with a peer or two and try to develop some friendships. We discussed how this could be challenging. "Yeah, all the girls are stuck-up, but I have one person in my math class I like. I'll talk to her." With decreased stress occurring due to being given the cue that she can proceed when ready, Greta relaxed her stance.

When Greta pictured her situation as being in a dark room and thinking she was a loner, it is no wonder she felt hopeless at times. When the focus turned to modifying her images and cognitions, Greta was a quick study. She learned that by creating an image of being alone but pursuing her dream of becoming an artist, she didn't feel shut off. Instead, Greta felt that she was disciplined in pursuing her artwork (a great reframing on her part). At one point, she said, "I can be shy and artistic, maybe even tolerate school." Thus, her thinking changed in the direction of being slightly more positive. She was aware, however, that the next step was to work with her parents on a more consistent basis.

Transitioning from Individual to Family Interventions

At some point, parents generally become part of the treatment plan with their son or daughter. There comes a point in counseling or therapy when an adolescent can directly negotiate and compromise with parents in a family session.

Family sessions focus on a blend of individual counseling efforts along with their interpersonal components. Major strategies to deal effectively with your teen in the family context include:

1. Seek partial compliance. If an adolescent is expected to be home by 9:00 p.m. or 10:00 p.m. during the school week and comes in one night at 11:00 p.m. and the next 10:30 p.m., you can see the attempt at compliance in the 10:30 p.m. arrival. Parents can then acknowledge the effort by positively commenting on their teen's progress.
2. Choose your battles; responding to all infractions will only serve to wear out parents and provide adolescents with a recharged will to challenge authority.

3. The blame game does not help either arguing party. Power struggles and control issues are inevitable. Given an adolescent's increased cognitive ability, they are now without question able to argue and use logic (most of the time). Parents do not have inexhaustible energy and resources at their disposal; therefore, choosing the right battle is important with any teen. As a parent, try to maintain at least some communication with your teen. Such an open stance is not only helpful in general, but it also prevents role modeling the silent treatment, which you do not want your child or teen to learn.

4. Behavioral contracts can also be productive. The contracts are useful because they require establishing a plan with rules and consequences (positive and negative) ahead of time. A good contract is one that both parties (parents and teens) can live by. For example, with shy and withdrawn teens, the contract may focus on talking more with others as a goal. This goal would contrast with an already outgoing teen who instead needs limits on their extensive cell phone conversations and texting.

Typical Parent-Teen Contract Items:
1. I will bring one of my friends over to the house once or twice a week.
2. I agree to introduce the friends I bring home to my parent(s).
3. Parents and teens agree to converse with one another in a respectful manner. Examples include no name calling, threatening, disrespectful tones, or sarcasm.

When contract terms are met, be sure to reward your teen with various privileges, such as hobby purchases, recreation opportunities, room redecoration, and driving the car (if licensed, obviously). Although you'd be surprised. I had one twelve-year-old in family counseling who was caught driving his parents' car. When an officer pulled him over and asked him what he was doing, he said, "My parents never told me not to drive the car."

Consequences for not adhering to a behavioral contract can involve the removal of a privilege. I have found it helpful to include the teen in a discussion with their parents concerning which privilege should be removed for what infraction. This builds compromise and negotiation skills for the adolescent (and sometimes the parents).

Case Vignette
Family Adolescent Counseling Session
The next case vignette includes a family session with the same adolescent, Greta. The treatment describes how the main areas of clinical focus and therapeutic goals are incorporated to help the entire family. Once again, modalities from the BASIC-ID offered in the assessment section will be in bold print for easy identification. In meeting with Greta and her parents, it was agreed by all that many of Greta's struggles were, to a greater or lesser extent, normative. The term normative refers to the usual development of an adolescent as she was trying

to assert more independence and wanted her parents "off my back." A major non-compliance problem that emerged in this regard was the parental expectation of Greta not staying in her room so often and not skipping school, as the parents had found out she was doing. Greta said, "I know I should go to school and get out more, but sometimes it's just too hard." She was able to explain to her parents that the individual counseling was helpful in her learning to shift perspective and that she now saw herself in a more positive light.

Her parents listened well but were not necessarily buying Greta's newfound optimism. They had a point. Greta would need to work hard to socialize even a little more and to remediate her slipping academic performance. In discussing shyness as a personality trait and not a disorder, the parents grew more tolerant. In fact, the mother described being very shy as a child herself and could relate. The father, on the other hand, was slower to warm to the idea that many people are quiet and reserved in their approach to others and not all that outgoing. His questions "Can't she just talk with five to ten people a day? Wouldn't that solve it?" were telling. In time, he was able to recognize that his more direct approach to others is not universally shared by everyone.

Partial compliance was gained when the parents agreed that if their daughter hung out with them in the family room, if only for a little while, retreating to her room on occasion would be okay. Referencing her grades, my input was that a contract for improved performance could be implemented. Greta initially didn't like the idea of a contract, but when I told her that it could be termed an agreement, as in, if you work on certain things, then you get to have privileges, she went along. I reminded the parents that while grades are important, Greta's problematic shyness, withdrawn behavior, and depressive symptoms needed to be prioritized. I used the term *problematic shyness* to distinguish it from shyness in general, which was a positive feature of Greta's personality. The family agreed that shyness became problematic for Greta only when she pulled back to the extent that she wouldn't talk with anyone, even those peers who approached her to talk.

Greta's parents learned to communicate more with her and essentially became role models for open discussion, including working through arguments and conflicts. As things improved, Greta became happier and somewhat more engaged at school. Power struggles with her parents decreased. I recommended that she find an art group at school or somewhere in the community that would likely be able to provide her with support and possibly friendships. Finally, Greta's contract or agreement included social items, such as talking more with peers each week at school, inviting one or two classmates over to her house, and initiating contact with an art group or other interest gathering of her choice. Privileges earned for completing these social goals included, wait for it…alone time (at her request), financial support from her parents for some art supplies, and redecorating her bedroom.

The Residential Therapy Process—Individual and Family

Interventions for an out-of-home or residential therapy placement mirror those offered in the office counseling process for individuals and families with one important added component: intensive program structure and staff and peer support. Virtually all residential programs benefit from utilizing the power of group counseling. In addition, the use of socializing agents or peer-mediated approaches, including staff, parents, teachers, and friends, is ideal. Residential placement would only be indicated if the adolescent is not only shy but severely socially anxious and has overall poor coping skills and judgment.

Adolescents who are excessively shy and withdrawn, as well as meeting the criteria for social anxiety disorder (SAD), may benefit more, at least initially, from individual counseling or psychotherapy versus a therapy group. In time, group counseling or therapy can be utilized and is often helpful in improving social skills using positive peer influence. Significantly, shy teens who also meet the criteria for social anxiety disorder are oftentimes capable of incisive insight, so assignments wherein they write about their own motivations can be helpful. For example, an autobiography can be suggested with the teen reflecting meaningfully about their past difficulties related to shyness and then sharing their story with the group.

Highly structured programs can contain serious acting out or significantly detached behaviors in teens. While negative teen reactions are curtailed, staff can provide education and support to promote more adaptive or constructive coping. Behavioral contracts can be used to focus attention on learning and then maintain positive thoughts, feelings, and actions. For example, a teen can be rewarded for accomplishing a specific contract item that reads, "Patient will remain abstinent from all alcohol and drugs while attending the entire treatment program." In the continuum of care from outpatient to residential or even inpatient treatment, the degree of structure, consistency, limit-setting, and positive peer interaction are all increased. Social skills are easier to learn in a structured setting when other, more mature teens who are also in the treatment program can act as peer guides. Quality-intensive adolescent treatment programs also provide an opportunity for the teen to internalize self-regulation and enhance their self-image. The structure of residential and inpatient treatment allows control of the adolescent's lifestyle to the extent that alcohol and drugs will, of course, be eliminated during any stay. How to turn adversity around is the main question for many adolescents whose circumstances indicate more intensive treatment is needed.

Because problems occur in a context, it is important to work with parents along with their adolescent at appropriate junctures in outpatient, or if needed, more intensive, structured settings. Whether parents take on the assignment to help their shy and socially anxious teen informally or turn to outpatient or residential treatment options, the assessment and treatment guidelines detailed above can be followed to create life-changing improvements in their shy, socially anxious, and withdrawn teen.

Chapter 8

Developing Effective Social Skills

Improving Current Social Skills

Social skills involve making eye contact, expressing interest, initiating a conversation, and taking turns talking. Smiling often and using your sense of humor help. Social understanding is important as well and is more involved. To understand social situations, an individual needs to first observe the interactions taking place, then place them in some type of recognized social role. For example, when walking into a completely new situation, a shy person can first monitor what is going on. Then, if it is recognized that people are in a casual mode and talking about what they are going to be doing for the weekend, it can be easier to jump in.

In terms of helping a shy person with their social skills and understanding, role playing different ways to initiate and maintain a conversation is a productive approach. This can be done by watching a family member, friend, or social buddy interact with others. Another strategy is to first observe television, movies, and social media interactions, such as chatrooms or discussion groups. This initial approach to increasing your social skills is likely to be less anxiety arousing than immediately making face-to-face contact. Importantly, social media can also have a downside by increasing loneliness if the shy individual feels left out of interactions taking place online. The important thing is to get out there in the world while also getting into favorable online interactions that are positive in nature.

Case Vignette
Increasing Social Interactions

Vick was a teen who was seen as an inpatient, meaning he was in a secure hospital facility that provided an adolescent treatment program. He was a very quiet and depressed individual, whose shyness resulted in visible blushing when others tried to talk with him on the adolescent unit. At the same time, Vick was skilled and very aware of his tendency to scoot away from interactions. He once remarked that if someone said more than hi to him, he would consider it undue elaboration. Thus, Vick would use humor to disarm people while simultaneously keeping others at a distance. One main goal in working with Vick was to move him toward more social interaction while allowing him to recognize that his wit and humor had their place. The trick was to get him to use his way with words to attract others, which he did want. We agreed that this would also help him decrease his tendency to distance himself from others. It was tough, though. When asked why he wouldn't ask his father to visit, he commented that "I think my presence alone is one of his top three agitation triggers." He followed this by flatly stating "just kidding," a frequent refrain Vick would make after one of his more caustic lines.

There was another side of Vick that needed attention, and that was his sensitivity, a personality trait that often accompanies shyness. There is nothing wrong with being sensitive, and most would agree that it can be a refreshing asset in a world that can at times be as bitter and cold as a winter day in Iceland. The downside is that a person's sensitivity can enter the high end of the range, referred to as hypersensitivity, and sometimes cause problems. In Vick's case, he would extend his heightened sensitivity into the world, and it would then combine with a feeling of guilt. For example, during one therapy session, he described having somewhat of a dull, dampened Christmas break from school. When asked what the several low points were for him during such a usually more joyous time, he related a sad observation. He softly said, "I remember riding in the car with my mom and dad when we drove by a Christmas tree lot. It was cloudy with snow flurries; the whole place had those strings of lights around it they put up. The owner, I think it was the owner, was standing there, and he wasn't selling any trees. No one was stopping. I just felt really bad for him."

Vick was able to process his experiences that dealt with sensitivity and, at times, guilt. He learned to accept that he could continue to be sensitive but not mull over things that clearly weren't his responsibility. True to form, he didn't decrease or eliminate this hypersensitivity without a characteristically dark, humorous remark. "You know, NASA did send a dog into space once. They wanted to see how it would do, but without any plan for its return. Wasn't that sad?" Yes, it was. In time, Vick became more open with others, and he enjoyed role-playing different social situations during the counseling or therapy sessions, which in turn helped his daily interactions.

Social Skills Training

1. Learn to express positive and negative feelings constructively. For example, a simple phrase could convey both positive and negative feelings. "I felt happy visiting my niece yesterday but got really bummed when our time together ended."
2. Learn to communicate effectively. Short, clear statements are a good way to start out. For example: "I enjoyed visiting the train museum with you last week" is preferable to "Sure, I liked that train museum. Did it occur to you that it's way different from a train of thought or even a wedding dress train? How wild is that?"

3. Find and build an ongoing relationship with two or three outgoing, positive peers who could be your social buddies, akin to study buddies. As discussed in this book, a reliable and dependable social buddy can show you the way in terms of role modeling. You can watch how to start and carry on effective conversations, as well as when to gracefully excuse yourself.

4. Use assertion techniques. Assertion involves owning your reactions by using "I" statements, sometimes usefully combined with "when you." By using sentences or phrasing that include the words "I" and "when you," you are taking responsibility for your own behavior, and the result is usually a less defensive response by the other person. That is, when we take responsibility rather than coming across as blaming in any way, the other person typically responds more favorably.

    a. Check out these short sentence examples:
        i. "I feel hurt when you don't listen to what I'm saying." Instead of "If you'd just listen more, I wouldn't get my feelings hurt."
        ii. "I feel uncomfortable when you push me into activities I don't like." Rather than "If you'd stop pushing me into these activities, I wouldn't feel so uncomfortable."
        iii. "I appreciate it when you hear me out on things." Rather than "Not hearing me out on things doesn't really help me in being more appreciative."

    b. Reversing the "I" and "When you" order also works well, for example:
        i. "When you raise your voice, I get a little annoyed." Better than "Your raised voice is annoying, as I'm sure you're aware."
        ii. "When you ignore me, I feel rejected." Preferred over "Wouldn't you feel rejected if ignored. I sure do right now."
        iii. "When you listen, I feel heard and respected." Rather than "Feeling heard and respected is important, can you listen better?"

5. One place to start toward the goal of increasing your social skills is to ask yourself, "What is important for me to do socially this week?" Next, write down two or three things that come to mind. Being self-permissive, you can advance any social things you didn't get around to for the next week and try again. Forward progress is the goal.

6. An effective strategy to improve your social interaction awareness (which may surprise some) is to watch TV, movies, and online shows. Importantly, this time you're now watching with a critical eye. Notice how the characters are talking and interacting with each other. What does their body language express? Which types of speaking styles are appealing to you? Which characters do you admire, and which annoy you in terms of their social approach and response style with others?

    It can be entertaining to notice that even in old shows like Mr. Ed (the talking horse), he was fairly polite when he "talked" with his owner, Wilbur. Conversely, my mom would caution me not to talk like "those Mafia characters" in the movies who always seemed to drop the "Th" at the beginning of their references to others, as in: "Dese guys, dose guys, or dem guys," rather than the more customary "These guys, those guys, or them guys," with the "them guys" not much better.

7. If you are feeling anxious or tense about going to a new and different event, gather some details about the venue first. For example, ask "Who usually shows up for the party. Is it employees only or are friends invited?" and "How long do people usually stay?" Once attending, focus on the other person, which usually helps to make you less self-conscious, at least during the interaction.

General Strategies for Increasing Social Skills

1. Social skills development as problem solving. One example would be the solitary mastery of a task or hobby, such as baking or playing cards. Then, a shy individual can share their task or hobby knowledge and skills with others. Such a *learn one, do one, teach one* sequence can serve to increase social interaction skills. For example, Alisa learned to knit from her grandmother. She made a nice scarf that her friends liked, and then she taught her sister how to make one.

2. Using a permissive or selective approach, the shy individual can work on social skills at times while learning that at other times it is okay to withdraw when feeling taxed or tired. Another issue regarding practice opportunities for social skills is that a depressed child or teen may find rapid social skills training too demanding at times. Therefore, they need considerable support and encouragement before introducing quick-type interventions.

3. Recognize the couple's dyad dance of pursuer/distancer and the individual blame/defend dynamic. For example, in the pursuer/distancer dynamic or dance, one person may pursue a discussion when the other person distances or wants to leave. In the blame/defend sequence, a person may find fault with another, but the other person defends their position. Clearly, these actions occur often in human relationships, and if you know you're in one of the pursuer/distancer or blame/defend loops, you can pull out of it to get back to improved communication.

4. Use a *think-feel-act* sequence when facing challenging social experiences. First, think about what you want to say and consider how you want to say it (e.g., a soft tone, some smiling). Second, feel the emotion you want to put into what you're going to say, such as enthusiasm or more of a sensitive conveyance of your topic. Third, act by going forward with the social encounter, be it a talk or attendance and involvement at a meeting, while trying to stay through the experience.

5. You always have a choice. For example, to engage or remain quiet; to use a safety behavior or not. In *Successful Shyness*, there are many practice opportunities you can try out that will help you move from safety behaviors to engaging more in social activities that you desire.

6. Practice confident shyness. One example is letting people who question you about "being too quiet" know you are sometimes shy or reserved and need time to warm

up. Keep taking steps to warm up to social situations a little quicker. Practice builds patterns that can create a newer, more comfortable, or familiar social pathway for yourself. Many shy people, for instance, have learned to allow themselves a warm-up time. Following a warm-up, they are then able to stay in a given social interaction longer while speaking up. Finally, they can process how they did afterward, asking themselves what went well and at what points they may have felt uncomfortable.

7. Recognize that there are several behaviors you can increase without having to work on shyness directly. The following behaviors will improve your social skills and, in the process, attract others to you: focus on active listening; support others; trust others; and engage in mutual respect.

8. As mentioned throughout *Successful Shyness*, finding a social buddy or social mentor can help if you are shy in new situations or will be interacting with unfamiliar people. The social buddy (as one equipped with good interpersonal skills) can go along with you or watch from a distance. In this way, they can give you valuable feedback on how you did in a variety of social situations. The social buddy can let you know how you came across in terms of body language, eye contact, or even the tone of your voice. If we don't know the reasons a particular interaction didn't go well, an observing social buddy can provide specific examples of how to operate more effectively in the future.

Strategies to Deal with Social Anxiety

1. Acknowledge the anxiety you feel. A constructive self-statement about noticing your own anxiety level rise could be, "I can feel my anxiety, but it's okay because I know this is the way I can mobilize myself and be more aware in the upcoming social situation." You can also say to yourself, "If my anxiety climbs up further, I'll slow my breathing down more and loosen up my muscles a little. No one will notice anyway."

2. Ask yourself what might be linked to the anxiety, such as repeatedly asking (under your breath) the *what-ifs*? For example, a shy individual who is socially anxious might ask themselves, "What if I ask this person out and I end up stuttering or can't think of anything to say?" Or "What if I stumble slightly walking into the room?" Decreasing the what-ifs is always a good strategy.

3. In general, if the anxiety is real or warranted, take a conscious breath (slightly slower and deeper is good), then proceed in the manner you think is best given the situation. For example, Juan was concerned about his internet technology position at a small firm that was going to downsize, and his manager had just called him in for a discussion. A friend leaned over and said, "You're indispensable in any computer-type work; don't sweat it." Ironically, the word "sweat" was a trigger for Juan as that has been a concern of his: "What if I sweat? They'll notice I'm nervous." Juan was able to focus his breathing and say to himself, "I've been working on this.

So, what if I sweat? A lot of people do, especially in tense situations. I'm just going to go in and maintain my relaxed breathing."

4. If the anxiety is overblown or imaginary, let the associated thoughts related to the anxiety simply go by. There is no need to try and stop the thoughts. This is an acceptance of the anxiety and the situation you are entering. An example in this realm is when Chen, a shy man, was going over his wedding vows and practicing what would be a semi-public yet hopefully positive experience. Suddenly, an odd and distressing image came to him, one in which the wedding venue's ceiling started to cave in. Yes, anxiety can fuel some strange mental gymnastics. Chen said to himself, "I've had these 'out there' images before, and like many people, I know it can happen before a big event." He then switched gears and commented to himself, "I'm turning my attention to how my best man is holding up. He gets more anxious than I ever do."

Direct-Action and Shyness

Ask yourself what you have missed out on due to being shy. Broad areas that are typically affected include family, friends, school, work, and hobbies. If staying away from social activities and your avoidance strategies haven't worked for you, take the next step. Direct-action or exposure to that which you've been avoiding can help you move through it. Why? Because with direct-action, you can act as if you know what to do and then follow through. For example, if you've been faced with doing a brief presentation at school or work and your shyness calls for a retreat or avoidance of the task, you will likely pull back. If instead you move forward and, through direct-action, take on the presentation (even if nervous), you will benefit from this approach. The presentation may turn out well, in which case you can congratulate yourself. On the other hand, it could turn out not so well, but you can still congratulate yourself. Why? Because with either result, you can offer yourself praise because you've acted instead of avoiding it and learned that the task was endurable. It's not always pleasurable, but you did indeed move forward. It's the old saying, "You've got to learn to walk before you can run," or "Practice makes perfect." The latter saying I'd prefer to modify to "Practice makes improvement." Who really cares about being perfect anyway? It is usually unattainable; we are humans. Thus, may we all have the courage to be imperfect while we are working on improving.

By way of summary, we want to move toward our social goals and not avoid them; it should be mentioned that avoidance can work—yet usually only in the short run. For example, if someone would like to attend a gathering but also really wants to avoid a potentially crowded social situation, they may feel a strong sense of relief by not going. Ultimately, such an individual may lose the opportunity to recognize that, by taking direct-action, they may have attended the event. Further, during the event, they may have been somewhat socially anxious but then, at some point, noticed that much of the initial discomfort had faded. Future events will then present themselves as an opportunity, and the individual will likely feel more confident and less hesitant about wanting to attend. This common sequence of slowly decreasing habitual avoidance and associated discomfort allows us to venture forth in a way we would like to live. For example, I saw one client, Hector, a forty-five-year-old business owner, who dreaded going to monthly chamber of commerce meetings in his affluent suburban community. At one point, he said, "Many people there seem phony, and I have to get up each time and describe my business. I get anxious right away, even when I'm talking, I wonder if others think I'm phony." Hector then proudly announced, "I feel like leaving but end up staying to the end of the meeting." We discussed whether, by staying each time, the social anxiety he experienced lessened. Hector pondered out loud, "My tension has lessened, and I wonder if I give people a break and assume they are genuine versus phony, things might get better still." Good work, Hector.

Evaluating Your Level of Shyness and Taking Direct-Action

When you evaluate your own level of shyness, you may want to reflect on what comments from others have come your way. As pointed out in the assessment section (Part 1), many of these statements seem overly vague and therefore aren't that helpful. Common examples include "don't be so shy," "are you just shy?" "you need to be more confident," and the vaguest, "you seem detached." In the practice opportunity below, thinking about and writing down positive personal or social goals to work on can help put you on a constructive track to effectively manage shyness.

Some social science writers have even proclaimed that "being shy is being selfish." This sentiment seems to stem from the notion that shy people are overly concerned with or worried about looking stupid. The implication is that if the shy person were less self-absorbed, they could offer their talents more freely to the world. Also, there is speculation that most shy people feel that there is a spotlight on them. There is a clinical term or phrase for this called "imaginary-audience phenomenon." If we think that we are always being observed, as many shy people self-report, even if it is in their imagination, who wouldn't become self-conscious? I suppose, coming from this perspective, the treatment would involve "getting over yourself," or, kindlier, trying to spend some time focused on others may do wonders.

To view your shyness more realistically, assess for any false equivalences you may be making.

1. Looking nervous = looking foolish
2. Blushing = being unprepared
3. Withdrawn behavior = disinterest
4. Speaking softly = timidity

Shyness involves excessive anxiety or, at the very least, heightened concern over negative social evaluation. There can be a lot of suffering for the individual who desires interpersonal contact but, at the same time, feels the need to avoid it. Useful questions to ask yourself include, "What is my anxiety costing?" and "What would it be like if I didn't have so much anxiety?" As is discussed throughout the assessment and treatment sections of *Successful Shyness*, one goal is to reduce arousal. At times, you may be concerned about specific thoughts that increase anxiety and may impede your ability to interact more with others. Should this occur at any given time, consider the following four ways you can effectively deal with virtually any thought:

1. You can ignore it; thoughts and feelings aren't facts.
2. You can accept it; if it's accurate, simply retain it.
3. You can acknowledge the uncertainty of it; not everything is black or white.
4. You can agree with it wholeheartedly; this thought or feeling rings true.

Choosing an accurate way to consider your thoughts usually results in more realistic ways to proceed and also helps to lower arousal. In discussing thoughts with one client, I do recall him remarking, "My thinking brain sometimes goes offline." This can be a constructive gift when going to sleep. Any other time, I suggest getting back online if you're concerned about your thoughts, particularly in social situations, and mentally reviewing the above list.

Many, if not most, shy or socially anxious people become stressed before a social encounter, which is a type of anticipatory anxiety and hesitation. If you can assess your level of anticipation as low, medium, or high, you have a way forward. One helpful strategy is to lower your arousal and anticipation levels, if needed, via relaxation methods, and then go ahead and try taking direct-action. In time, you will be able to effectively manage shyness by using direct-action more frequently. One way to look at the process is that "to get over it, you learn to go through it."

A useful technique you can use on an everyday basis, especially if you're wondering why you're acting a certain way, is to simply ask, "What is maintaining this behavior?" For example, if you find yourself almost always leaving large meetings, you can ask yourself what has maintained this habit. Is it that you can avoid talking with others because most of these types of situations have made you anxious? Or is it that you simply find the background noise in such circumstances too overwhelming? Whatever the reason, once you know what is maintaining a particular behavior, habit, or routine, you can go about making adjustments that will be more helpful to you overall. By taking direct-action toward a personal or social goal, you're going to build confidence in yourself and be able to respond more effectively in social situations.

Practice Opportunity
Personal and Social Goal setting
List several personal or social goals for which you'll take some action steps. For example, a common personal goal is simply "I want to increase my confidence." A frequent social goal for those who are shy (along with millions of others in the world) is "I want to decrease my anxiety in social situations." Below each personal or social goal that you've listed, indicate a

direct-action that you took. A simple direct-action step you could take would be, "I'm going to practice my relaxation procedure to decrease my anxiety."

1. Personal or social goal:_____
   Direct-action taken:_____
2. Personal or social goal:_____
   Direct-action taken:_____
3. Personal or social goal:_____
   Direct-action taken:_____

As you work on creating personal and social goals that fit your needs, a few pointers can help the effort. The one saying that keeps coming to mind is "A goal without steps is a wish." Thus, first set your goals, and then list objectives or steps that will help you reach your goals. Steps are really just specific things you can do to reach a goal. As long as you're at it, creating goals in positive terms is the best way to go. For example:

1. In the next week, I would like to improve my eye contact with others when in conversation. Versus: In the next week, I would like to stop looking away from the person I'm talking with.

The positive goal regarding improved eye contact is more easily processed by the brain because it is focused on the desired behavior you're wanting to achieve. It is what you want to do rather than something that you don't want to do, which in this example is looking away from the other person in conversation.

2. I will spend twenty minutes each day rehearsing what I want to say at my up-coming interview. Versus: I will spend twenty minutes each day rehearsing for the interview, if needed, and I don't have errands to run.

Recognize that what you say to yourself can and will affect how you respond to a given interpersonal situation you are facing. Thus, making realistic positive self-statements can help. For example, say to yourself, "I practiced for this interview, so it is likely to go better than if I didn't do any preparation at all." The focus of counseling or psychotherapy is to help guide positive self-statements into a constructive action plan. Basically, techniques are used that support you by having you constructively change your thoughts, feelings, and behaviors in the direction of meeting your goals and thereby improving your daily life. Of course, as this book emphasizes, working on the various practice opportunities is a form of self-help that parallels that which is accomplished in professional therapy.

Speaking of psychotherapy or counseling, many people have asked, how do you know you've improved on a goal and how do you maintain your progress? I would say that significant progress toward a goal has occurred when there is improved psychological and physical functioning. For example, Lucy, a thirty-year-old law enforcement officer, was concerned that she would blush when talking with her peers, no matter the subject. She learned that if she just went ahead and talked about things that she was familiar with, her tension would go down, she would feel more comfortable in time, and she wouldn't notice her face "getting red" as she put it. In general, diminished symptoms such as social anxiety, improved interpersonal relationships, and enhanced satisfaction in and outside of the home are all signs of goal attainment.

In general, an individual's ability to respond to complex social interactions with emotional balance varies widely. It is admirable to try and remain in emotional and physical control, to the extent you can, given a difficult situation or set of circumstances. In a word, may we all strive to develop equanimity, which has been defined as mental calmness and composure, particularly in stressful situations. This is a high-bar goal to achieve, but we can approach it. In general, goals that seem unattainable we call aspirational, meaning we aspire to meet them and wish everyone their best for the effort entailed. Use self-compassion along the way because most personal and social goals take time.

Learning by Direct Experience and Observation

There are two major ways to learn: (1) direct experience and (2) observation. An often-used example of direct experience is that of a child who accidently places their hand over an open stove flame. The experience is indeed direct and painful, with the learning not to do it again being immediate. Regarding observational learning, here is a simple practice opportunity to try out: Start by observing someone you know who you feel is socially adept or has an easy manner in conversation with others. After you watch the interaction, write down each step you feel helped to make their social interaction sequence effective. For example, Jasmine watched her friend Akira talk with a girl who was well-known for being kind of pushy. She noticed that Akira kept her voice even and did not argue with the other girl. Near the end of their conversation, Akira also nicely said she had somewhere to go, and the pushy acquaintance seemed to be okay with it; there was no meanness. Jasmine observed her friend handle a difficult conversation with relative ease. She then felt she could imitate some of the calmness with which Akira handled things.

Practice Opportunity
Observing Others in Social Interactions
Watch or observe an interaction or two by someone you know who is handling themselves well and who you might even say is being socially adept. List the positive behavior you saw on the left. On the right, indicate each step you feel helped their social interaction go well or was effective.

Jasmine's responses:

Observing Someone in a Conversation
1. My friend talking with a pushy girl

Steps That made the Interaction Effective
Akira kept her voice even.
She did not argue with the pushy girl.
Akira remained nice and excused herself.

List the positive behavior you saw from someone you know on the left. On the right side, jot down the steps you feel helped the interaction to be effective.

Observing Someone in a Conversation
1._____

2._____

Steps That Made the Interaction Effective
_____
_____
_____
_____
_____
_____

After you've evaluated a person's communication style, consider engaging in your own covert rehearsal, which simply means going over how you would like to come across to someone else. This is something you would do before your next overt or real-life conversation, using a style you find appealing. Should an awkward conversation occur, which happens to all of us, process what you felt was problematic with a trusted friend or family member. On the caustic yet humorous side, I did hear one definition of a good friend that went something like this: "A good friend who is trustworthy is one you ask to come over to your house at 2:00 a.m. and to bring a shovel, and they agree, without asking any questions."

One psychological principle worth pondering to facilitate effective social interaction is that "self-disclosure begets self-disclosure." For example, if you find yourself in line at the post office and comment on the weather to the person in front of you, they may agree with you that it is nice outside. Yet, if you add "It seems like nice as it is, we sure haven't had much rain, and I get sinus problems," and the person may respond in this hypothetical, "Really, I get sinus issues too, especially when it stays dry. And, by the way, I know a good allergist." A more unlikely self-disclosure sequence would go something like this: "Didn't I see you at the train platform last week? With the price increase, I might just work from home." The bystander you initiated the conversation with then responded, "I wouldn't worry about the money. I just won the lottery. Would you like to share it with me?" All humor aside, you will be surprised at what happens if you bring social interaction into a more self-disclosure range, sharing something personal when appropriate. Notice that oftentimes other people will indeed respond in kind, sharing more of themselves than just the time of day.

In general, the use of persuasion in social settings can be powerful. For instance, people can be socially persuaded that they possess the capabilities to master difficult situations. In fact, simply getting support from others and being encouraged to follow through with being more social can lead to or facilitate effective performance. To review, observational learning, which is a main component of psychology's social learning theory, includes the careful observation of others. For example, by closely watching someone competently execute a social interaction task, you can learn how to be more effective when you attempt that same task. For example, participating in a work meeting is a common activity that many, if not most of us, have gone through. Watching videos of live work-setting meetings and their agendas and structure can help. Or simply ask a friend how their meetings go at work and what's involved. This can help you perform better when it's your turn to participate in one. Finally, after successful completion of an activity, task, or practice opportunity, you can more easily recognize that you're creating and developing improved confidence and self-efficacy.

Case Vignette
Using Observational Learning

Duran was an enthusiastic young adult I saw in individual counseling for what he described as "choking" in his favorite sport, which was basketball. Friends of his would get together for a pickup game after college classes, and it would often turn competitive. Duran was known to shoot free throws well, that is, until he couldn't hit the basket if he tried. Thus, by choking or experiencing an immediate drop in performance, Duran became perturbed at best. "Why should I even play if I can't shoot a damn free throw?" was his lament. In working with Duran, I felt that due to his rising social anxiety and his complaint of being embarrassed over his basketball play, it might be a good idea to step back a little. I asked Duran if anyone had ever filmed his free throw shots on their smart phone. He said, "What would I do that for? It seems egotistical." I explained that it was an action plan that would involve two steps. I said, "First, have someone film your free throws, no matter how good or bad, then watch it. Next, watch an NBA game where someone goes on a hot streak and makes every free throw shot."

After Duran played around with the idea and did some filming, I asked, "What did you observe? What was different about your form and what you saw from the NBA player?" I then commented that if you can keep what has worked in your form and incorporate a few tips or techniques from watching the NBA player's performance, you'll improve. As a follow-up, the next time I saw Duran in session, he said that he had played a couple of times in the preceding two weeks. At first, his performance at the free throw line was worse than before, but then it steadily improved. Checking in with Duran's overall experience, he remarked, "Well, the first time I got back on the court I was thinking too much about how to do it. My free throws were really off. Then, when I started to relax, you know, slow my breathing and all, it got way better." The sequence of observing yourself first with help from a peer, then watching another who excels at the same activity, can accelerate learning skills, both personal and interpersonal.

To summarize, there are advantages to having someone show you how you're doing—in this case, during an activity—and then watching or observing how effective others are at doing the same thing. This will help your own performance improve. Observational learning, or modeling, as it is sometimes referred to, can even be lifesaving. Take, for example, the numerous safety videos we've all been exposed to over the years. It is indeed instructive and advantageous to watch someone else who, unfortunately, gets clipped by a car while jaywalking on a busy street, rather than go out and try it ourselves. We might even universally ponder, "I think I'll use the crosswalk instead."

The Important Role of a Social Buddy

Shy individuals can benefit from role models. Looking up to people in real life, on film, or online can help guide the way. We can follow the lead of role models in social situations by observing them and then practicing how to come across to others more effectively. Clinical research has shown that social learning approaches that describe the imitation of positive, proactive role models (live or from media sources) can be very constructive. Because shyness, as well as social anxiety, starts early, I would recommend finding a social buddy for a shy child, as well as for a teen, or adult. As discussed throughout *Successful Shyness*, a social buddy can be immensely helpful.

To review, like a study buddy, the social buddy can provide a positive role model about how to act in various social situations with better ease. Of course, a social buddy needs to be chosen carefully, with assets such as reliability and dependability important. An individual who is social yet highly manipulative and will not be there for you in a pinch, turns out to be less desirable as a choice. In a slightly different and more sarcastically humorous vein, a shy teenage girl once asked her dad about finding an outgoing, reliable, and dependable boyfriend. His brief response was exactly the same as one I've heard from a coach before: "Just make sure he doesn't do anything that's dangerous, illegal, or immoral, and you'll be okay."

Concepts and Methods for Effective Social Responding

1. Develop social support. You can reach out to friends and family, as well as groups, including church, synagogue, or mosque, and hobby. or interest-related meetings. In general, finding a group in the community that you like and can get involved in will be helpful as it can foster mutual support.
2. An overarching goal is to decrease distress and increase functional capability in social situations. Let's break that down. Take Logan, a middle-aged lab technician, who would become anxious any time he was to meet a new client at his work. He also felt socially anxious when being introduced to just about anyone. To decrease his distress, Logan produced a workable plan. He would meet the new client and try to find a topic of common interest, be it a news story or some other local matter of which many people were aware. When it came time to meet a new person, he would proceed in the same manner; that is, Logan tried to find a common theme

to break the ice. After any new interaction, he would take a short break and jot down a note about what went well and what could be improved in terms of these initial interactions. In a relatively short time span, Logan was able to increase his functional capability by more easily communicating with new contacts, knowing that he could take a brief time afterward to process how things went.

3. Develop specific goals and objectives (or strategies) to meet the goals. Juanita, a thirty-four-year-old banker, wanted to meet more people, especially after work. Yet she wasn't sure how she would achieve this goal over the next two or three months. With feedback, she learned that the goal of meeting new people was straightforward enough, but how to go about it? In individual counseling, she learned that objectives need to be specified to meet any goal. She also learned that objectives can be permissive and flexible. Juanita came up with the following: "I'm going to meet one or two new people every week over the next three months or so." Thus, she was able to provide steps to meet her goal, but not assign herself objectives that were too rigid or demanding of her efforts. It worked.

4. Develop social-emotional skills, including interpersonal effectiveness and emotion regulation. Examples of interpersonal effectiveness include engaging with others directly and sensitively with a balance between expressing your own interests andasking others about what floats their boat. Emotion regulation is a skill that boils down to not getting too hotheaded in social interactions that involve sensitive topics. In this regard, you can use the rational override method, wherein you remind yourself to speak with the voice of reason while recognizing that you may need to tone it down if you find yourself becoming too loud or emotionally charged. "Let's talk about this a little later. I hear what you're saying, but right now I need to calm myself down a little" works well if remaining calm is too hard to maintain in the heat of the moment.

5. Increase social self-esteem. Interestingly, Duke University psychologist, Dr. Mark Leary, found that social self-esteem rises with any increase in acceptance: "Would you like to come with us to the beach?" Self-esteem, on the other hand, can fall with any criticism: "You're wearing that?" One implication is to aim to interact with those who are positive and caring, but some measure of criticism will still likely come our way from time to time.

6. Control or influence? In dealing with others, recognize that the aim is not to control people, but if indicated, it is perfectly fine to influence and encourage their positive behavior. The distinction between control and influence is that control involves telling someone to do something your way. Influence, on the other hand, especially when constructive, offers well-meaning suggestions to follow.

7. Learn when *beating a strategic retreat* can be appropriate when a particularly difficult social interaction deserves a break. Viola, a young college student home on break, had just finished washing her car when her neighbor Jamal, not known for

his sensitivity, remarked that she missed several small spots. She responded that she spent a lot of time and effort on the car and would appreciate some praise, not just some nit-picking criticism. Jamal then countered, "Can't take any constructive feedback, can you? I was just trying to be helpful." Viola was getting more frustrated, noting to herself that Jamal seemed to make unsolicited negative comments often, and she was tired of it. In counseling, she commented that she was proud of herself when she simply responded, "Jamal, I've heard you, and right now I'm going to run an errand that I almost forgot to do. By the way, your zipper is open."

8. On direct-action (exposure). Think of engaging in direct-action or exposure as beginning with one of the easy, or simple practice opportunities, such as asking one or two people over to your place next week. More challenging behaviors that will help you manage your shyness can be learned in time. For example, staying with friends for a social gathering that takes place over a weekend. Importantly, you may occasionally encounter a setback in that you end up avoiding a planned social situation or backing out of a practice opportunity. Not to worry. There will always be another chance to engage in the near future. Think of a setback or temporary failure as a fact of life. This is where a sports analogy can help. Consider a basketball or football game in which a player misses that final shot or field goal. Failure to win occurs immediately and with finality in such a game—not to mention that thousands of fans in the stands and at home just witnessed the event. But wait. Notice that the players usually recover from the loss in a few days or so and are ready to suit up and play the next weekend. Their setback or brief failure was dramatic and public, but indeed very temporary.

9. Set reasonable timeframes to meet your goals. Pay attention to the expression of positive emotions, which are generally better received than negative expressions. For example, if one individual says to another, "I appreciated our talk last week. Let's meet again soon." This positive expression of emotion goes better than, "I haven't talked with you since last week. Don't you want to meet again?" That is a negative expression.

10. Shyness can increase in those interpersonal situations that are relatively unstructured. For instance, consider a party with people from different backgrounds, and you're not aware of the event that's being celebrated. One way to begin increasing social contact is to choose the get-togethers you attend and find ones that are at least somewhat structured. You can do some reconnaissance—find out who will be there and what the occasion is for enjoying each other's company. It is perfectly okay to start slow and proceed to larger social goals when you are ready. Setting realistic expectations is the way to go rather than targeting a goal that may be too hard to meet, at least initially.

11. If a child, or adult, for that matter, falls down, you are likely to help that person get back up right away. By analogy, shy people can benefit from self-help and counseling because there is sometimes demoralization. Wanting to talk with others and

socialize but instead hanging back can be emotionally painful. Working on yourself via self-help or seeking out professional counseling are ways to be helped up after your well-being has fallen. We can all benefit from a morale boost from time to time in response to difficulties we're experiencing. Self-help such as offered in this book, as well as many others on shyness, can facilitate the development of positive motivation and offer structure and encouragement to meet your effective shyness management goals.

Creating a Social Situations Hierarchy List

A hierarchy is basically a structure to rank items from low to high in terms of easy to more challenging situations regarding your engagement in social interactions. Listed below are common social situations that shy individuals find themselves concerned about. You can read over the list of examples, then create your own list that includes those social situations that you are concerned about, from easy to more challenging. Once you've created a hierarchy from the examples given, or ones you've come up with yourself, use direct-action or engagement in the task to try them out. Go from the easy ones you've identified to the more challenging social situations. Make a note or two afterward on the results of your efforts.

Social Situation Hierarchy Examples:

1. Talk to someone that you know and see in a store or in your neighborhood.
2. When someone does something you like, give them a compliment.
3. Initiate a conversation with someone you know as an acquaintance or friend.
4. Join a conversation that has already started and wait for an opportunity to give an opinion.
5. If your opinion in a conversation is different from someone else's, ask them to explain their view in a little more detail (this will demonstrate that you're actively listening).
6. Call one or two friends, classmates, or coworkers whom you haven't talked to in a while and ask them how they are doing and if they want to get together.
7. Invite a friend over and ask them if they would like to join you in a social activity.
8. Go out for an activity with a group. Movies, sports, concerts, lunch, or dinner are examples.

Practice Opportunity

Creating a Social Situation Hierarchy

In counseling, Michelle, a thirty-four-year-old optometrist, reviewed the social situation hierarchy examples listed above and decided to try out number three. This one deals with initiating a conversation. The results of her effort are offered below.

List a social situation from the hierarchy on the left. On the right, indicate what type of results you had following your social involvement in the activity.

Michelle's responses:

Social Situation Hierarchy	Results
Initiate a conversation with someone	I started a conversation with a coworker. I got her talking a little and that helped me to talk. It was good.

Use the eight-point list above or create your own list, which includes those social situations you are concerned about participating in. Go ahead and engage in the social situations you've identified, each at your own pace. Start with the easier ones first, then move on to the more challenging ones that you've identified. List the social situation on the left and then a brief note for your results on the right.

Social Situation Hierarchy   Results

1._____   _____

2._____   _____

3._____   _____

4._____   _____

5._____   _____

6._____   _____

7._____   _____

8._____   _____

Learning Social Skills Using the BASIC-ID

Using the BASIC-ID model described in the assessment section (Part 1) of *Successful Shyness* and discussed in the treatment section (Part 2) involving an individual adolescent counseling session can be helpful in a variety of situations, particularly when structure is needed. As described below, in the case of Amirtha, she was able to use the structure of the BASIC-ID to help her pursue a meaningful social goal.

Case Vignette
Using the BASIC-ID to Provide Structure

Amirtha, twenty-eighty, was a shy, reticent graduate art student who was unsure of herself when discussing her work with others, even when they expressed admiration for her ink drawings. Using the BASIC-ID, she learned in counseling to break down her concerns. Regarding behavior (**B**), she acknowledged that she would rather stay in her off-campus college apartment than attend an art gallery show with her friends. The idea of a social buddy was brought up, and Amirtha expressed curiosity along with mild interest.

As has been discussed elsewhere in this book, one way to learn social skills is by enlisting the support of a social buddy. I further explained to Amirtha that a social buddy could be an acquaintance or friend. It could be an individual that didn't mind going to one of the art shows offered around town and could role model social interactions if Amirtha would just invite her along. She thought about it awhile (cognition, **C**) and announced that one of her friends was likable enough and that, "She talks with anyone and everyone, and I find her somewhat tolerable." I said that this friend could help and to be sure to bring her along for her direct-action of engaging socially at the upcoming art show. This action would cover the interpersonal (**I**) dimension of the BASIC-ID.

Note that the BASIC-ID model does not need to be followed in order (the filing order in Amirtha's social buddy work is BCIADSI, but it is helpful to use each letter element to comprehensively view almost any social situation). Next, Amirtha was able to recognize her affect (**A**) or feelings in that she experienced a slight rise in anxiety and tension (drugs, **D**, or biological factors). The biological aspect rings true in this case, as is the development of physical symptoms associated with anxiety and tension. Her discomfort would rise whenever she thought about an upcoming art show to attend, but now there was also some excitement that a more social person could "teach her the ropes."

In terms of the sensation (**S**) dimension of responding, Amirtha was pleased to have developed a keen eye for colors, which had the ability to lift her emotions. She felt as though her art through imagery (**I**) was a way to stimulate positive visual experiences in herself and those who saw value in her work. On the other hand, she felt that her social buddy could only help with talking because "she's nice and I like how she communicates with others, but she doesn't know jack about art." We laughed, and I said, "Maybe you can help her out by helping you socially by teaching the basics of art appreciation."

In this case, Amirtha was able to use the elements of the BASIC-ID to provide her with structure so that she could ground herself while pursuing the individual goal of attending and engaging in art gallery shows with the help of a social buddy. As her interpersonal world expands and her comfort level with others in a variety of social situations improves, Amirtha hopes to have her own art collection displayed in public. Good going.

Practice Opportunity
Using the BASIC-ID for a Social Goal
Now it's your turn if you'd like to use the BASIC-ID model detailed in the Assessment section of Successful Shyness to help you with a social goal of your own. Each section of the BASIC-ID will also be summarized below to include its core elements.

Briefly write out your social goal here:

_____

_____

B is for behavior. Many people are doers in that they like to use action to get things done. Others tend to think and reflect more before engaging in more direct behavior. Shy people may tend to hang back more than others. Consider where you are on the dimension of action or reflection.

        Action before reflection   Reflection before action

What behavior are you wanting to act on and how much reflection do you want to engage in before you act?

_____

_____

A is for affect or feelings. People are emotional at times, yet feelings may not be expressed openly by many. Shy people are likely to suppress emotions if they feel they will be critically judged for expressing certain feelings, but not always. Shy people may be quite direct with those they know well and do not fear harsh evaluation from. Consider whether you openly express emotions or tend to control expression.

        Suppressing feelings   Expressing feelings

What affects or feelings are you concerned about when working toward your social goal? Are you comfortable expressing your feelings first to yourself and then to a trusted friend, or do you feel like suppressing your current feelings might signal a better social response? For example, Ted wanted to go to the movies with his friend and felt as though the time was right to express forgiveness—forgiveness over the sense of temporary abandonment he felt when his friend ditched him last week to attend a concert with someone else. He decided to express his forgiveness while holding back on, or suppressing, the anger he felt over the ditching event until their relationship was back on cruise control.

_____

_____

S stands for sensations. Many people seek out sensory experiences, such as food, music, art, and other adventures in the world. The shy may like all of these sensory delights while not always being in tune with how withdrawing and isolating from social contact can dampen sensory stimulation. In other instances, the shy may sometimes consider being home alone, or cocooning, to purposely lower heightened sensory experiences, such as at a large social event.

Low Sensory seeking   High Sensory seeking

Describe for yourself if your social goal includes low, medium, or high sensory seeking. For example, if Jada were to accept a date from her new boyfriend who wanted her to go sky-diving with him and his friends, a lower trajectory sensory opportunity could involve stating, "Thanks for asking, and I'm happy to come; I'll be watching you the whole way from near the airport taxiway."

_____

_____

I for imagery. Mental imaging is a type of daydreaming or fantasy somewhat apart from thinking in words or planning. Visualizing real or imagined experiences can be a common activity for shy individuals that often involves creativity. In general, people vary widely on their daily use of mental pictures.

Low Imagery   High Imagery

Many social goals involve visualizing how the experience may unfold. You may have low imagery or high imagery. Recognize that shy individuals can generally imagine different ways a social situation could go. Your job is to visualize, with low or high imagery, how things could go positively.

_____

_____

C is for cognition or thinking. Many people, including shy people, like to think about things analytically and to problem solve by thinking things through. Cognition, or thinking, is also the engine we use to plan things. Some people are simply not as analytical in their approach.

Low Cognitive focus   High Cognitive focus

A high cognitive focus could involve thinking about expectations and how you might plan and even problem solve an upcoming, potentially complex social situation. Or you can simply choose a low cognitive focus and think about one simple social goal, such as how to say "Hi" to your neighbor who is well-known to be irreparably cranky.

_____

_____

I stands for interpersonal relationships. How social are you? For the shy, this is not a trick question—it so happens that shy individuals would like to be more social, but for various reasons, as discussed in this book, tend to hang back. For example, too much avoidance or withdrawal will necessarily result in being less social. Of course, you can be low social in general but still have close family and friendships, as well as intimacy.

Low Interpersonal   High Interpersonal

Do you have a social goal that involves low interpersonal contact or one that involves high interpersonal contact? An example of low interpersonal contact would be waving to a friend while driving. High interpersonal contact could include making a presentation to coworkers on a new safety policy to be implemented.

_____

_____

D stands for drugs and biological factors. Bad habits do occur, and for the shy, drinking or other drug use can be used to provide a social lubricant. The downside of such use is that it may result in not working through some anxiety to get to the other, more relaxing side. In other words, alcohol and drugs can only temporarily block discomfort and tension, and they may well bounce back. It may be better to learn how to manage situational stress so that it won't negatively affect your engagement in social activities. Other biological factors that can be enhanced come from getting enough sleep, eating well, and exercising.

Low health awareness   High health awareness

Will your social goal be easier to reach if you have high health awareness and follow through with getting enough sleep, eating well, and incorporating regular exercise? Or might you consider using alcohol as a method to decrease interpersonal anxiety (lower health awareness) instead of engaging in, for example, focused breathing and muscle relaxation to produce a calmer response?

_____

_____

Additional Social Skills Treatment Goals

1. Learn new social skills in general. For example, initiate conversations with new or unfamiliar people. Watch how others begin, maintain, and then close conversations.

2. Be specific with your goals. For example, "I will increase my social interactions with peers, family, and acquaintances over the next five days." Also, to prevent becoming overwhelmed, break down your goals into short-term, intermediate-term, and long-term efforts.

3. Volunteer at organizations. Make sure you allow yourself time to warm up in each social situation. In other words, at your own pace.

4. Find someone shier than yourself and coach them on the ways you've learned to be more comfortable with managing shyness. You can also share effective ways that work to be more social that have helped you in different situations.

5. Learn to put a warrior perspective on avoidance by combating early withdrawal from activities that are stressful. The main reason is that these activities may be enjoyable for you once you stay longer and work through some discomfort. If a particular set of circumstances becomes too stressful, you can always give yourself permission to pull back. For example, note that fighter pilots have an ejection seat to escape, yet I suppose that is an altogether different kind of highly stressful set of circumstances. A more apt example would be when a politician is presenting and answering questions. When the audience doesn't like the responses and turns hostile, it is not unusual for the politician to take cover by stating they have another meeting to attend or a flight to catch.

   Remember that old behavior is better established than new behavior. In this case, the well-known psychological phenomenon essentially means that coping strategies such as withdrawal from interpersonal relationships may be well learned and part of your established repertoire. More recent behaviors, such as staying in a social situation longer, even when somewhat anxious, will take several encounters before this new interactional behavior becomes easier. Again, be understanding and use self-compassion during this relearning process. Mark Twain's old saying in several different variants comes to mind once again: "Giving up smoking is the easiest thing in the world. I know because I've done it thousands of times." Twain was obviously well aware of the tendency to fall back on old behaviors.

6. Incorporate this constructive three-step model to help you move forward in managing shyness successfully: (a) face your fears; (b) visualize competence; (c) set practical goals with small incremental steps. An incremental step, for example, could be as simple as asking a friend to go to the movies with you. Later, you can work up to asking the same friend to go on a one-day hike, which may have been your first intention. Think of that saying, "small shoes for small feet." No need to rush into things too quickly. Another relevant analogy, since I seem to be currently preoccupied with mobility, is: "A journey of a thousand miles begins with a single step."

7. Take time for self-care, including well-being, self-compassion, and promoting your own brand of positive future thinking. Dr. Kristin Neff, a psychologist who studies self-compassion, has discussed three essential elements. First, a person can use mindfulness, which includes a nonjudgmental, open stance that sees and accepts the present moment. Second, self-kindness is important and involves treating yourself with warmth and positive regard. Third, common humanity appreciation allows us to recognize that we are all connected, and while success may come our way, failures are also a part of life. Considering failure as a unique concept involving learning has its advantages. Many people have recognized and appreciated the fact that failures can be helpful in ultimately becoming successful.

Particularly relevant for the shy, be aware that failure is okay; it is a critical part of working toward your social goals because you can learn from your mistakes. I recall a time when my dad asked me to play the trumpet at the beginning of a Boy Scout troop meeting. I was hesitant, shy, and concerned about how I would perform. The song was easy enough, and I had practiced it before, but I hadn't had much experience in front of an audience outside of my immediate family and friends. I started the number and immediately fumbled some of the notes. I wasn't sure what to do, so I simply stopped. I started over from the beginning of the musical sheet, and no one laughed. This surprised me at the time. I had learned that even public failure isn't necessarily a big deal. Credit goes to my dad as he later told me that starting the song over and continuing was a great way to follow through.

Practice Opportunity
Making a Contrary Decision During a Social Goal

Describe a time when you made a decision that was contrary to a social goal that you were working on. What factors and chain of events led to your decision? For example, Lester, a forty-five-year-old software engineer, wanted to initiate conversations with female peers more often, be it at work or when he was just hanging out with others on the weekend. He made a simple social goal, which was to begin at least one conversation with a female coworker over the next week. When Lester approached a woman at work who was new to the job to ask her how she was doing, he abruptly changed his mind and went back to his desk. When asked about the contrary social goal decision, he said that he wasn't sure what to say. The factors and chain of events that led to his decision were relatively straightforward. Lester said he was busy with a report that he had to get out, and this probably contributed to his uncertainty as to what he wanted to say or how to initiate any dialogue. His solution for next time was to close any loops with projects that he was working on or busy with, then slow his breathing and try again.

In the lines below, you can list a social goal as well as the decision you made contrary to that goal. Next, you can gain more clarity on the reasons you took an alternate action or direction. Describe the factors and chain of events that led to the decision that was contrary to your original social goal.

Lester's responses:

<u>Social Goal</u>
Initiate more conversations with female peers.

<u>Decision Made Contrary to Social Goal</u>
Returned to desk rather than initiate a conversation.

<u>Factors and Chain of Events That Led to Decision</u>
Busy with a report, became uncertain, not sure how to initiate.

Below you can list a social goal as well as the decision you made contrary to that goal. In the third section, you can list the reasons you took an alternate action or direction. Describe the factors and chain of events that led to the decision that was contrary to your original social goal.

<u>Social Goal</u>

_____

<u>Decision made contrary to Social Goal</u>

_____

<u>Factors and chain of events that led to Decision</u>

_____

8. Stay in the present when you can, and worrying about things will retreat. This strategy is what the term mindfulness implies. A present focus keeps distractions away. I've always thought mindfulness to be an interesting term, though slightly "overdone" in a way. That is, few people strive to operate mindlessly. While I'm on the topic, I do recall some people saying, after not being "present" or making a slipup, "I forgot myself," which is at the very least an interesting phrase.
9. Occasionally, bring a friend along with you to social events. Have your friend stand away from you, across the room, for example. After the event, ask your friend for honest feedback about how you were coming across in social interactions. This method can be a beneficial way of gaining perspective on how any of us operate socially. The main reason for the friend's remote but active observation is because when we are in the situation, we don't want to be self-monitoring our own behavior too closely.
10. Importantly, in certain social interactions, shyness may not be the problem you are experiencing. For example, at times it is necessary to set limits on demands other

people may be making on your time or available energy to interact. It is not easy for anyone to confront another without some initial hesitation, particularly when you value the relationship. However, boundaries are important to establish with some individuals who may otherwise become too dominant or intrusive at times.

11. Learn the concept of *negative effect reciprocity*, which simply refers to the fact if you give someone a hard time (as in close relationships with family and friends), you can expect that they will reciprocate by giving you a hard time back. It is, of course, beneficial to break out of this loop by returning to the high ground of positive statements. It reminds me of what one senator said about those in Washington who are ethical and do take the "higher ground while traveling to their work." He remarked, "They are not bothered or burdened by heavy traffic."

12. Practice reframing: Virtually any negative comment you may consider making to someone else can be reframed into a positive statement. For example, a typical statement from a parent to a teen is: "This room is a mess." It can be reframed as an affirmative statement, which is usually more helpful. For instance, something in the form of a request: "I would like you to keep this room clean" is more positive and pleasant to hear. Indeed, this type of positive request will usually generate more compliant behavior. For a little humor, there is one comedian's take on messy rooms where he quotes his mom as being an authority. "My mom was an expert on pigsties, because she would tell me that my room was the worst pigsty she had ever seen."

13. Use social support: Seek out those who can understand your feelings and struggles. In turn, be responsive to their needs. Over time, these actions will build trust and mutual support. Be aware that as you become more social, interacting with others will sometimes include disagreements or conflict. When this happens, a constructive approach can be as simple as direct discussion to address the breakdown. You can even initiate the conversation as an example of learning to lead the way. For instance, a simple statement such as "Looks like we're having some friction over this issue. Let's talk about it," can get the ball rolling. Finally, if you're feeling significant loneliness, this is a particularly important time to reach out—family, friends, and even talking more with a peer or acquaintance can be very helpful. The overall goal is to increase social support.

14. Use perspective taking. For example, June went to her high school English class teacher to ask why she got a C on her midterm. She usually got As so she was extremely disappointed. Ironically, it was April Fool's Day when she went in to ask the teacher if her low grade was a joke; it was not. When she reviewed her actions with her guidance counselor, the feedback she received was helpful. The guidance counselor asked June how many times she had received a low grade, and she responded, "Just twice. That's it." The guidance counselor then offered that over June's years of test-taking, "twice" only represented less than 5 percent, and in

general, she performed very well. Thus, gaining some perspective on the situation was valuable to June. The guidance counselor then took time to congratulate June on her social skills, especially given that she spoke up to or asserted herself appropriately with her teacher, an authority figure.

15. A good ongoing goal for shy, sensitive individuals is to maintain a realistic positive outlook while not slipping into doom and gloom. Another way to look at this type of goal is to replace negativity bias with realistic positivity. Negativity bias is the tendency to look at things in more pessimistic terms than the reality of a situation warrants.

Case Vignette
Working with a Negativity Bias

Darius, a fifty-four-year-old radiology tech, was a client who tended to find the negative in most situations. While working with him, it became clear that some of his negative pronouncements, such as "If I go to the after-work party, everyone will just ignore me" turned out to be inaccurate. For direct evidence, Darius was asked what happened at his most recent after-work party, and he acknowledged that, in fact, most coworkers engaged him in conversation. It appeared that Darius was using negativity bias to prevent some measure of disappointment should his social situations turn out to include being ignored. I suggested to him that he could flip his self-message, by thinking of the positive possibility that others would interact with him favorably in most social situations.

Darius came up with the self-prompt "My next social interaction will go well if I try" as a way to be more realistically positive about his future interpersonal opportunities. It worked, to a degree. Darius mentioned in a session that being positive could help, but he sometimes slipped back into a "negative place." We reviewed how old behavior is better established than new behavior and what setbacks are to be expected. I reminded Darius that he had made progress in his social behavior and that "being negative about his negativity" isn't worth the emotional energy investment. Clinically, we call this "having a symptom about a symptom," for example, getting uptight about being anxious. As is true for all of us, Darius needed a healthy dose of self-compassion and the maturity to recognize that some imperfection versus perfection is actually a preferred goal in life.

16. Be wary of the *intolerance of uncertainty* sentiment that some individuals, particularly those who are generally anxious or socially anxious, sometimes live by. For example, if you enter an unfamiliar social situation and aren't sure how the interactions are going or where they're headed, the intolerance of uncertainty might

kick in. If it does under such circumstances, you may just want to leave. At the risk of being uncertain as to how to proceed, social anxiety, including tension, can increase, making the plan to avoid interacting and skip the scene more compelling. The way out is to accept some measure of uncertainty, as things may turn out better than you initially expected.

Case Vignette
Dealing with the Intolerance of Uncertainty

Amir, a forty-seven-year-old hospitalist with an exacting style in his work as a busy inpatient physician, sought out psychological consultation at the recommendation of a colleague. In counseling, it became clear that his perfectionistic tendencies seemed to be in response to his intolerance of uncertainty. That is, Amir wanted to do everything right, so he became anxious, especially with his medical team, if procedures weren't done in a certain way. He confided that he was shy and, for various reasons, didn't like unpredictability. Thus, he strove to structure his work, including conversations and his personal activities, in such a way as to minimize disruption.

In discussing the implications related to the intolerance of uncertainty, Amir acknowledged that he needed to "check all the boxes" before proceeding with any tasks. When asked what drove this behavior, he said he often asks himself, "What if this?" or "What if that?" happens. Thus, we had our work cut out for us given a serious case of the "what-ifs." This type of self-questioning can be expected in those individuals who are socially anxious to the point that they want all their interactions to go smoothly. With Amir, it meant precision in interacting with his medical team, family, and friends. In working with Amir, he understood the concept of the *courage to be imperfect* and was given tasks in which he would interact with others with the focus off himself. He strove to actively listen more while thinking about what they wanted to say to him. Amir did this rather than ending up in the "what if this doesn't go well?" loop. In general, when we focus on the other person, our own thoughts, preoccupation, and questioning tends to dial down.

Amir tried hard and made good progress in becoming less questioning of outcomes before they even happened. That is, until one day in session, he asked, "What if I don't ask myself enough about what-ifs?" The best clinical intervention that came to my mind was to say, "Hey, just tell yourself to snap out of it." Recognizing the preposterous lengths to which our minds can travel on negative autopilot, we both laughed at the human condition, as well as my attempt at humor with a flippant comment.

Social Strengths and Weaknesses

After trying out some conversations with others, take a few minutes to review your strengths and effective patterns of social responding. Also, ask yourself if there are any weaknesses or behaviors you would like to change or modify. Some people do well by simply applying, shall we say, Midwestern social sensibility, as in say "Hi," "Bye," and, "Nice to see you."

> **Case Vignette**
> *Recognizing Social Strengths and Improving Weaknesses*
> Take Atticus, whom I saw in individual counseling when he was a young adult starting out in sales after college. His supervisor had told him that he needed to learn how to engage potential clients. Atticus took this to mean he had to use more "gift of gab," as he put it. Working on his existing social strengths, he was able to identify that he could easily talk with others about his hobbies. On the downside, Atticus said he tended to shoe gaze or look down when talking with others. His supervisor told him that when he was young and in sales training, his boss just told him to make sure he smiled when talking with others. We both had a laugh when Atticus pointed out the irony of his supervisor's comment when he saw a poster in the back of the company's accounting office that read: "Smiling is contagious, which is frowned upon."

Practice Opportunity

Identifying Social Strengths and Weaknesses

List which social strengths have served you well in relating to others. Next, list those social weaknesses that you would like to improve on.

Atticus's responses:

Social Strengths
1. Working on using the gift of gab more, or being motivated to speak up
2. Being able to talk with anyone about hobbies if they were interested

Social Weaknesses
1. Needing to improve direct eye contact with others when in conversation
2. Smiling more when in communication with others

Evaluate your own social strengths and weaknesses. First, list which social strengths have served you well in relating to others. Second, list those social weaknesses that you would like to improve on.

Social Strengths

    1. _____

    2. _____

    3. _____

Social Weaknesses

    1. _____

    2. _____

    3. _____

Improving Social Skills When Difficulties Emerge

The good news is that because shyness can be driven by difficulties in social interactions, learning social skills to improve those interactions is an effective overall strategy. Indeed, sensitivity to comments or criticism by others can be addressed in social skills training. For example, role-play exercises in a supportive environment can help. An easy way to start is by watching a role model present the desired behavior in a particular social interaction. Next, you can go ahead and try it yourself and play out the role that you've just observed. That is, just imitate the role model's actions (verbal and non-verbal) and see how it goes. Also, feedback from others whom you've chosen to casually watch or observe you from a distance can be especially useful. Basically, these helpers can provide feedback following the social interaction sequence you just had. For instance, a friend might offer the following: "Ok, good with your voice and posture. Now try a little more direct eye contact next time."

In developing effective social skills, it is easiest to start with a relatively simple social interaction and then progress to more complex ones. Pay close attention to what you can tolerate in terms of anxiety. That is, if your social anxiety climbs too high, go back to a simpler social interaction, one that is relatively short. Relevant postevent feedback can include these prompts to yourself: "What worked?" "Were there any difficulties?" "What could I try that would increase the chances of a positive experience?" You can keep notes on all your practice opportunities, which will provide you with a useful gauge of your overall progress. When you see the gains that you're making from your written notes, it can be very reinforcing in and of itself.

Take Shanice, a sophomore in high school, who came up with her own "social exercise" as she called it during one individual counseling session. She tasked herself with talking to three or four peers she had never met before. She had one of her friends watch how she was doing from some distance away. Shanice did well in terms of finding some common talking points with several peers yet felt intimidated by one girl who was older than her. She became tense and anxious. Shanice thought about it and decided to stick with simpler social interactions by initiating conversations with peers that were around her age for the time being.

Removing Yourself from Toxic Social Situations

Communicating effectively with others has many advantages, including forming rewarding relationships at home, school, work, and in the community. However, there are times when you may want to remove yourself from a particular social situation that has become toxic. A typical toxic social situation is one in which people are starting to raise their voices too often or cut one another off repeatedly. One strategy that can work well is to have a special phrase handy that communicates something like, "Let's tone it down, or maybe I just need to take a break here." If you're becoming anxious due to any rapid escalations in a face-to-face interaction, the standard "I want (or need) to leave to catch some fresh air" also works well because it's often true. At other times, it may be appropriate to exit a social situation politely if you find yourself becoming too irritated with how the interactions are going. In general, try to foster a positive social orientation with the hope of developing a constructive support system over time. Communicating with people that we care for usually goes better from the get-go. Thus, encourage mutually rewarding friendships by being sure to ask others out for an activity, especially if they have asked you out previously. Gathering a support system, which can involve as few as two people, ensures that many, if not most, of your social situations will be toxic free.

Chapter 9

Specific Topic Areas in Shyness Responding

Social Interaction and Anxiety

Very few people are comfortable with *social homelessness*. A lack of family, friends, or romantic relationships in your life can be remedied by reaching out. One useful strategy is behavioral activation, which is exactly what it says—put yourself out there by literally getting up and getting going. For example, you could call someone on the phone or initiate a visit with someone you haven't seen in some time. Psychological research has shown that behavioral activation can help improve focus, mood, and self-confidence. Examples of behavioral activation include exercise, engaging in hobbies, and family get-togethers or community events. Speaking of hobbies specifically, if you want to decrease your social anxiety, consider joining an activity or project with friends or peers. Examples include a musical group, card playing, a golf outing, bowling—you name it. When we are engaged in an activity that requires our full attention and concentration, we are able to suspend our worries, preoccupations, and self-consciousness. Of course, our social anxiety may return despite our best efforts, but less and less as we begin to extend our comfort zone into activities we choose to participate in and benefit from. Events that we don't choose but would do well by being involved in, such as school or work meetings, may also be a little easier once you've learned how to interact with others more often.

Social interaction is also a form of behavioral activation and can become stressful at times. Shy or socially anxious individuals who are reluctant to engage in conversations can relate to a three-phase sequence that often occurs. First, there is a hesitation to initiate. Second, a shy person can feel overloaded by social stimuli, which can then result in freezing or flooding. The freezing response refers to a type of shutting down that others may, mistakenly, interpret as detachment or aloofness. A flooding response (which can cause or aggravate freezing) occurs when an intense social situation results in the individual (shy or not) being overwhelmed with feelings or emotions. Third, after a conversation, the shy may obsess over any real or perceived criticism they may have received. Thus—as effective generals know—it is sometimes okay to simply beat a retreat, at least temporarily, and to fight again when circumstances permit. That is, stop a direct-action sequence if it gets too stressful, and sticking it out is causing too much of an anxiety spike. You can pull back, again temporarily, while setting your sights on trying again very soon in a new conversation or other social situation.

Kiara was a twenty-year-old modest student who rarely asked questions in class and described the reason as "being shy." This was slightly surprising, as she was now a senior in college with such high grades that one would assume class participation had contributed to them. Who knows? She may have had professors who valued less talking in class as preferable to more. Tension over an upcoming job interview resulted in her coming in for counseling. Her main concern was whether she could socially "perk up" in her words. This is an example of someone who is shy but would like to learn to be more outgoing for a specific purpose, namely the all-important job interview process. Kiara watched successful job interview scenes online and talked with several of her friends to get pointers on how to proceed. This form of observational learning is an effective method, especially to learn new social skills. One thing that she found interesting in her discussion with others that she didn't expect was that it is okay to ask the interviewers a question or two toward the end of their meeting. Ultimately, Kiara did well enough in her job interview efforts yet self-reported that her anxiety remained high mostly toward the beginning of a given job prospect. She could calm down when her breathing slowed, and she was able to relax her neck and back slightly during the actual interviews. She even commented, "No one seems to notice when I go through my relaxation steps." Good progress was made.

Shyness and Dating

As a shy person who wants to be effective in dating, first learn the local social situational cues and norms. For example, it can be explained by noting that, in some ways, it's like paying attention to a foreign culture. The meaning of bowing in Japanese is an expression of courtesy and respect. These days, I suppose, a local American social cue may be an acquaintance looking up from a smartphone when the shy person says hello. Making supportive and empathetic responses while dating is a good way to reinforce the duration and quality of any romantic relationship, given that it has gained some traction from the beginning or outset.

If you tend to be rejection-sensitive, be careful not to *trust test* too much in dating situations. For example, checking up on the consistency of someone's statements, their whereabouts, or what they're doing can erode a developing positive relationship. How to break the rejection-sensitivity cycle centers on three main components:

1. Be aware of when it occurs by using situational awareness. For example, if you're sensing you may be rejected in a certain social situation, consider that further interaction with the other person may not be productive and move on. Alternatively, perhaps you notice that you feel this way in too many social situations, even neutral ones, such that you may want to hang in there. You can try to socialize again with a little more openness and assertion on your part.

2. Surround yourself with supportive family and friends. Those close to you can give you feedback on whether they think you may be overreacting in a certain set of

social circumstances. Family members and trusted friends can be there to provide you with both feedback and encouragement. Your job is simply to ask for support when faced with an uncertain social situation.

3. Work on feeling more confident in a variety of social situations. Chronically shy individuals tend to become more inhibited. They tend to withdraw from many social situations and leave or escape from those encounters they can't completely avoid. In general, as psychologist Dr. Bonnie Jacobson put it, the goal is to "get the shy people to be more comfortable in their own skin." Once calmer, you will come across more effectively. It takes practice, as most worthwhile things do.

Part of what you're trying to do to manage shyness effectively, especially for dating purposes, is learn to be calmer and more relaxed. A quiet, reserved stance is a personality asset that still allows you to reach out to others, especially when it is favorable for you to do so. Also, being a good listener will draw others to you and can be a pleasant surprise to many in our modern, fast-paced world.

Another approach is to be extroverted when it's appropriate. For example, a shy individual may not meet as many prospective dates if they remain relatively isolated and withdrawn from social contact. If the same individual can act more outgoing by hanging out with others and going to various social activities, even very temporarily, they may meet their goal of finding a date. The next step is taking the plunge and initiating contact with someone you're interested in. Dates can lead to more enduring romance and intimacy, a major benefit in the effort to be (or act) more outgoing, as in *situationally extroverted*. You're playing against type (a normally quieter you) for an important reason. Basically, this action plan of being more extroverted is meant for a purpose, namely dating. A more permanent outgoing stance than a situational one is simply not necessary. Who wants to play against type for long? That is, we are all more introverted or extroverted, more shy or less shy, and so on. Thus, the plan is to use something other than your "ordinary or usual" personality style when it may work best for your goal.

Somewhat tangentially, but relevant to the balance between social and solitary, I'm reminded of an obituary I read in an Iowa newspaper. The long-ago piece was short and piercingly succinct. It read: "Jim was well regarded in the community. He enjoyed spending time with his family and friends and listening to the radio." I assumed that Jim had a gift for being social, especially with family and friends. He also relished his alone time and the solitary pleasure that a welcoming radio could provide.

Cautionary Dating Tips
For teens and adults, helpful tips for dating, whether shy or not, include the following:

1. Check them out first.
2. Ask other dates if appropriate.
3. Ask your friends about them.

4. Note their verbal and nonverbal behavior.
5. Date in small groups first.
6. Date in public.
7. Take separate cars initially.
8. Give a family member or friend your timetable.
9. Communicate directly and assertively.
10. Be familiar with emergency services (including 911).

Shy individuals are likely to be effective at following these tips in that they involve careful observation, talking with those you already know, and following through with cautious action. The one behavior that is important to get things started is to reach out to friends and family and let them know you're interested in dating. By using the tips related to increasing social support, you can counteract the observation that many shy people tend to suffer in silence. As psychologist Dr. Zimbardo, a leading expert in shyness, has put it, the shy can imprison themselves by not reaching out. Shy individuals aren't the only ones who experience significant physical and emotional pain at various points in life, but the inward direction and hesitancy to express yourself to others can compound distress. Psychiatrist Dr. Karl Menninger has used an apt analogy we can all relate to: "When a trout rising to a fisherman's fly gets hooked and finds himself unable to swim about freely, he begins a fight, which results in struggles and splashes and sometimes an escape…In the same way, the human being struggles with the hooks that catch him. Sometimes he masters his difficulties; sometimes they are too much for him. His struggles are all the world sees, and it usually misunderstands them. It is hard for a free fish to understand what is happening to a hooked one." In the case of shy individuals, others may see the hesitancy and inhibition in their interactions yet not know of their internal emotional pain or its extent. Just as there is physical pain, emotional pain can be very real.

Relevant to the shy, emotional pain can be brought on by social rejection, and the line between experiencing physical or emotional pain is very thin. In other words, both types of pain are just that—painful or hurtful. One main solution, as is discussed throughout this book, is to practice different strategies and techniques to become more comfortably social. But first, a little more detail from emerging research has found that brain circuits that process physical and emotional pain overlap. This finding should not be surprising in that we have one overall nervous system. To minimize the complexity, the neural signatures of physical and emotional pain will continue to need clear identification. The challenge for the shy focuses on not allowing feeling stung emotionally, which results in the common overreaction of pulling back for too long socially. The solution, to reiterate, is to get out there and interact when you're ready, or, as they say, "take the risk." It can be rewarding.

Case Vignette
Dating and Situational Shyness

Levi, a twenty-year-old college student, found himself at a relatively small four-year college in southern California. He came in for counseling during one of his breaks due to his "hang-up over dating," as he put it. Levi was quite extroverted or outgoing in most of his interactions with others. He said, "I don't know what it is. When I see a girl I'm attracted to, I just freeze. It's as if the spreading wings of the angel of death are fast approaching." First, I asked Levi if he was a drama major, and he responded, "How did you know?" Then we got down to business in terms of working on relaxation methods to slow his rapidly rising reactivity. This increase in vigilance almost always occurred right before he would introduce himself to someone who he thought he might like. Next, we worked on situational talk. Dealing with simple topics about how things are going is a great way to start a conversation. In time, Levi practiced talking with many different young women about any number of things and expressed that it did indeed get easier with practice. Finally, he was able to ask several different students that were in his same classes to do some things—casual dating, really—and was proud of himself. An important thing that Levi learned was to "lower the demand characteristics" as we clinical psychologists put it. That is, simple and easy conversation is the way to go, rather than demanding of yourself that you always find something important to say.

Embracing Uncertainty

Another challenging strategy you could try involves embracing uncertainty. Basically, no matter what you've been saying to yourself, even something as simple as "I don't know if anyone I know will be at the wedding" doesn't have to be a no-go for the event. In fact, you can choose to go ahead and attend while recognizing your uncertainty. The point of this type of response is that you always have a choice about whether to proceed or not. It is a healthy emotional habit to go ahead and challenge uncertainty from time to time. Of course, if a neighbor's dog is barking and has bitten others before, maintaining uncertainty and active avoidance is a recommended strategy. This is true even if the pet's owner (with whom you'd like to socialize) says, "Oh, he's fine. There's been no lashing out at anyone for over two weeks."

In general, the next time you ask yourself, "Am I sure about this?" experiment with taking the next step to see what happens. No need to overworry. I'm reminded once again of the girls' high school cross-country team ,whose coach advised, "You can do anything you want, as long as it's not dangerous, illegal, or immoral." This type of admonishment does cover the waterfront with broad caution, yet leaves some opportunity for charging ahead, right into the land of uncertainty.

Focusing and Reframing

There is that clinical saying that is useful: "What we focus on, we amplify." When we think positively about a situation and concentrate on how well we would like things to go, we are encouraging a better outcome. For example, if an individual focuses on something as routine as getting to work on time, this action is amplified through daily prompts, with on-time attendance likely to follow. When we focus on possible negative outcomes, the associated thoughts become amplified. An example would be someone saying to themselves, "I was late yesterday. I think I might be late again. It's a habit." Of course, to reduce guilt, the same individual might add a convenient justification, such as "Most people are late from time to time. It's no big deal."

Reframing negative self-statements into positive ones is usually the way to go and can even serve the same end. For example, the "I was late yesterday..." phrasing could go better if the person being nonchalant changed their self-statement to "I would like to be on time more often, yet I know most of us who work are late sometimes." Does a negative self-statement and focus in and of itself necessarily result in a bad outcome? No, but focusing on what could go right with positive reframing is a better way to think about many future situations, particularly social ones. The focus often amplifies the prospect of a good outcome. As mentioned previously, one psychologist came up with a great prompt you can repeat to yourself: "Breathe in confidence, exhale doubt." Finally, you can prepare yourself for a problematic result by being (once again) positive: "I can cope with this not going well" is an example of a good self-statement that is realistic.

To extend the topic of things not going well, another constructive approach is to take a direct-action by starting a new social project that you indeed expect may not be easy. As an example, let's say you get asked to bowl with a group of friends but have never tried it before. In all likelihood, you can expect to perform below par, as in a few (or more) gutter balls. The best and most accurate self-prompt can be something like, "It's okay. I still like being with my friends, and I'll improve in time." Also, you can announce your circumstances to others in a constructive way to decrease your anxiety while letting others know your stance. For example, you could say something in a straightforward way, such as, "Thanks for inviting me. This may even be fun, but I have to let you know, I've never bowled before, so don't let me slow you down while I try it out." Finally, even if you fall below whatever standard you've set for yourself, take stock in Winston Churchill's quote: "Success consists of going from failure to failure without loss of enthusiasm."

Changing Yourself First

I've had shy clients remark that if others were nicer to them, they would speak up more. Interestingly, there is a higher probability of changing someone else's behavior, such as being nicer to you in social situations, if you focus on changing yourself first. This informal human law specifies that if you change yourself (basically your response), such as leading off by being friendly, the other person cannot (easily) stay the same. For example, the typically curmudgeon boss might turn slightly nicer in response to your consistently friendly approach. I suppose this is the reason they instruct customer service representatives, who are sometimes tasked with dealing with difficult callers, to remain friendly. That is, if the customer on the other end of the line is angry and escalating, a calm tone from the service representative might help deescalate things. However, when some people hear a controlled pseudo calm voice on the other end, especially when the caller has a valid complaint, it can be even more frustrating. Of course, a shy person could just use the assertive voice learned and state upfront, "Please don't use any pseudo calm manipulation on me while I'm venting. I might escalate."

Social interaction skills can be learned, and the change-yourself-first approach gives you a higher probability of success. It beats trying to get other people to change first, which is a lower-probability prospect. Although there is a concept, termed social exchange theory, that is relevant in that it calls for each party to change or adjust to one another's stance. I'm reminded of a T-shirt I saw a woman wearing as she was walking with her husband. The terse statement was entertaining while revealing at the same time as it read: I'll be nicer if you'll be smarter.

Specific Strategies to Effectively Manage Shyness

1. Work on your communication skills by talking more with your family and friends on a frequent basis. This approach doesn't always work with all family members and friends (maybe some are shier than you are). Not to worry, as I've informed clients, you only need one or two people in your family or peer group who will welcome some conversation.

2. Before initiating discussions with others, jot down a few talking points you want to cover, and then go over the list briefly before you enter the conversation. A good way to begin most conversations is to ask a question or make a comment. For example, "Do you like living in Anchorage, Alaska?" After this type of icebreaker (no pun intended), you could add a comment such as "I don't know about you, but I feel like putting on an extra pair of socks when it starts to hover around zero."

3. If you're not sure about a particular social situation, ask others about it, and then proceed when you feel you have enough information to go on. For example, I recall one time when I was invited to do a talk for a hospital group on alcohol and drug abuse. It turns out that the approach I took in addressing the subject was just about the opposite of the facility's desired one. Clearly, I should have talked with the person who invited me first, and then I could have at least incorporated any ideas they may have had on how they assess and treat substance abuse issues.

4. Smile and laugh more as you gain spontaneity in your interactions with others. You will most likely find that your conversations flow more easily when you open up.

5. Show up to any meetings (at work or socially) on time or early. This action provides an easy way to warm up and mingle. In the process, be nice and be sure to compliment others as appropriate. Something more than "I like your tie" or "Nice shoes." Some people used to think I was friends with the local meteorologist because,

coming from the Midwest, I'd always ask about daily conditions when greeting others. I wasn't being superficial either; the weather changes a lot in Illinois and Iowa, as well as in other parts of the country. Indeed, weather patterns affect our daily lives. I suppose a useful theme would be to talk about topics you're comfortable with and see where it takes the conversation.

6. Learn to take small steps toward being more social. Clearly, it is tough to make decisions in the face of uncertainty. Take it slow and approach each social practice opportunity by first considering short versus long conversations for starters.

Helpful General Strategies for Yourself and Others

1. Compromise and negotiation in your dealings with others are important and lend themselves to smoother, more effective social interactions. For example, if someone you know wants to go to a different restaurant than you do on a particular occasion, you can use the *go-along-to-get-along* strategy. Something like, "Sounds good to me, and next time maybe we can go to that new place I like by the lake, rather than your pick today, which is near the active volcano area."

2. Set limits with others. For example, you may want to let others know how much time you have available on a certain day. Be careful to set only those limits you can reasonably follow through with. For instance, if you set a limit on yourself, such as "I will not leave any social situations early, even if I get really anxious," you may not be able to follow through with such a high (and rigid) standard. I recall taking a CPR course in which the instructor used the phrase "slow is fast." Apparently a popular prompt among many paramedics and ER personnel, it does make a lot of sense. My interpretation is that when you are in a social situation that drives your adrenaline (and social anxiety), take time to breathe, then think about your current capabilities and limits. And then proceed.

3. Practice unconditional self-acceptance (U.S.A.), which simply means that you will want to be uniformly kind to yourself. The way I think of it is that you may have made a mistake, even a big blunder, but you're still a good person. Humans are fallible, and the prompt mentioned a time or two in this book is to have "the courage to be imperfect." Of course, this does not mean do whatever you want, then congratulate yourself for being a good person. Oddly, I suppose it is wise to impose some conditions on even unconditional concepts or practices.

4. Ask for what you want in positive terms. For example, "I would like you to lower your voice a little" is preferable to the negative "Your loud voice grates on my nerves." If we hear someone say to a child, "Don't be shy," wouldn't it be more positive and helpful if the adult flipped to the positive and simply said what they wanted: "I'd like you to speak up because I want to hear what you have to say." Interestingly, almost anything expressed in negative terms can be reversed to a more helpful positive statement. Another example is "Please have the dogs shake

themselves off outside." This works better than "If those dogs shake themselves off in the living room once more, I'm going to go ballistic." An added benefit of leading with the positive is that it lets the other person know what you want (lower your voice, dogs shake off outside). Telling someone something in the negative does not let them know what you want (a loud voice grates on my nerves, going ballistic).

5. Martin Luther King wrote a sermon in which he said, "Shattered dreams are a hallmark of our mortal life." We can take an important meaning away from this quote. That is, we don't always get what we have striven for, as some dreams can get dashed. Yet it remains in our interest to continue toward our goals. With shyness, there will be setbacks, and, at times, frustration with the intrusion of old behaviors. Not to worry, and, indeed, it is not as dramatic as shattered dreams. With consistent effort, positive changes will result, leading to successful shy responses.

6. Simple and effective strategies to work with your shyness:
   a. Avoid definitions; you are not always shy, so don't label yourself as such. For example, you could say, "I was being shy yesterday at the concert."
   b. Focus on others and show interest, compassion, and empathy.
   c. Bring a friend or a social buddy, but do not use a social shield.

7. What are some immediate benefits of successfully managing your shyness? List several main benefits. (Example: "I can meet more people that interest me.")
   a. _____
   b. _____
   c. _____

Old Behavior is More Established Than New Behavior

It is an informal human law that old behavior is better established than new behavior. The one vivid example of this that comes to mind is from a story my dad told me about his father, my grandfather. It was back in the time, around 1920 or so, that many were still riding horses in their agriculturally based daily lifestyle. Then early automobiles came, the Model T, and subsequently the Model A. As the story goes, my grandfather was driving his newfangled vehicle into an intersection, and the brakes weren't working efficiently at all. What did he do? He began to yell, "Whoa." Clearly, with years of telling a horse how to stop via the whoa command, this familiar old behavior was not going to work versus the new behavior of pushing down on the brake pedal.

Another, more current example related to shyness is when someone who has been quiet with others for years begins to speak up, which would clearly be a new behavior. Thus, falling back by being quiet, especially in a stressful situation, is to be expected from time to time. Or, a shy individual just learned to initiate conversations but is much more used to having the other person talk first. As the conversation begins with someone, it would be easy to see how there could be a pause. The new behavior of initiating doesn't kick in, and the shy person once again waits for the other person to respond first. It is important to note that returning to previous well-learned behavior is not a reason for personal recrimination. Take an individual who has smoked cigarettes for twenty years, then decides to quit. A week later, they relapsed by smoking again. Would we be surprised or judge such an individual as "failing abstinence." Let's see, twenty years of smoking (the old behavior) and one week of not smoking (the new behavior). I'd give the person a break and say, "Good for you, you've got a start. Now get back on the proverbial horse and ride." I would probably even add, "Great initial effort."

Shyness as an Asset at Home, Work, or School

Just as we're learning that managing problems associated with shyness can lead to being successfully shy, we can also take stock in the assets shy behavior already provides.

Case Vignette
Shy Behavior as an Asset

Isabela, a twenty-one-year-old actor, although shy, trained herself to project a "quiet presence" that worked well in various roles. Her reserved presentation projected a unique individual quality that helped her on set. Meanwhile, she noticed that when interacting with her friends, an active listening stance drew others close. Isabela received consistent feedback from friends and acquaintances that her ability to listen was appreciated, as they sensed her care and concern for their welfare. The combination of two different shy behaviors, namely having reserved accessibility in acting (which was genuine) and maintaining an empathetic listening approach in her friendships, were both important shy assets.

In the following practice opportunity, you can indicate how you've been able to use shyness as an asset at home, work, school, or in the community.

Practice Opportunity

Using Shy Behavior as an Asset

List one or two ways that you've been able to use shy behavior as an asset at home, work, school, or any other social outlet, such as in your local community.

As an example, here are Isabela's responses:

Shyness Behavior Used as an Asset	Main Result
1. Projecting a "quiet presence" in acting roles	This type of reserved presentation gave a unique individual quality to her work
2. Using an active listening stance with friends	Received appreciation from those she interacted with that they felt heard

In the following section, you can list one or two ways that shyness or shy behavior has worked for you.

<u>Shyness Behavior Used as an Asset</u>   <u>Main Result</u>

1. _____   _____
                                     _____
2. _____   _____
                                     _____

Practical Problem-Solving Strategies for Shyness

Shyness centers on a tendency to avoid social interactions due to discomfort, even though participation with others is desired. Self-consciousness arises from shyness due to concerns over being criticized or judged. Further, cognitive negativity (thinking about troubling scenarios) can create a reluctance to act. A couple of major literary references or examples of shyness include the characters Holden Caufield in *Catcher in the Rye* and Boo Radley in *To Kill a Mockingbird*. In both books, the characters are seen by others as shy, distant, or withdrawn, if not outright different. Yet, as each story progresses, these same individuals are clearly sensitive and caring toward others in the end, especially toward children. Thus, a problem with avoidance is likely to occur in shyness, but on the positive side of the equation, sensitivity to the concerns of others is a huge asset.

The following four strategies or tips will help with shyness problem solving:

1. Use positive coping statements. For example, a shy person thinks to themselves, "I've talked before a group before, and even though I was anxious, it worked. I can do this again and will bring a friend who can give me feedback afterward."
2. Work on increasing social support and connectedness. Disclosing shyness or a reserved stance to family and friends will usually bring acknowledgment, as they have likely noticed your behavior. Further, support and connectedness are likely to occur because people can relate to feelings of discomfort in social situations.
3. Disrupt any polarized or all-or-nothing thinking you may be engaging in. For example, Tai was very self-critical, and, with his shyness, he didn't like to venture out much on campus. He felt as though he needed to say the right thing to anyone he met, or else he shouldn't say anything at all. In counseling, Tai learned that such a dichotomous or all-or-nothing approach will not result in greater social interaction. He did want to be more social and was thus able to take the suggestion that just getting out on campus and talking with others didn't need to be perfect. He could relate to the notion that verbal communication is filled with pauses, temporary awkwardness, and sometimes miscues that everyone experiences from time to time. For proof, he was asked to be on the lookout for the phrase "I misspoke,"

which can be heard occasionally from most college professors, except for those who are still learning to acknowledge imperfection.

4. While we're on the topic of being self-critical, it is also important to learn how not to create another symptom of the first symptom (self-criticalness). In other words, if an individual is shy as well as highly sensitive, a self-critical symptom or stance can create another symptom—that of being anxious or depressed over being too self-critical. Clearly, a vicious cycle of emotional disruption generally follows. Not to worry, we can go to a practice opportunity that will help find a way out of this all-too-common symptom-about-a-symptom quandary.

Practice Opportunity
Avoiding the Development of a Symptom About a Symptom

As briefly described above, be careful not to create or develop a symptom about a symptom. For example, Diedre, a sixty-three-year-old retiree, was often self-critical (a symptom). At times, she would fall into a depressed mood (a larger symptom) over being self-critical. A way out of this negative loop is to use unconditional self-acceptance (U.S.A.). In time, Diedre learned to say to herself that even though she could get depressed, especially over her self-criticalness, she could usually rely upon her smarts and easygoing manner. These abilities were much larger aspects of her intellect and personality.

At one point in counseling, Diedre remarked that her episodic depressed mood could be a drag, but it certainly "didn't define her being" as she put it. She had learned unconditional self-acceptance (U.S.A.). Learning to distinguish your problems or separate them from your value as a human being is fundamentally important. Shyness, for example, can be a problem at times, but in no way diminishes your value as a unique individual with assets living in the world. We all experience successes and failures along the way; it's best to practice U.S.A.

List a symptom you have that is generally associated with your shyness on the left. On the right, list the symptom you've developed about that symptom. Finally, indicate what alternative response you've been able to come up with that gets you out of the symptom about a symptom conundrum.

Diedre's symptom responses:

<u>List Your Symptom</u>
1. Self-criticalness

Alternative Response:

<u>List Your Symptom About a Symptom</u>
Depressed about it. I don't like getting down about being hard on myself.
I can rely upon my abilities and by using U.S.A. I can be easy going about things

List a shyness symptom on the left. On the right, list the symptom that you developed because of your first symptom.

List Your Symptom

1._____

Alternative Response:

List Your Symptom About a Symptom

_____

_____

_____

_____

_____

Effective Shyness Self-Corrective Actions

Regarding your shy responding, you may already have learned ways in which to correct or alter certain behaviors to be more effective in social responding or to deal with self-consciousness. Think about what self-corrective methods or actions you have considered. More simply put, what have you tried in the past that has worked well for you? For example, if you attended some meetings at school or work and they went smoothy—how did that come about? What did you do (including possibly remaining calm, cool, and collected) that was helpful? Also, as you've noticed being anxious or tense from time to time before a social activity, have you ever slowed your breathing on your own or listened to some music to decrease stress?

Case Vignette
Self-Correcting Withdrawn Behavior

Catalina, a twenty-eight-year-old college graduate, worked in a high-end jewelry store chain and took pride in knowing the product line. The store sold a wide array of watches, bracelets, and rings. While discussing her shyness when she was in college, she noticed a change that she made after entering the work force. Catalina became aware that her work life seemed to bring her more spontaneity, along with "easy socializing" as she put it, with her regular customers.

Catalina said that she had worked through some of her shyness over the years by just "getting out there and talking." At the same time, she felt that she was more open with those who came into the store regularly because knowing them a little better brought comfort and trust. Basically, Catalina self-corrected her shy tendency to withdraw from conversation by putting her best foot forward, although with care. When she was able to see her customers over a period of time, she learned the benefit of familiarity in establishing a more outgoing stance. Catalina's self-corrective stance and the actions she took are detailed below.

Practice Opportunity
Taking Self-Corrective Actions

Self-corrective actions are listed on the left, with the results listed on the right.

Catalina's responses:

Self-Corrective Actions	Results
1. Getting out there and talking	Leaned how to be more comfortable around people when conversing
2. Putting her best foot forward	Leaned that familiarity with customers can help with openness.

List a few self-corrective actions on the left that you have used in the past that have worked well in your efforts to breakthrough shy responding in certain situations. List the results of your actions on the right.

Self-Corrective Actions   Results

1. _____   _____

                                                     _____

2. _____   _____

                                                     _____

Engaging in a Variety of Social Activities

Another way to learn interpersonal effectiveness is to involve yourself in several different types of social activities with acquaintances, peers, or friends. For example, Grant wanted to go to a new aquarium exhibit in town (number seven in the practice opportunity list below). Shy and hesitant, he did decide to ask a female peer, Rosa, who was in his college biology class. She agreed, and they both enjoyed the experience and the time they spent together. In a follow-up counseling session, Grant confided that one of his childhood fantasies was to be a fish in his aquarium at home. He commented that "it would be fun to look out at all the curious people watching me swim around." He said that he didn't share this fantasy with Rosa, to which I replied, "That's okay, perhaps when you get to know each other better."

Practice Opportunity
      Direct-Action in a Social Activity

Choose a social activity from the list below or add one or two of your own. Next, engage in that social situation; that is, take direct-action. Finally, jot down a few remarks on what went well and what didn't.

List the social activity on the left, who you brought along in the middle, and on the right, side indicate how you felt things went—basically the positives and negatives of the activity.

Social Activity	Acquaintances, Peers, or Friends	Post Activity Comments
1. Watching a TV show or movie		
2. Going to a restaurant		
3. Playing a board game		

4. Playing a sport
5. Taking a walk
6. Going on a hike
7. Taking in a concert, exhibit, etc.
8._____
9._____

Grant's responses:

Social Activity	Acquaintances, Peers, or Friends	Post Activity Comments
Taking in an Exhibit (Aquarium)	Rosa, a peer	Grant said he enjoyed the experience and time spent with Rosa.

Select one or two of the social activities from above, or ones you've chosen, and list the social activity on the left. In the middle, you can indicate an acquaintance, a peer, or any friends you asked to join you. On the right side, indicate how you felt things went—basically, the positives and negatives of the activity or situation.

Social Activity	Acquaintances, Peers, or Friends	Post Activity Comments
_____	_____	_____
		_____
		_____
_____	_____	_____
		_____
		_____

Another associated practice opportunity you can engage in following any social situation is to write down the persons, places, and things that increased your shy responses. Next, provide one strategy that you think may help you deal more effectively in one or more of the three domains. First, let's take a look at how Celia handled her increasing shyness.

Case Vignette
Dealing with Increased Shy Responding
Celia, a recently retired postal clerk, decided to take a walk with an acquaintance she met through a friend, and it went okay, but not great. The acquaintance was

Travon, the place was a hill with a view of the city, and one thing that increased Celia's shyness was the fact that both individuals tended to remain quiet. These long periods of mutual silence felt a little to moderately uncomfortable. In terms of a strategy, it may be that the acquaintance wasn't the best match, yet the location or place was nice and didn't seem to be a problem. Celia may have thought to yourself something like, "The thing that I could work on is filling in 'dead space' to keep a conversation going." In this effort, focusing on the other person by asking a relevant question or two is something Celia could try and that usually lowers shy responses.

Practice Opportunity
Social Situations that Increase Shy Responding
List a social situation. (1) Next, describe below what people, places, or things increased your shy responses. (2) For the problem-solving aspect, indicate a simple strategy that you could use to help deal more effectively in this type of situation (involving the domains of persons, places, or things) in the future.

Celia's responses:

Social Situation: Walking with Travon, an acquaintance
1. Persons, places, and things that increased my shyness responding.
   "We both remained too quiet, which was a little uncomfortable."
2. One strategy that can help me deal more effectively in one of the three domains.
   "Maybe the person wasn't the best match, but I think I could have asked a few more questions to keep the conversation going."

List a social situation that increased your shy responses and describe below it: (1) what people, places, or things were involved; (2) indicate a simple strategy that you could use to help deal more effectively in this type of situation (involving the domains of people, places, or things) in the future.

Social Situation: _____
1. Persons, places, and things that increased my shy responses.

   _____

2. One strategy that can help me deal more effectively in one of the three domains.

   _____

   _____

General Tips on Improving Aspects of Problematic Shyness
With the direct-action (or exposure) approach, you can get involved in those social situations that produce anxiety at a slow pace and in graduated steps. In time, with your relaxation

strategies on board, you will be able to experience less anxiety in these same social situations. An apt analogy would be dipping your toe in the water and withdrawing it for a while if it is too cold or uninviting. An example of a common occurrence involving the need for direct-action or exposure is when people want or need to fly but are afraid to do so. Truth be told, the only way to get over a fear of flying is to fly. With the clients I've had who learned to fly without fear (or less fear), I recommend the graduated steps approach. It works by having individuals start by taking a short one-hour flight (after breathing and relaxation exercises), versus a fourteen-hour international route. Things do work out better with a graduated approach to many challenging tasks; there is no need to go big or stay at home when it comes to learning effective shy responses in social situations.

Regarding social activities, the challenge, though, is to keep at it within the graduated approach action phase. This will allow you to stay in the social interactions you've decided to pursue a little longer while your anxiety decreases. With anxiety diminishing, even a small amount, your urge to avoid other similar social situations will also decrease. In general, as your comfort level rises and your avoidance behavior recedes, your social participation will be more engaged and effective. In time, you will be able to tolerate more social situations and circumstances for longer periods. One way to think of direct-action is that it is a strategy wherein you're practicing a social interaction skill in real life. The end game is that through this process, you will be able to spend more time enjoying people, places, and things.

Those with shyness and some measure of social anxiety can sometimes appear to others as aloof and judgmental. One reason for this stance by others is that they notice that shy and socially anxious individuals can be preoccupied and not focused on others. Of course, what might really be going on is that the shy and socially anxious appear more detached because they are concerned about how they might be coming across. Outwardly, this shy stance can look like aloofness, if not outright arrogance, to others. Essentially the opposite of how shy people feel, which is usually more discomforted and uncertain as to how to proceed. Rather than being arrogant, many shy individuals self-report that it is their self-consciousness and inhibition that can get the best of them at times. The best tip here is to experiment with just speaking up a little more and see what happens.

However, there is one aspect of being judgmental that may ring true when it comes to shyly responding in familiar social situations or circumstances. To this point, it is interesting to observe the shy and socially anxious when they are among those that they know well. That is, the shy and socially anxious can at times be dominant, even bossy, and quick to judge those that are close to them, such as family members or friends. Perhaps this makes up for all the times that shy individuals were inhibited, pulled back, or withdrawn from people outside their inner circle. Of course, this may be true for all of us to some extent. Think of it as a human law (an informal one) that we are more real within our families or with close friends. One main reason is that home is often a safe place where we can let our hair down and be ourselves.

Chapter 10

Shyness Interventions Related to Broad Personality Features

Introversive and Extroversive Strategies Related to Improving Shy Behavior
An interesting study summarized in a major psychology periodical publication with the title "Fake It till You Make It" described how acting extroverted for a week can be helpful. The main research finding from the study found that by engaging in extroverted behavior, such as being more assertive or talkative for a week, study participants reported increased well-being. The research study was published in the *Journal of Experimental Psychology* and used the term "forced extraversion," which simply refers to being more assertive, talkative, and spontaneous. This outgoing behavior, which was practiced for a week, helped both introverted and extroverted undergraduate study participants. By the way, this book uses the more popularized spelling, extroversion, rather than extraversion.

Shy individuals have sometimes been referred to as socially introverted, which makes sense if by introverted, you mean quiet and preferring close relationships to high contact with many different people. In general, it is important to recognize that introverted individuals who are normally quieter and reserved can indeed be extroverted or more outgoing at times. As mentioned earlier, introverts may or may not be shy. The concepts of introversion and extroversion are detailed throughout the assessment chapters of *Successful Shyness* for your review. Conversely, those who are extroverted can be caught being quiet, even reading in some isolated library somewhere, fully content alone on at least some occasions. For those who are shy, deciding to engage socially has as its pivot point whether such interaction may cause distress. If possible, emotional discomfort is anticipated in an upcoming interaction, then the goal becomes how it can be lessened or managed more effectively.

For example, I recall way back when I was in elementary school, each student in my class had to do an oral report on a historical figure. I was stumped on how to proceed. My dad, in retrospect, was clearly unaware of my early shyness, suggested I choose *Black Beard the Pirate* and dress up in a costume to tell tales in front of the class. Apparently, he meant this as a serious suggestion, and I remember feeling like running away. There was no way I was going to do anything more than get up and read a few lines about pirates in general. I was distressed but got over it when I reduced my own ten-year-old geared assignment to something much less dramatic. It was an early shyness management effort, I suppose. Based on what I know now, I sometimes wonder or fantasize if a compassionate school psychologist could have helped me back then: "Please excuse this student from doing anything dramatic in terms of an oral report as he may well have a genetic predisposition resulting in an exaggerated inhibitory response style, coupled with high social anxiety." Or perhaps a more characteristic form of help from the early sixties: "No need to excuse this kid. Have him stand up there and do it; it builds character. If he pees in his pants, that's what the school nurse is there for."

Going back to the "Fake It till You Make It" research, an interesting development in the design occurred. When the study individuals were asked to switch and practice introversive behaviors, including being quiet, deliberate, and reserved for a week, decreased well-being was self-reported. The lower well-being result for the "introversion acting week" was experienced by study participants, whether they were generally extroverted or introverted. While this study was limited to US undergraduate participants, it is interesting to speculate that when we try on a new set of behaviors, in this case, acting extroverted for a period of time, it can work. Learning to be more connected with others takes a certain amount of reaching out, and if we can accomplish this by acting more extroverted, even if generally introverted (and/or shy), a new skill has been learned. There is a term in clinical psychology referred to as *functional autonomy*, which refers to gaining an independent and rewarding behavior by first practicing the new behavior. For example, if you aren't particularly interested in tennis but decide to play with a friend and, through practice, begin to like it, what happens? Essentially, the new behavior has become functional, enjoyable, and autonomous or independent. This is another instance of "fake it till you make it," or the more nuanced phrase would be "practice makes perfect," or at least more enjoyable. For shy people, reaching out to others to have more interpersonal connection may at first be accompanied by some discomfort, but in time it can become satisfying. *Successful Shyness* includes many practice opportunities that can make reaching out and being more social easily attainable.

The Shy Extrovert

An effective strategy for the shy extrovert may be to visit with friends but also to leave time for more solitary activities, such as reading a book or starting a hobby. Whereas an outgoing individual may not seem shy to others, they can be, and it is hard for them because they would really like to be more social. It seems that shy extroverts are affected by their own self-consciousness just like any other inhibited person. The difference is that those who are shy and outgoing most likely have their discomfort arise in some but not all social activities. Goals for shy extroverts include directly addressing unmet wishes for social connection. Strive for interpersonal connection on terms that fit your style yet try to remain flexible and open for offers initiated by others. Interestingly, research has shown that encouraging and engaging in social relationships in the school setting or workplace can decrease bullying by others. It may be that if bullies, who are forever looking for easy targets, see that you have a decent social support system, they stay away. Straightforward problem solving includes asking yourself how you can improve your social world on a daily or weekly basis.

Internalizing and Externalizing Coping Styles

Are you an internalizer or externalizer? These two coping styles are prominent, with either style having its pluses and minuses. Interestingly, if we have features of both styles, which most people do, we will be more effective in dealing with others in our daily lives. The internalizing and externalizing coping styles are also discussed in the assessment section (Part 1) of *Successful Shyness*. These two prominent coping styles are summarized here as they relate to interpersonal responding. In short, whether you tend to internalize or externalize more will impact how you interact with other people.

1. Internalizing coping style: Individuals who cope by internalizing issues or problems are often described as self-critical, inhibited, and introverted. Let's break down these three major components:

a. Self-critical. You may get down on yourself frequently for actions that you feel could have gone better. At the same time, you may help others who are struggling.

b. Inhibited. You may often find yourself pulling back due to an internal sense that it isn't necessarily a good idea to put yourself out there with others. Shy people seem to be more inhibited than others, and it may largely be due to their concern over social judgment. That is, they may feel more sting from even slight criticism or rejection in a given social situation.

c. Introverted. As discussed in other sections of Successful Shyness, introverted behavior is often characterized by spending comfortable alone time, high self-awareness, and taking your time in making decisions.

If you can relate to this style in your own social responses, you can use various practice opportunities in *Successful Shyness* to learn self-awareness strategies to develop insight. Next, focus on interpersonal skill-building activities. Those who internalize emotions or *act in* are often described as overly controlled. Regarding self-help or meeting with a mental health professional, if you have an internalizing coping style, focusing on insight, as mentioned above, can be very productive. Ask yourself why you relate to others in the way that you do. Next, engage in interpersonal skill building, such as effective communication (see below), to improve socializing.

2. Externalizing coping style: Individuals who cope by externalizing issues or problems are frequently described as impulsive, action or task oriented, and extroverted. These three main features are briefly summarized as:

a. Impulsive. You're likely to act quickly, sometimes without careful deliberation, and lack inhibition. On a positive note, you're poised to be adventurous.

b. Action or task oriented. You're comfortable taking action and can get tasks done.

c. Extroverted. As addressed in this book, the main features of extroverted behavior include enjoying social company, preferring to talk out problems, and being generally optimistic.

If you feel like this coping style fits, you can use *Successful Shyness* practice opportunities that focus on present concerns and how to decrease distress. Next, concentrate on practical methods to extend empathy and compassion to others. Those who externalize emotions or *act out* are often described as under controlled. Given an externalizing coping style, self-help work or seeing a mental health professional who focuses on the problem at hand is a constructive way to go. Learning ways to resolve any relationship concerns or disputes can be beneficial. While you're at it, given an outgoing stance, try drawing out a shier friend or acquaintance who is also looking to interact with others in a kind and compassionate manner.

Whether you tend to use an internalizing or externalizing coping style, when you make mistakes (everyone does) while pursuing a goal, be sure to use self-forgiveness. It is not necessary or even desirable to have just right experiences, which is simply too perfectionistic. To be more specific, the phrase just right experiences refers to the need for things to look or be a certain way. Thus, we can all give ourselves a break by aspiring to have constructive experiences in whatever we do, with mistakes or setbacks along the way just part of the process. To me, the phrase "constructive experiences" is a worthy modification and a more relaxed stance than having to accomplish our goals in just the right fashion or perfectly.

Social Isolation During Pandemic Times

From the get-go, the devastating effects of the recent Corona virus, or more precisely, the disease it causes, COVID-19, presented the world with a curious action phrase—"social distancing"—meant as an intervention. Clearly a call to arms to stop the spread of an oftentimes deadly virus, the phrase is one that which under ordinary circumstances we would not recommend that a shy or withdrawn individual follow. The opposite phrase, "social engaging" would fit the picture better for those who are shy and socially anxious in terms of getting out there and interacting more with others. But, with a pandemic calling for relative personal isolation, this apparent dilemma can be at least partially resolved by having both shy and non-shy socially engage online.

Of course, most of us are aware that the social distancing the Centers for Disease Control (CDC) has recommended refers to physical distancing, yet many shy individuals may have taken advantage of the lack of public interaction and skillfully retreated to their home comfort zone. Not to worry, in times of a pandemic, we want to prioritize physical health because to ignore the safeguards put in place to protect it could mean illness or even death. Since almost everyone has been affected by COVID-19 in one way or another, regaining social skills and communication capabilities will be a goal everyone can appreciate. In fact, most individuals can now recognize how shy people must feel when they are expected to be effective socially right off the bat. That is, many people have commented on experiencing awkwardness in social situations because pandemic social isolation has resulted in their being out of social interaction practice.

Online Use to Socially Engage During a Pandemic

The internet can be used via social media to extend a shy person's interpersonal interests online. At the same time, one caution for the shy is the possibility of overusing the internet to not engage but instead remain relatively detached from others. Nonetheless, reliable, trustworthy online sites that educate about shyness and social anxiety can be helpful to those desiring more information. Further, valid internet-based counseling and psychotherapy sites are available and can help in reducing symptoms, such as significant avoidance associated with shyness and social anxiety. Chat and discussion groups, as well as online support, can be helpful as a way for the shy to communicate. On the other hand, as referenced above, those who are shy and socially anxious may use online services, such as various forms of messaging, to avoid potential discomfort with more direct forms of communication.

To summarize, there are many common forms or mediums by which we communicate with others. For example, email, instant messaging, video conferencing, telephone, mail, and of course face-to-face interaction. Again, using direct-action or exposure to increase more overt or open types of communication can definitely help the shy. It is important to *start slow and go slow*, particularly at first. This apt phrase essentially means that short encounters with others in conversation are preferable to longer ones. Such limited, informal conversations are also a way to begin reaching out socially as opposed to first trying out a one-hour presentation to the public. Initially, going slow allows social skills to improve over time, with more face-to-face and other direct interactions taking place as confidence builds.

The Optimally Adjusted Personality

Whereas there have been many, many signs and symptoms associated with personality difficulties articulated in clinical research and among the lay public, over the years, I've noticed that it has been much harder to find out what's right with us in terms of personality functioning articles. After searching long and hard, I found the below list on optimal personality features to be a breath of fresh air.

Use the optimally adjusted personality list originated by two clinical psychologists, Drs. Zeklow and Bennett, to help you choose a positive social buddy. Such an individual can help guide you in the world of social interactions and would ideally embody many of the following attributes:

1. Genuinely dependable and reliable
2. Sympathetic and considerate
3. Productive
4. Has the capacity for close relationships
5. Has insight into their own motives and behaviors
6. Behaves in an ethically consistent manner

7. Straightforward, forthright, and candid
8. Adopts a giving stance with others
9. Arouses acceptance and liking in people
10. Has high aspirations

Of course, you can also endeavor to use the above personality features as goals that are attainable now or in the future for yourself. If you do, chances are that your daily lifestyle will benefit, and you will attract others to your social world in the process.

Effective Lifestyle Choices for Mental and Physical Health

1. It is important to get at least adequate exercise and sleep to help deal with stress and stay healthy. Include a nutritional diet, and you will benefit from these effective lifestyle choices. Let's start with exercise. Even simply walking can help bring down anxiety and tension. Sports activities can help, including cycling and swimming. Yoga and muscle relaxation exercises can also be highly effective. A wide array of research on sleep has made it clear that a good night's rest is pivotal to mental and physical health. How refreshing to know that when we allow ourselves to get enough sleep, we are indirectly contributing to our overall daily productivity, be it at school or work. A balanced diet will support a healthy immune system and provide us with extra energy to better meet our short- and long-term goals.

2. One way to improve mental health is by spreading it to others. This can be accomplished by developing the interpersonal skill of empathic listening. This type of listening can be a shy person's asset, one that is noticed and appreciated by others. An active communication stance is an important aspect of empathic listening and includes clarifying what others have said to better understand their viewpoint. For example, Dante was with a friend who appeared upset. He asked what was troubling his friend, who responded, "It's my boss. He's a real perfectionist and doesn't give anyone a break." Dante empathically commented, "That sounds like a tough situation. Whatever your boss is doing that is so uptight, maybe you can work around it. I support you."

3. The phenomena of *initial resistance* comes to mind when trying to minimize any negative impact on mental and physical health. Basically, initial resistance can be honored. That is, initial resistance is simply an issue to recognize and quickly work through. For example, initial resistance can occur when you don't want to go in for a swim because the water feels a little cold, even when the air temperature is ninety degrees. But notice that, after your realistic initial resistance, you decide to take the plunge and find that in only a few minutes you're enjoying yourself. The mental and physical stress of holding back gets extinguished, and you can tell because you feel more comfortable and relaxed. The point is to work through initial resistance to get to the other side, which is a positive goal. It reminds me of one thing I've

always pondered. People have often said in different contexts that "change is hard." I'm not so sure about this as an absolute. Change I don't like is often hard (even after working through initial resistance), but change I want and look forward to doesn't seem hard at all.

Going back to the concept of initial resistance in action, in social situations, you're somewhat in initial resistance mode when you allow yourself time to warm up. This is perfectly fine, and as you acclimate or adjust and basically get familiar with a social situation, the initial resistance often fades. My suggestion is to allow yourself what mental health professionals call *distress tolerance*. In other words, human beings are designed to handle some measure of discomfort to get to the other side—namely, calmer interpersonal responses in social situations. As a lifestyle, being calm and even interacting with others will, in time, improve both your mental and physical health. After all, as it is often said, we are social beings and, to a greater or lesser extent, depend on one another's goodwill.

Another way to go is to try powering through initial resistance—don't wait for motivation. For example, have you ever thought about walking, running, or riding your bike, but just didn't have the motivation? Then, somehow, you decided to get out there anyway, and after a short while, you enjoyed your walk, run, or bike ride. What happened was that you worked through your initial resistance. It's called initial because this type of resistance doesn't last awfully long, thus you can plow through it, motivated or not. The same goes for managing your shyness. For example, start that conversation with an acquaintance and see if you feel better after you've talked for a while.

Psychological resistance is somewhat akin to the concept of resistance in physics. I took physics in college. It didn't really stick with me, although I do recall a few important concepts applicable to everyday life. One natural law is that a stationary body tends to remain stationary, while an object in motion tends to stay in motion. Thus, when we get off the couch (stationary), we are altering our physical world by entering an activity (motion). It works every time, or more realistically, most times. I suppose the awkward analogy to communication would be that if you start talking to someone, you might find yourself talking longer with them than you thought you could. Another important physics proposition, which I may have mentioned in another context within this book, seems to me to be an overarching one, namely that "the laws of physics are unforgiving." The sad implication and truth of this probable fact is that no matter how good a person you are, if you are not careful, you could tumble down the stairs at the same rate of speed as the vacuum cleaner you just let go of. But I digress again.

4. Response prevention refers to not bailing or dropping out of a social situation. That is, once you've engaged in a direct-action, such as joining in on a conversation, you don't want to quickly leave or escape the situation, even if anxiety rises. Basically,

you're preventing the response of leaving, even if you're a little uncomfortable (especially initially). Equipped with the strategies and techniques *Successful Shyness* offers in the practice opportunities, you'll be able to hang in there for a while. By staying in the social situation, your reactivity will settle down, and relative calmness will ultimately prevail. However, if your discomfort rises too fast and becomes too burdensome to handle, you can always take a break and return to the social situation. I recall in older movies that a character would confidently announce, "I need to get some air." It seems a totally socially acceptable option—just get back in there once you've slowed your breathing and calmed down somewhat.

By way of summary, by taking direct-action and staying in a social situation through any initial resistance, and sometimes slight to moderate anxiety, you will get to the other side. By using response prevention or preventing the response of "I'm out of here," you will gain confidence. Again, you can use your best judgment. If a social situation becomes overwhelming or too toxic, sometimes leaving is the preferred choice. To maintain a lifestyle of mental and physical health while staying in sometimes challenging situations, we want to have self-compassion on our side, which is the next topic.

5. Take time out each day to self-sooth or practice self-compassion after having made progress toward your goals, whether you've had setbacks or not. Consider this self-compassion reflection: In general, it sometimes takes a long time to develop a complex-type psychological issue or problem. Regarding shyness, it may well have started when young by keeping distance from others while at the same time remaining physically close to a parent at social activities. In general, and without trying, you may have learned that by avoiding potentially difficult social interactions, discomfort could be minimized. With avoidance rewarded by not having to engage socially, the beginnings of a life-long pattern may have developed. By allowing self-compassion and acceptance, you can give yourself a break. You can allow for a calm or patient stance in the knowledge that positive change, including effectively managing your shyness, will come step-by-step.

Chapter 11

Effective Communication Strategies

Tips to Improve Your Conversation Skills
1. Maintain direct eye contact.
2. Encourage others to interact by asking a question or two.
3. Remember names.
4. Use active listening.
5. Use empathic responding.
6. Use an open communication style.
7. Attend to your own and the other person's nonverbal behavior: eye contact, head and facial movement, body posture, and vocal quality.
8. Summarize what the other person has said and ask for clarification on anything that you did not initially understand fully. This action reflects genuine interest in what the other person discussed.

Another important effective communication technique, termed self-disclosure, deserves further commentary because it can really help deepen relating to others. I call this learning the art of balanced self-disclosure. For example, if someone states they've had many chronic physical issues or problems, you could share (if you want to disclose in this particular interaction) that you have long dealt with, say blushing or excessive sweating. As discussed earlier in *Successful Shyness*, there is an informal clinical human law that self-disclosure begets self-disclosure. What this means or implies is that if you mention to someone that you find yourself standing right next to that it is raining harder, they may simply agree, "Yes, it is." If, however, you expand on the sentiment by further commenting, "It is really raining harder. It sure rained a lot from where I came from in Saginaw, Michigan." A surprising match of your self-disclosure may be made with a comment such as "Yeah, I know what you mean. I grew up in Oregon, and it seemed like it rained almost daily in the fall and winter."

Structuring a Social Conversation
One way to structure an entire social interaction or conversation sequence includes using the following three main steps:

1. Observe how others have had conversations in your area of interest.
2. Mental rehearsal can help you go over how you want the conversation to flow.
3. Active interaction involves going through with the conversation in a focused manner.

Post Communication Debriefing of the Conversation Sequence

After you have put yourself out there and initiated a conversation with someone, allow yourself time to go over the interaction you've had. First, go over the following areas with yourself, then with someone you trust to gain helpful feedback.

1. How do you feel the conversation went?
2. Was your anxiety or tension level low, medium, or high?
3. How do you think the other person responded to you? Favorably or unfavorably?
4. If you were to have the same conversation again, is there anything you would change in terms of your approach, body language, eye contact, or closing the interaction?
5. Finally, consider how you would like to deal with this type of conversation in the future. Ask yourself, "What worked well in the social interaction I just had?"

Case Vignette
Observing Successful Social Interactions

For example, Gwen, a twenty-seven-year-old military veteran, was motivated to watch a socially skilled peer in a conversation, but she was very isolated and couldn't think of anyone. We problem solved this minor dilemma in counseling and came up with an alternative. Gwen would watch someone on a TV show whom she admired and felt she could benefit from how the actor came across. If memory serves, I think she chose Laura Prepon from *That '70s Show*. Referring to one episode, Gwen commented, "She was having an argument with her dad, and I liked how she was direct, but not in a bossy way." Gwen also commented that the actor stood straight, maintained good eye contact, and even smiled a few times, even though she was a little upset. Gwen was able to incorporate the positive features, both verbal and non-verbal, of the actor's interaction, even though it was taken from the TV alone. To think of it differently from watching a live conversation, I suppose you can rewind and view a TV or online social interaction as many times as you want, which is one advantage.

Practice Opportunity
Observing a Socially Skilled Individual

Watch someone you consider to be a socially skilled peer in an active interaction or conversation with another person. This peer could be an acquaintance or someone you admire from afar. As you watch the conversation, write down a few of their interpersonal actions that you view as effective. Indicate what made an impression on you in the successful interaction that took place.

Gwen's response:

Socially Skilled Individual	Effective Interpersonal Actions
1. TV actor from That '70s Show	The actor in the scene was direct yet respectful. She had good body language—both posture and eye contact. She handled things well, even though a little upset.

Observe an individual or two that you view as socially skilled, or someone on TV or the internet. List a general description of the individual on the left and what effective actions you were able to observe from their social interaction on the right.

Socially Skilled Individual	Effective Interpersonal Actions
1._____	_____
	_____
	_____
2._____	_____
	_____
	_____

While not mentioned often enough in articles or books on shyness, a time-out from social interaction can be beneficial. You can even take a short break during a given interaction. For example, if you are getting too anxious while talking with a particular individual, you could simply state that you need to use the bathroom or get some air, then go to calm yourself for a few minutes. Use focused breathing or some other rapid way to de-stress. When you've relaxed to the point where you can return to the conversation, go ahead—approach the person once more and reengage. Alternatively, I read one advice column that stated, "Your fear of speaking up is on you. Get over it and use your voice." While I'm sure this type of suggestion is well intended, it fails the compassion test and ignores how taking a brief break from a taxing speaking interaction can help someone proceed. I suppose my best suggestion would be not to listen to all the varied advice out there. Even if accurate, standard-type recommendations are rarely able to take into consideration an individual's particular situation or set of circumstances.

To summarize, in taking a break from a particular conversation, an apt phrase you could entertain would be something like "strategic social interaction temporary detachment." It's way too long, though. How about the straightforward self-statement, "I'm going to take a brief break"? The point is that avoiding that which you would like to do, such as engage in a desired conversation, is not an example of effective responding in the long run. However, strategically detaching or taking a temporary break can be a constructive avenue or coping method on the way to successful shyness.

Important Communication Elements

When you are communicating with others and trying to form some type of relationship, follow the popular psychological guidance of using:

1. Genuineness
2. Unconditional positive regard
3. Empathetic understanding

Try not to worry too much about some of those who have apparently good outward communication and general social skills. In fact, some of these individuals may overdo it with their loud and verbally forward manners. As they say in Texas, "He's all hat and no cattle." The most effective overall communication pattern to learn is one in which you convey genuineness and unconditional positive regard. That is, a positive regard that doesn't involve judging the other person. Finally, use empathy combined with active listening to really understand the other person, including their interests and concerns.

Because empathy is so important in everyday interactions with each other in society, it deserves a detailed appraisal for the shy and non-shy alike to incorporate into our daily communications. In the dictionary, empathy is defined as a psychological identification with experiencing the feelings, thoughts, and attitudes of another. In practical terms, here is how you can put empathy into practice:

1. Imagine the other person's perspective.
2. Read their emotions.
3. Try to understand the other person in general.

To expand on the important interpersonal concept of empathy, we can focus on three main realms. First, there is what has been called cognitive empathy. This term expresses an ability to understand how the other person thinks; we see and understand their point of view. Second, emotional empathy is described as the ability to feel within yourself the emotions that another is experiencing. This type of empathic response is an immensely helpful skill in establishing rapport. The third form of empathy is titled empathic engagement. Once we're able to consider how someone thinks and relate to their feelings, being helpful is next. That is, we can intervene as we have sensed the need, and are now in a compassionate posture to act.

Because shy individuals are generally sensitive and very aware of their interpersonal environment, empathy or empathic responding can help you initiate contact. For example, you may see someone struggling with their luggage or getting their car keys out of a purse. A simple "I've had that happen almost weekly—can I hold your drink while you find what you're looking for?" can be a helpful, empathic response. In general, when we are responding with empathy, we are maintaining an other-oriented perspective versus a self-oriented one in which we've become too preoccupied with our own thoughts or what to say.

Another way you can express empathy while being effective in your communication with another person is to follow this straightforward three step process:

1. Ask more questions of the other person to express interest.
2. Listen longer to the other person's responses.
3. Pay more attention to other people in terms of what they say and do.

In fact, psychological research has shown that the brain chemical oxytocin, which has been termed the *social hormone*, does seem to be released more when we maintain eye contact and respond to soft physical touch. Thus, human social interactions have a way of increasing oxytocin output, which in turn makes for mutual empathy and helping behaviors. Good news indeed.

When we use effective communication strategies combined with empathic responses, good results can be expected in time. To reinforce your efforts as a shy individual, practice what you're most likely already good at:

1. Use active listening to appreciate the other person's point of view.
2. Ask open-ended questions.
3. Provide nonverbal cues such as nodding affirmatively (as in up and down).

Open-ended questioning is particularly important because it draws the other person out and allows them to respond in more detail. As an example, a classic sequence would involve asking a teen how their high school day went. If you lead with, "How was school?" the answer would most likely be a predictable "fine" or "okay." A more open-ended question may get a broader response, such as "I hope school went well today. Tell me about the highlights." When dealing with others in general, it is helpful to find similarities or common ground rather than focus on differences. For example, two people may have quite different tastes in music, but their love of going to concerts is something that each person shares.

To summarize, using genuineness, unconditional positive regard, and a healthy dose of empathy makes for effective communication in our everyday world. When we are willing to listen to other people's experiences and believe they are valid, we will gain another perspective or take on things. The shy can excel at the expression of empathy as long as they learn to follow the guidelines of reaching out a little, listening, and responding to others with compassion. Short, everyday situational-type conversations and circumstances can be the forum for trying out newfound effective communication skills.

Exploring Broad Communication Styles

In our efforts to communicate effectively with others, it can be helpful to explore several major communication styles in general. Virginia Satir was a well-known and creative family therapist. She identified five main communication styles people tend to use from time to time:

1. The blamer. Blaming someone or something else becomes routine. Others may respond by becoming defensive or arguing back.
2. The placater. This style is used by those who are concerned about how others view them. These individuals are often referred to as "people pleasers."
3. The super-reasonable. This type of communication can seem almost computer-like. The individual responds in a very correct and proper manner, yet with little emotion. Ironically, there can be a high degree of underlying sensitivity, but individuals with this communication style may often appear cold or unfeeling.
4. The distractor. Irrelevant topics may be brought up in this communication style. A range of emotions can be expressed, such as anger or guilt, but they seem to serve the purpose of avoiding a sensitive issue. Worse, there can be an attempt to throw others off through manipulation of their feelings.
5. The leveler. This communication style is what we would like to use, as it is characterized by being assertive yet empathic. Levelers demonstrate emotional balance in dealing with others. Mutual problem solving can more readily occur by using this style.

To summarize, the first four communication styles can be problematic, and yet we may find ourselves slipping into one of these styles based on who we are talking to and what the subject matter involves. So, what is the most adaptive and helpful communication style when dealing with others? It is the fifth communication style, that of the leveler, which is optimal to use in interacting with others simply because it is balanced and congruent. Leveling considers the feelings of both people in the conversation. Clinical research has shown that when we are congruent with what we are talking about, assertive, allow for some self-disclosure, and strive to develop mutual respect, our communications will go as well as can be expected.

Practice Opportunity
Working with Your Communication Style
Take a look at Satir's five main communication styles, as detailed above, and circle the one you tend to use most, as listed on the left. On the right, circle which style you would like to use more often in the future.

Predominant Present Style
1. The Blamer
2. The Placater
3. The Super-reasonable
4. The Distractor
5. The Leveler

Preferred Future Style
1. The Blamer
2. The Placater
3. The Super-Reasonable
4. The Distractor
5. The Leveler

If you're feeling brave, you could ask a family member or friend to identify which of the five communication styles they think best identifies your efforts. You may be surprised if their selection is different from your own. Not to worry; we all use these different communication styles at times. It is thought that, if you agree with the clinical research, the leveler communication style seems to be the way to go in most situations. As a humorous aside, I do recall a wife complaining to her husband in a couple's session, "You don't take blame for anything" to which he responded, "Whose fault is that?" I hoped he could develop the self-awareness in time to identify his chronic-blamer communication style and learn to change to another more constructive predominant style (that of the leveler).

Assertive, Aggressive, and Passive Communication Styles

1. Assertive behavior: open, calm, confident expression of wants and needs. Any action that also respects the wants and needs of others equally.
2. Aggressive behavior: words or actions that coerce others to give in to the aggressor's preferences. Any action that takes away the rights of another person. Goals are achieved at the expense of causing negative feelings in others.
3. Passive behavior: allowing one's own rights to be ignored. Any action that yields to the preferences of another person while not asserting your own wishes.

Details of Communicating Using Assertion as a Preferred Style

Assertive behavior is the most adaptive and preferred of the three interpersonal communication styles, with the main features detailed below. If you become anxious around others often enough, you may begin avoiding many social interactions. Unfortunately, such pulling away from dealing with others can result in social skill deficits simply because you've had less opportunity to learn how to communicate with others. One way to improve interacting with others is to use assertions. Assertion involves responding to others in a direct manner and expressing yourself openly while communicating your preferences. It is important to contrast assertions with other less effective ways to respond. Take aggressive behavior, which involves words or actions that coerce others to give in to the aggressor's preferences—not good. Or consider the opposite of aggression, as in passivity or submissiveness. A passive type of responding to others can allow one's own rights to be ignored. It may be appropriate to put another person's preferences first at times, out of courtesy, but not to the point that you are no longer able to assert your own preferences or wishes as appropriate.

To help your efforts toward successful shyness, it can be useful to remind yourself that effective social interaction is highly related to well-being. Fortunately, we have a straightforward course of action in dealing with others by simply implementing a positive, assertive stance in matters. Let's look at some different types of assertive responding as researched by psychologist Dr. Eileen Gambrill, which you can turn into helpful practice opportunities:

1. Positive assertion. When you plan on taking the initiative.
   a. Initiating conversations: You can start a conversation with simple situational talk. Example: "It sure has been rainy again this week. Do you think it signals the end of our epic drought?
   b. Maintaining conversations: You can use listening as well as speaking skills. Example: "I like what you're saying about the benefits of traveling internationally. What places have you enjoyed the most?"
   c. Ending the conversation: Be direct, even enthusiastic, about future contacts. Example: "Very nice talking with you. I'll be back here tomorrow late morning; drop by if you like."
   d. Asking for a favor: Be clear about what you want and provide the reason for your request. Example: "I really appreciate your watching our house last year. We're going on a short vacation later this month. Can you look after our place again?"
   e. Complimenting others: Offering praise to others is something most of us welcome. Example: "You really look great; your exercise program is something."
   f. Showing affection: When indicated, a pat on the back or a hug can offer compassionate non-verbal communication. Example: "I'd like to give you a hug. Your talk on being affectionate and compassionate with others when appropriate was great."
2. Positive assertion. When someone else plans on taking the initiative.
   a. Accepting compliments: Listen to the compliment and then thank the person. Example: "Yes, I've been trying to slow my pace down a bit, thanks for noticing. I appreciate the positive feedback."
   b. When another person starts the exchange: Listen to what the other person has to say, then respond directly. Example: You can use the answer-question guideline: "Yes, I come here often; how about you?" With this method, interest in the other person is shown.
   c. Responding to requests for a future meeting: Say yes when you want. Also, push yourself a little if you really do want to say yes, but being apprehensive causes you to hesitate. Example: "I'd like to come over to your place for the barbeque, but I'm not sure I'll be free that evening. You know what? I can make it happen. Thanks for the invite."

In general, be aware of your verbal and nonverbal behavior. Being pleasant will encourage others to engage more. For example, smiles, good eye contact, and open body posture all help. These actions are important for another reason—with extroverted, non-shy individuals, they do not always perceive how anxious a more reserved, shy individual may be internally. Quietness can be interpreted as aloofness by an outgoing person. Thus, being a little more open, anxious or not, helps the other (extroverted) person know you are giving the interaction a green light.

3. Negative assertion. When you're involved in taking the initiative.
   a. Disagreeing with others: Use "I" statements rather than "you" statements. Example: "I understand your point, yet I think there is another way to look at this issue." Not, "You clearly don't know what you're talking about given your point of view on this issue."
   b. Resisting interruption: Once again, the use of "I" statements comes in handy. Example: "I'd like to finish my thought."
   c. Apologizing when you're the one at fault: Provide a straightforward "sorry." Example: "I know this was your favorite sweater; sorry for misplacing it. I'm going to look for it as soon as I get home."
   d. Admitting ignorance: No one can know everything. Acknowledge this fact as appropriate to the interpersonal context or situation. Example: "It's true that I know a fair amount about wines, but no, I'm not aware of what particular type of wine Plato drank."
   e. Ending unwanted interactions: Make direct statements that you need to leave the conversation. Example: "Sorry to interrupt, but I have something else I need to get to." Also, here is where the broken record technique can be used, particularly with a persistent person. Simply repeat your statement worded slightly differently: "Really, I've got to get going."

4. Negative assertion. When someone else plans on taking the initiative.
   a. Refusing requests: Clearly and politely decline the offer. Example: "I actually like your sales pitch on the sunglasses, but I really don't think I need a third pair at this time."
   b. Resisting temptations: You don't need to please everyone, including yourself, on occasion. Example: "I'd really like to go on that trip with you this weekend but need to stay here and take care of my child. There's no time to find a babysitter."
   c. Responding to criticism: Agree with any truthful aspects of the criticism. Example: "Yes, you have a point. I was talking loudly. I'll tone it down."

The SAEB Model

Let's say that things haven't gone so well in social activities at times, even though you've made progress along the way. There is a social interaction model that can be used to help things out. It is called SAEB. This convenient acronym, which can be particularly effective with automatic thought processing, stands for symptom, automatic thought, emotion, and behavior. To use this model in everyday communication situations, consider the following everyday situation common communication concerns.

Everyday Situation Communication Concerns
1. Flubbing a presentation.
2. Appearing too nervous.
3. Stuttering occurs during a conversation.
4. Blushing and someone may comment on it.
5. Forgetting what you wanted to say.
6. Shaking (particularly of the hands).

Case Vignette
Using the SAEB Model
When you are facing a familiar troubling situation, you can use the SAEB model to effectively sequence through and manage a social interaction. For example, take number four above: blush, and someone may comment on it. Alana came to counseling because she experienced anxiety and tension when in conversation with just about anyone. Alana worked in a library and, as a young adult, would run into many different people and situations when at the front desk. At one point, she stated, "I can feel my face warming up, and I then know I'm blushing." In grade school, more than once, she was teased by others with remarks like "Are you embarrassed again?" or "I just asked you a question. You don't need to blush." Alana described feeling trapped because the blushing wasn't something she could hide or "make go away" from her response when anxious.

We reasoned together that the best strategy may be to get on the front end of the problem. Using the SAEB acronym, we first fleshed out (no pun intended) the S = symptom of anxiety and consequent blushing. Next, we went over what Alana's A = automatic thoughts were corresponding to the symptom. She said, "Here I go again. I'm blushing" and "I don't want to blush; they're going to say something" were the most frequent thoughts that popped into her head when in conversation. Regarding E = emotion, Alana lamented that she sometimes felt slight dread (if any dread can be considered slight) when approached by others to discuss something. Finally, we reviewed her B = behavior, which was to oftentimes limit speaking in a conversation if she felt her anxiety and related tension were rising too fast.

In terms of problem solving, we produced a simple disclosure statement she could use if she felt her face was warming. Alana practiced different versions of saying something like "Sometimes, I blush. It's just something that happens, like on auto when I talk." In time, she was also able to adjust her internal automatic thinking to simple statements, such as "I'm blushing. Big deal. I'll just tell them I sometimes blush" or "I'm probably blushing now, and I bet other people do too." Alana learned to manage her interpersonal communication re-action (blushing) effectively via the SAEB approach and felt less anxiety and tension as a result.

Practice Opportunity
Using the SAEB Approach to Everyday Situations
Below is listed the everyday situation communication concern (number four) and SAEB detail for Alana's work on adjusting her automatic thoughts to be more positive, yet realistic, regarding blushing in conversations. The everyday situation is listed on the left, with SAEB details on the right. The new automatic thought statement is then made, one that is more positive, yet accurate.

Alana's responses:

Everyday Situation	SAEB
4. Communication Concern: Blushing during a conversation.	Symptom: Anxiety, blushing
	Automatic Thought: "I don't want to blush."
	Emotion: Slight dread
	Behavior: Limit speaking

New automatic thought that will help going forward: "I'm blushing. Big deal. I'll just tell them I sometimes blush."

Your turn if you like. Just choose one of the common communication problem situations above (everyday Situation numbers one through six) or one of your own, and use the SAEB model to better manage your thoughts, emotions, and behavior while interacting with others. You can list the everyday situation on the left, with SAEB details on the right. Next, the new automatic thought statement can be made. Strive for one that is more positive yet accurate.

Everyday Situation	SAEB
Communication Concern: _____	Symptom:_____
_____	AutomaticThought:_____
	Emotion:_____
	Behavior:_____

New automatic thought that will help going forward:

_____

_____

Increasing Communication Skills
There are a variety of ways to increase your communication skills. The main goal of effective communication skills is to learn how not to shy away from the conversation. One important

dynamic in social relationships involve the ability to compromise or negotiate with people. Put another way, try to be positive, recognize when you are rigidly holding onto an opinion, and, as St. Augustine profoundly offered, "Hear the other side." When initiating conversation with others, it may be obvious (if not humorous) to avoid toxic questions such as "What are you talking about?" or "Are you serious?" and the proverbial "Are you kidding me?" A simple "Good to see you. How are you doing" can be an effective opener. Many conversations can benefit from being personal and considerate in your remarks, and fortunately, you will then notice most others responding in kind.

To make things relatively easy, you can breakdown a social interaction that you want to have by learning how to think contextually. In other words, separate an upcoming conversation into its meaningful parts.

Meaningful Social Interaction Parts
1. What are the elements of the conversation you will have?
2. How do you envision it starting?
3. What will be the main topics?
4. How do you want the conversation to end?

Practice Opportunity
Effective Communication Skills for Conversations
Ashok had an upcoming interview with a potential employer and wanted his initial conversation to go well. At thirty years old, Ashok felt his college education in computer science should be put to better use. In counseling, he expressed being shy but also said he "needed to do something" because he felt he had been employed at too many "soul-sucking jobs." A recruiter found his resume online and was excited that he had extensive computer programming skills. A position was opening at a large national company, and an interview had been scheduled. We reviewed the four questions you can ask yourself to breakdown a future conversation into its meaningful parts (listed above). This was a guided approach in our individual counseling to provide structure and add context to help Ashok organize his thoughts. He came up with a plan that provided for a straightforward approach to practicing for his face-to-face interview.

On the left, list the anticipated social interactions or conversations you want to breakdown into the four meaningful social interaction parts. On the right, include the responses you want to make for each of the four social interaction or conversation parts. With this practice opportunity, you're just making notes on how you want to respond, subject to change based on whatever social circumstances you may engage in. Some individuals like to keep an outline using the four meaningful social interaction parts and their anticipated responses with them to informally rehearse.

Ashok's responding:

Meaningful Social Interaction Parts	Response
1. Main conversation elements	Talk about my background and experience in computers. Also, some personal information and goals.
2. Starting the dialogue	I will thank the interviewer for the opportunity to apply, and tell him what it means to me.
3. Main topics to include	Computer science education and qualifications for a full-time position.
4. Ending the conversation	I will ask the interviewer if they have any more questions and then ask them how they like the company

Offered below is the same structure to follow if you would like to come up with a plan for a conversation that is important to first map out before meeting face-to-face.

Meaningful Social Interaction Parts	Response
1. Main conversation elements	_____ _____ _____
2. Starting the dialogue	_____ _____ _____
3. Main topics to include	_____ _____ _____
4. Ending the conversation	_____ _____ _____

Practice Opportunity
Positive and Negative Behaviors in Social Situations

Both positive and negative behaviors in social situations have consequences. For example, a simple positive behavior could be smiling more often in conversations, which may be rewarded when the other person responds in kind. A pleasant interaction is the result. A basic and familiar negative behavior in social situations occurs when someone may have poor eye contact with the other person, and it cuts a conversation short. I saw a young man, Keith, in counseling who complained of people not talking for a very long time with him. He said this occurs even though he's a generally "likable" guy by his own personal appraisal (and that of his mother). Keith also described himself as responsible and trustworthy. Indeed, he struck me as personable, even affable at times. It turns out that he did have a few peculiarities in his approach and manner with others. In an office setting, I noticed that Keith was loud, as in a louder than average speaking voice kind of way. He also tended to look downward every time he finished saying something, but he didn't seem to be aware of it. We discussed his positive social behavior, which included his engaging interpersonal style. I gently confronted Keith about his downward gaze problem. He said that he had never thought of himself as a "show gazer," but acknowledged that this could be negative if his aim was to extend conversations. He accepted the feedback well and said he would work on his body language.

List a positive behavior or two that you've used in communication with others and what results have occurred. Similarly, list one or more negative behaviors in talking with others and describe how things turned out.

Keith's responses:

Positive Behaviors in Social Situations	Results
1. "I'm likable with others."	"They sometimes seem to notice."
2. "I'm responsible and trustworthy."	"People will listen to me."

Negative Behaviors in Social Situations	Results
1. Unaware of loud speaking voice	Shorter conversations
2. Downward gaze after talking	Others are puzzled

Below you can input your responding with a positive behavior or two that you've used in communication with others and what results have occurred. Similarly, you can list one or more negative behaviors you've noticed in talking with others and describe how things turned out.

Positive Behaviors in Social Situations	Results
1._____	_____
2._____	_____

Negative Behaviors in Social Situations   Results

1._____   _____

2._____   _____

How the Outgoing Can Help the Shy

Regarding what I've termed a social buddy system, it explains how an outgoing, action-oriented individual can learn to relate to and help a shy and likely socially withdrawn individual. The shy person can interact with a few peers and choose one who can serve as a helpful social buddy. Just as someone might benefit from having a study buddy to master difficult course content, the social buddy can help with how to interact with others more easily. Basically, the social buddy is in a role model position, and the individual who is shy can observe how the more social peer navigates the beginning, middle, and end of a variety of social interactions.

For example, Amara was a freshman in high school who was coming in for counseling due to slipping grades and a complaint that she had few friends. When the subject of a social buddy came up, she seemed receptive. Amara even had someone in mind, but when she mentioned that she would have to wait until her friend Esther was released from juvenile hall, I suggested she needed someone sooner. Who did she know was social, kind, and had earned the respect of her fellow peers? Amara chose Ariana. Her reasoning was that their names both started with an "A." When I asked if she had any other criteria, I was pleased that she said, "Ariana would be a good role model." In the weeks that followed, Amara learned to shadow Ariana from a reasonable distance and was able to pick up on how Ariana would socialize with others. She noticed that Ariana usually began her conversations by greeting others with a smile and asking how they were doing. In time, Amara was able to imitate and rehearse those behaviors she felt were consistent with her own style of relating, just in a more outgoing manner. She had a few setbacks yet was able to become more social and friendly with others as her school year progressed.

Three Tips on How the Outgoing Can Help the Shy

1. For the outgoing, offering to observe a shy friend or peer's social interactions and then providing constructive feedback is a good way to help. Take Nathaniel, who noticed his friend Joshua was nervous around their mutual friends and didn't talk much. It seemed odd because whenever Nathaniel and Joshua were together playing video games, Joshua sometimes talked non-stop. Nathaniel brought up this apparent social contrast between their own talkative dyad and then observing Joshua not speaking up with others. Joshua said that he was just shy "when there are a lot of people." Nathaniel offered to help by first role modeling how he joined in on conversations. Next, he let Joshua know he would watch him when he tried to strike up a discussion with their same friends so that he could provide feedback.

    Joshua was game, and they worked on their participant-observer roles this way for a couple of weeks. Joshua became more observant in general. He noticed that

Nathaniel initiated conversations or participated in existing discussions just by asking a question or two and being genuinely interested in the responses he got. When Joshua tried the same approach, Nathaniel watched from some distance and gave feedback that things were going better. Specifically, Nathaniel praised Joshua for using better eye contact, asking questions, and listening to those he was talking with attentively. Successful shyness comes together in steps by using your own personal strategies and techniques and those offered in this book, as well as many others on shyness. It is also a good idea to reach out and even rely upon others to help you in your efforts.

2. By being a social buddy to the shy individual, you can role model real-life interactions. Just pick a social activity that both of you attend together that includes positive social relationships. The social buddy can take the lead, and your shy learner can observe the way in which you respond to others and even get involved as the situation warrants. There are many hobbies and sports activities as well as community events that allow for easier socializing. Larger events, which might appear intimidating at first, can be easier because you can be more anonymous in the crowd. Try different events where you can introduce a shy individual to people in different social situations and contexts until individual preferences are met.

3. Provide advice, feedback, emotional support, and companionship to a shy friend or peer. I've left this point intentionally short, as the one sentence provided, taken to heart, is all a shy person may need from you to blossom.

Specific Strategies to Draw Someone Out of Their Shyness

1. Reach out to the shy person because they may not initiate a conversation. Come alongside them while going to a social activity together. Use empathy. Build emotionally supportive and compassionate responses with the shy person. This type of warm reaching out will definitely help the shy. It might also help you to counter your own feelings of frustration when dealing with a shy person. Frustration can occur, as it is sometimes hard for a more outgoing individual to figure out or understand the reasons a shy person may be so reticent and inhibited. If you've grown up with and gone to school alongside a shy friend, there is one activity that can stimulate dialogue. Go to a few places you recall visiting together when you were younger. When you see these sites, you'll often find that certain features are much smaller than you expected, such as tiny chairs for students at a local elementary school. At the same time, because you may have been traveling to one location or another with adults (usually parents) when you were young, now that you can venture out as peers, it will be different. You can see how one place you visited is remarkably close to another, something that you've never previously put together before. Simply talking with others about shared experiences brings out the shy and the outgoing alike.

2. When you see a shy person step up and be more direct with others, you can provide social reinforcement by offering praise and encouragement. The shy individual who has learned to speak up for themselves is making progress. Do not rescue the shy person by talking for them. Instead, allow flexibility by not forcing anyone into a particular social situation.

3. Empathize with a shy individual and their struggle, but do not commiserate or agree that the social situation or circumstances cannot be changed. Most social encounters can be modified, unless, of course, the social setting involves a trip to the DMV or airport security line.

4. Encourage the shy individual to join any groups that share their interests. There may be initial resistance to doing so, but many shy people become loyal members of a group once they've tested the waters and found support. Bonding through a group activity is an easier way to get to know people than a more random approach.

5. In general, positive peer relationships encourage cooperation, emotional closeness, and prosocial behaviors. Interacting with friends and peers makes social skills easier to develop and use. Learning to communicate more directly with others can foster self-confidence along and increase positive social contact. Individuals who can communicate effectively and strive to resolve conflicts are more likely to be accepted by others and build more mutual friendships. Through friendships, shy individuals can learn to:
   a. Interact with each other more, which can help the shy person contribute to joint decision-making, express empathy, and broaden their social perspectives.
   b. Appreciate the satisfaction gained from mutual social support.
   c. Develop constructive interpersonal skills with others, including peers and coworkers.
   d. Build confidence and self-esteem as well as mutual respect with peers and friends.

6. Learning ways to develop emotional closeness with others can also be highly beneficial. One effective way to bring about closer relating is to frequently express empathy, basically being sensitive to others and their concerns. Another focus can be productively spent on simply getting to know people, making sure to communicate or share compassion and sensitivity, as well as learning to problem solve together. This may take some time, but it is worth the effort.

7. Shy people oftentimes do want to interact, basically share that recessed, extroverted side of themselves, but feel awkward and self-conscious or just don't know how to proceed. As was described and included as a practice opportunity for three major types of conflict in the Assessment section of this book, the one conflict that shy individuals often have is that of approach-avoidance. Shy individuals want to be social (a desire to approach and interact with others) but tend to hold themselves back (avoidance of others) due to the discomfort they experience.

One implication for all of society is to reach out to those who don't necessarily look like they want to interact but may very well have a reserved type of accessibility. That is, talk with shy people and initiate discussion, and you may find that they come alive in terms of their interactions and, more broadly, social activity engagement. Of course, reaching out to the shy this way is indeed preferable to assuming that the individual is being aloof, cold, or arrogant, which is usually not the case. I would like to quickly add that shy people have a responsibility in these social interactions as well. Not surprisingly, for the shy, the one big social task is to try not to come off looking aloof, cold, or arrogant. If someone doesn't really want to engage, then it's a good time to back off and go about your business, which is easy enough to do.

Tips for Those Who Are Shy to Help the More Outgoing

1. Spend time with the more outgoing person and share solo activities that you've enjoyed. You can allow for quiet time, such as walking or gardening together, for example. Because outgoing people are so people-centered, they can usually use help from the shy in learning how to organize their non-social interaction tasks, such as appointments or homework scheduling. You could suggest a few good books to an outgoing person that you've become acquainted with—a book with colorful characters in it, for example, not the federal tax code.

2. Give feedback to an outgoing person once you've established a relationship. Let them know if you see instances when they may be talking with others too loudly or don't recognize other behaviors that are distancing friends or peers.

3. Help an outgoing friend or peer take time to do detailed work, such as studying or working on a project. You can role model solitary concentration on a task, and then both of you can do something social after the work is done.

4. Introduce a more outgoing friend or peer to your family to increase socializing even further. In this regard, as discussed elsewhere in Successful Shyness, choose a friend or peer that you've discerned is both reliable and dependable. I'm reminded of the sitcom *Leave it to Beaver* where the friend of the family, Eddie Haskell, would always address the parents as Mr. and Mrs. Cleaver, then denigrate them behind their backs to his peers, Wally and Beaver. Of course, the parents, Ward and June, were well aware of Eddie's high capacity manipulation abilities.

Chapter 12

The Stages of Change Model for Shyness

In this chapter, learning the stages of change conceptual model can provide you with a practical roadmap to help you focus on present and future goals, less on the past. The names of the six stages of change are precontemplation, contemplation, preparation, action, maintenance, and relapse. The first goal for the shy individual is to recognize that there are several stages to the change we want to make. The goal is to be able to take effective direct-action in our efforts to reach out more to others and experience the satisfaction of social interaction. Using the stages of change model researched and popularized by psychologists Drs. James Prochska and Carlo DiClemente will provide you with a useful guide in progressing toward reaching your goals. For example, a common goal for those who are shy is to learn effective ways to socially interact with others.

Case Vignette
Using the Stages of Change Model
A detailed example using the six stages of change is provided below, using a case vignette format involving Nadia, who wanted to move from an isolative stance in her life to having more social interactions with her peers.
    Nadia's responses:

Six Stages of Change

Stage of Change	Definition	Goal
1. Precontemplation	Not considering change	Begin thinking about change

An example of an individual in precontemplation is Nadia, who is shy and withdrawn. She hasn't given much thought to socially interacting with others and prefers to spend most of her time studying in college. A goal for Nadia at this point is to begin to think about what it would be like for her to socialize from time to time. She had recently mentioned to her dorm roommate, "I would like to get out a little more; you know, do things maybe with your friends."

<u>Brief Summary of Precontemplators</u>: They may not yet think there is a problem, so they aren't considering any immediate change.

<u>Stage of Change</u>	<u>Definition</u>	<u>Goal</u>
2. Contemplation	Beginning to consider change	Identify pros and cons

Nadia attended individual counseling at her college student services center and started to discuss with her psychologist opportunities to get out more. Basically, she had begun to consider a change in the direction of socializing with other peers around her age. The pros she mentioned included removing herself from the "four walls" that she explained were in effect "closing in on her." Two cons she brought up with her psychologist were that she wasn't sure what to say to others if she did socialize and that the thought of proceeding would make her anxious.

Note that no actual change in Nadia's behavior has yet occurred. This is how the change process works. We first get into our consciousness the idea of change, then we roll around with the pros and cons. Thus, Nadia has gone from the precontemplation to contemplation stage of change. You may now recognize that the change process, for most all behaviors in fact, is not automatic, but generally follows six main stages or steps. There was an old expression presto chango, which was often used as a magician's command. Change, as we all know, is not so fast or easy. In a positive vein, this six-stage process gives people time to adjust to any changes they are wanting to make and shows them how to follow through. Next up is the preparation stage.

<u>Brief Summary of Contemplators</u>: They know their destination and how to get there but haven't yet started (or may procrastinate—who doesn't?).

<u>Stage of Change</u>	<u>Definition</u>	<u>Goal</u>
3. Preparation	Preparing to make a change	Set a start date for the change

Nadia has now set her sights on going out with her roommate's friends for a Friday night movie. She has set the date one week in advance, and everybody, including her own room-mate, is looking forward to the show she chose. Nadia has prepared to make this change and is now optimistic about participating in what is hoped to be a pleasant social activity.

<u>Brief Summary of Preparation</u>: In this stage, people have gained momentum and are making preliminary steps toward change. They have likely resolved some ambivalence regarding their planned project and are getting ready to take action.

<u>Stage of Change</u>	<u>Definition</u>	<u>Goal</u>
4. Action	Engaging in the new behavior	Set dates to work on change

Nadia and friends acted by simply going on the group movie outing and enjoying themselves. They agreed to get together in two or three weeks to do something together again. The only negative view was from her roommate, who said if they saw another Rom-Com movie, she would walk out because it was "killing brain cells."

Brief Summary of Action: People are busy, and change is visible. Caution: Action is not always change; sometimes it's just running in place, which you want to avoid.

Stage of Change	Definition	Goal
5. Maintenance	Maintaining the new behavior	Evaluate ongoing progress

Once action is taken, in this case Nadia venturing out into the social world, the behavior will need to be maintained. That is, one movie doesn't make for strong social connections. Nadia can evaluate how the evening went at the movies, then go forward by maintaining a social activity schedule over the weeks to come.

Brief Summary of Maintenance: Changers consolidate their gains and work to prevent relapses.

Stage of Change	Definition	Goal
6. Relapse	Relapse happens; work on it	What caused the setback?

The last stage of change is closing out or termination, and oftentimes relapse. And we all tend to relapse from time to time with falling off a diet being a classic example. What do we do? Getting back on the proverbial horse and riding is a good idea. In other words, if relapse is part of the change process, Nadia can go back to any of the previous stages, especially if she becomes isolated again, and reflect on what may have caused the setback. She can ask herself how she went from social action back to withdrawn behavior. Nadia can review the contemplation and preparation stages, then act on new social activities when she chooses.

Another way to view the relapse stage is to simply view it as recycling to an earlier stage in the change process. The saying "going back to the drawing board" seems an apt description. In other words, moving back and forth between earlier stages is fine as that is how the change process works. As mentioned above, another well-worn saying applies: "If at first you don't succeed, try, try again." While difficult for all of us, successful change that is meaningful usually includes some measure of persistence and patience.

Brief summary of relapse (sometimes after the termination of meeting a goal): Stages of change occur in a predictable sequence (one through six). Relapse, setbacks, or recycling to earlier stages in the change process occur regularly.

Practice Opportunity
Using the Stages of Change Model
Think of a goal that you would like to pursue and use the six stages in the change model to facilitate your progress along the way. Once you complete your intermediate goals toward the change you would like to make, you've achieved your final goal—accomplishment of the

change you wanted to make. This practice opportunity will allow you to gain familiarity with using the stages of change model in any new efforts toward effectively managing your shyness.

Each of the six stages of change is listed on the left. On the right, you can summarize the results you obtained for each of the stages.

Nadia's responses:

Six Stages of Change

Stage of Change	Results
1. Precontemplation	Haven't given much thought to socially interacting.
2. Contemplation	Considering socializing with peers around my age.
3. Preparation	Set a date to go to the movies with your roommate and friends in one week.
4. Action	Went with friends to a group movie outing.
5. Maintenance	Will schedule other social activities
6. Relapse	If I become isolated again, I will go back to a previous stage and progress from there.

Think about a change you would like to make and break it down through the six stages of change as you proceed from precontemplation to action and maintenance. Of course, you can allow for the relapse stage at the end if it happens—and it oftentimes does (usually to an earlier stage of change as a new beginning point).

Six Stages of Change

Stage of Change	Results
1. Precontemplation	_____ _____
2. Contemplation	_____ _____
3. Preparation	_____ _____
4. Action	_____ _____
5. Maintenance	_____ _____
6. Relapse	_____ _____

Alternative Understanding of Experiences and the Stages of Change Model

Many individuals find it helpful to examine alternative ways to understand their feelings and experiences. This process can provide a different perspective on dealing with discomfort or distress and lead to a calmer response. An alternative understanding of experiences and gaining perspective can be particularly helpful to shy and socially anxious individuals. Further, using the stages of change model or process in this context can help you mobilize toward direct-action. For example, Kylie was a young adult aspiring to be an actor. She had taken drama classes in high school and college, but since moving to Hollywood, she found it difficult to get the acting experience and helpful supervision she needed. Kylie knew that she had to propel herself forward in such a challenging career arena. On top of her desired acting trajectory, she acknowledged in counseling that she was shy and would withdraw from social contact from time to time. An alternative understanding of her experience was offered in an early therapy session that I had with Kylie. I explained that millions of people are shy, and because shy individuals are observant and good at "reading the room," this might help in any future acting efforts. Also, she should try to get feedback or perspective from others on how they approach acting, especially if they are otherwise quieter or shy.

When asked how she arrived at acting, even though she was shy, she said many TV and movie characters that she had watched over the years seemed to be the quiet and brooding type. This was the kind of character role in which Kylie said she would feel at least somewhat comfortable, even confident. The direct suggestion I gave her at this point was to be, in fact, direct. I said, "Try telling a prospective mentor what you told me, something like, 'I've done some acting, and being shy myself, I think I can learn to successfully take on the role of a quiet but strong character and do it convincingly.'" Kylie's self-esteem seemed to rise when others offered encouragement and support. Kylie used the stages of change model to move from contemplation to action. She was able to pursue auditions on a near monthly basis, confident that her shyness was an asset. May she do well in her future acting efforts.

Three Main Areas of Focus for Dealing with Interpersonal Situations

In this next section, we'll take a look at integrating the three main areas of symptom reduction, conflict resolution, and skill building when working through any interpersonal situations or set of circumstances.

1. Symptom reduction. Focus on decreasing tension and anxiety; avoidance responding.
2. Conflict resolution. Work through interpersonal role conflicts and disputes.
3. Skill building. Learn problem-solving skills; assertive responses.

The above three-step process is a good treatment guide if you want to use a self-help approach or decide to see a healthcare professional. In the first step, you can learn to decrease symptoms such as anxiety and avoid activities. In the second step, you can work on conflict resolution by talking with family and friends when communication difficulties arise. The third step promotes skill-based training, such as assertion, which can facilitate effective communication you would like to have with others.

Case Vignette

Symptom Reduction, Conflict Resolution, and Skill Building for Social Situations
Lynette, a forty-year-old bakery shop manager, described becoming anxious and tense when dealing with certain customers who were regulars at her store. In counseling, she described wanting to avoid these regulars at times because "they always want to talk my ear off." Lynette learned how to use progressive muscle relaxation (PMR) and focused breathing to lower her anxiety and tension. One role conflict Lynette identified involved wanting to be customer friendly while at the same time trying to run her business efficiently. "I don't mind talking with customers for a short while, but I get anxious when I'm expected to carry on a conversation and people are waiting in line to make their purchases." While working with Lynette, it became clear that she would benefit from creating an informal script she could use to resolve her role conflict. She came up with, "Nice talking with you, but it looks like I need to see what these other customers want right now." Lynette also talked with her family and friends about her tension and stress at work, and they all agreed that "polite but firm" was the way to go. Lynette worked on being more assertive and, with practice in session, was able to provide better eye contact and open body language while speaking clearly and not too fast. Her tension and anxiety slowly decreased as she was able to speak up a little more and serve her customers in a more efficient manner, all while remaining relatively calm.

Practice Opportunity

Using Symptom Reduction, Conflict Resolution, and Skill Building
After going through a difficult interpersonal interaction, take a few minutes to evaluate the experience through the lens of the three-step process listed below. The three main areas of symptom reduction, conflict resolution, and skill building are listed on the left. In the middle section, summarize what you were able to do or not do during the social situation. Finally, indicate or describe what you could do next time to help yourself in any future difficult or complex social encounters.

Lynette's response:

Main Area	How I Responded	What I Can Do Next Time
1. Symptom reduction	Tense and anxious with customers	Use PMR and focused breathing
2. Conflict resolution	Tended to avoid some customers	Talk with customers briefly
3. Skill building	Too passive with some customers	Use assertion

Think of a time when you were going through a difficult or complex interpersonal interaction. The three main areas of symptom reduction, conflict resolution, and skill building are listed below on the left. In the middle section, summarize what you were able to do or not do during the social situation. Finally, indicate what you could do next time to help yourself in any future difficult or complex social encounters.

Main Area	How I Responded	What I Can Do Next Time
1. Symptom reduction	_____	_____
	_____	_____
2. Conflict resolution	_____	_____
	_____	_____
3. Skill building	_____	_____
	_____	_____

Chapter 13

Cognitive Behavioral Therapy (CBT) Concepts and Strategies for Shyness

CBT Concepts

1. Using CBT, we can be on the lookout for our own biases in perception and interpretation. In general, CBT involves modifying negative thoughts or cognitions (including biases), being aware of feeling states, developing a positive coping plan, applying skills learned in actual distressful situations, and providing self-reinforcement. One way to think of CBT is to consider one of its central tenets: "The way we think affects the way we feel." Importantly, the way we think can be accurate or inaccurate. So, what can you do? Simply look for the evidence to see if your thought is true, accurate, or at least in the ballpark. Another quote relevant to the power of our thoughts comes from Marcus Aurelius: "Our life is what our thoughts make it." Clearly, it is important to examine our thinking, which can be a good thing, but there is also no need to overdo it or get too thought preoccupied.

Case Vignette
Where's the Evidence?

Jada had taken a college course in world history from a professor she viewed as totally unreasonable. "This guy was out there, always quoting historical figures in his lectures, people no one has ever heard of." She also commented, "He gave me a low grade on a test, and when I asked him about it, he went ballistic; I swear he would make Attila the Hun look calm and reasonable by comparison." The issue Jada had was that she was going to take another history course and predicted that the professor, a different one, would be just as hard to deal with. When asked how she came to this conclusion, she said, "History repeats itself." I don't think she was being sly, but she made a prediction that was likely biased based on her previous professor's behavior. When asked where the evidence was that a new professor would be anything like her former one, she acknowledged that she didn't have any "hard data." In a subsequent session, Jada was able to recognize that her thoughts on her previous professor influenced her next course offering in a biased way. She developed a plan wherein she would "wait and see" how the new professor would respond to students. Jada also reflected on the danger of overgeneralization. "I guess not all history professors are apt to be overly detailed, obsessed with esoterica, and flip out when a student asks about a test grade."

Case Vignette
Another Exploration to Find the Evidence
In this very brief vignette, Amira, a twenty-two-year-old first-year medical student, complained of her fear of failure, even on a single lab assignment or test. A common thought she had was, "I'm going to fail this lab." Understandably, she then interpreted this thought as not good at all. "It means I might psych myself out to fail rather than do well." Her following emotion was one of high anxiety and even dread. In a simple exploration of finding the evidence for her dire prediction, Amira could find only one or two examples in her entire college career when she did not do well on a test. When Amira then considered the thought "I usually always do well because I study," she was able to calm herself somewhat, with the accompanying emotion being one of only slight apprehension.

2. Negative cognitive triad: Negatively biased self-statements and appraisals concerning the self, the world, and future. We've all had negative thoughts that have caused us distress. When anxious and depressed, a poor self-image can emerge, in which there are more sweeping negative views of the self, current experiences, and the future. The way out of negativity is to take stock in yourself and use a strength-based approach that increases positive thoughts that are true and consistent with your values. These more proactive, goal-oriented ways of thinking and being in the world can constructively guide us in social situations.

Case Vignette
Dealing with the Negative Cognitive Triad
Mable, a forty-year-old travel agent, described feeling shy and insecure at times when working with her manager. More broadly, she complained of low self-esteem. "Maybe I shouldn't be doing this anymore. I'm not as fast on my feet as the other agents. I get down on myself." She was also developing a negative outlook on the world, complaining of too much crime in places she was helping people travel to and from. "I don't know if the chaos going on out there is ever going to end." Finally, she wasn't too big on the future. Mable reasoned that

since she had to work for so many more years, it might be too expensive for even a travel agent to travel at some point.

In working with Mable in individual counseling, we agreed that it would be productive to tackle each aspect of the negative cognitive triad separately. First, with her low self-esteem and her associated negative view of her own feelings, we wanted to look for evidence. In fact, Mable may have been slowing down a tad compared to her younger colleagues in the workplace, with which she was disappointed. When she considered another perspective, she agreed that she was also more experienced than many at the travel agency. Indeed, clients gave her direct feedback that they were pleased with her courteous and helpful manner. Thus, Mable was able to balance her view of herself to include not only negatives, such as her currently lowered self-esteem, but also positives, including being experienced and appreciated in her occupation. Second, when we looked at her view of the world "going bonkers" as she announced in one session, other possibilities were discussed. With some perspective taking, Mable was able to appreciate that most of her clients enjoyed their trips to various places in the world, just as she did when she was able to travel afar herself. While not trying to sugarcoat things but acknowledging that the world has its share of huge problems, Mable was able to conclude that her daily life has been moving forward relatively "error-free," in her words. Third, when discussing the future, she was able to have some hope that, because things were not as dark as she originally perceived them to be, she could look forward to a better tomorrow.

3. One cognitive distortion that is helpful to correct for is overgeneralization, wherein you may view a negative event as a never-ending pattern of defeat. There are many others. Among the more common cognitive distortions are the following:
   a. All-or-nothing thinking. This distortion involves the tendency to look at things in black and white, or absolute terms.
   b. Jumping to conclusions. You may leap to the opinion that people are nearly always going to react too negatively to your conversations. Or you consistently predict that things will turn out badly.
   c. Magnification or minimization. With magnification, things get blown out of proportion, unrealistically. In minimization, this type of thinking results in shrinking the importance of things, but inaccurately.
   d. Personalization. This is when you blame yourself for something for which you weren't entirely responsible.
   e. "Should statements." In this cognitive distortion, an unrealistically harsh self-command comes to the fore with criticisms of "I should have done this" or, in regard to others, "They should not disagree with me."

f. Misattribution. One way to think of making an accurate attribution versus a misattribution is to make sure you give yourself credit when credit is due, rather than become your own worst critic. As discussed in the Assessment section of *Successful Shyness* (Part 1), you can examine whether a particular social situation went well enough that you could make positive, accurate attributions.

Given the significant number of ways in which people can make cognitive distortions, it leaves us wondering if there is any way out. There is. Simply be aware of the ways in which we may be affected by various biases and try to self-correct for them when it's important. We are humans, allowed to make thinking errors, and can take some satisfaction in the knowledge that everyone else does from time to time. A great resource on the matter of thinking and its twists and turns is *Thinking, Fast and Slow* by Dr. Daniel Kahneman. This psychologist won the Nobel Prize, not in psychology but in economics, by demonstrating how our thinking is affected by any number of biases and that if we proceed carefully, we'll be better for it.

> **Case Vignette**
> *Attributions and Misattributions*
> Consider the various ways in which attributions and misattributions can be made in an everyday experience. Gabrielle, a thirty-four-year-old mortgage broker, went to a party and said to herself that she interacted reasonably well and plans to do so in the future. Thus, her attributions would be internal (interacting reasonably well), stable (she could continue interacting in the future), and global (interacting effectively in what will be a variety of future social events). Gabrielle's optimistic attributional style can easily be contrasted with a more negative one if she had misattributed her actions such that her social interaction efforts were external (based on luck, as in, she would have felt that it was just that the people she spoke with were especially easy going). Further, her success in social interaction was unstable (based on this party alone, but unlikely to interact this well again). Finally, a specific versus global type of misattribution was made (if she felt this party was successful in terms of interacting only because she was in a good mood).

4. Challenge negative thoughts. For example, are the thoughts realistic? Are they balanced? Take time to evaluate your thinking in different situations, and if you find it to be too biased or negative, come to a more realistic appraisal. Another way to look at this approach is that CBT involves changing faulty thinking to a more accurate cognitive response.
5. "We feel what we think." Discover your faulty assumptions or dysfunctional beliefs. Ask yourself, "Where's the evidence for these thoughts?" Work on correcting any biases you've recognized. Restructure your negative thought patterns toward less

biased appraisals. This process is commonly referred to as cognitive restructuring. When we clear up biases in our thought process, good things can happen. Take it from the famous psychologist Dr. William James, who said, "The greatest weapon against stress is our ability to choose one thought over another." I've assumed that Dr. James meant that when our thinking is clear and accurately positive (versus unnecessarily biased in a negative direction), we will be healthier.

6. Major CBT treatment goals include problem-solving and behavioral activation. Decreasing cognitive distortions (thoughts) and lowering physiological reactivity (behavior) are associated objectives to reach these important goals.

CBT Strategies

1. Thought stopping is one technique that can be used to loosen the strength of repetitive cognitions, or, in a word, rumination. Take Therese, a forty-three-year-old ICU RN who is excellent at her hospital job but would worry almost every night. She would become preoccupied with the thought that one of the IV lines that she had set up for a particular patient might have a kink in it. She would check on the patient's IV functioning at the beginning of her next shift to routinely find the IV in working order. In counseling, Therese learned that when she began to ruminate about her work procedures, she could tell herself, "I'm going to stop obsessing. Things are really okay. I would get a call if there was any problem." This simple and accurate self-statement would cause her repetitive worry cycle or rumination to end.

2. Guided imagery. Successful imaginal rehearsal can help by picturing yourself responding effectively in a social situation and then trying the same behavior in a live situation.

3. Graduated exposure, and this book's preferred term, graduated direct-action, can help the shy individual ease into potentially tension-producing social situations. For example, you could start with an easy social activity, such as making small talk with friends. In time, you can work up to leading a meeting or making a presentation in a class.

4. While the shy individual is staying in a social situation and coping with some anxiety along the way, the term response prevention applies to not leaving the situation. The shy can learn to stick it out, equipped with an escape route only if needed. In other words, the response that is prevented is leaving or escaping the social situation prematurely. Not to worry, theaters have fire exits, and people can use "I forgot to feed my dog" if the social interaction gets too hot or uneasy. Of course, this excuse should be used judiciously. That is, 1) you should have a dog, and 2) bring a picture of your pet along so as to remove any doubt.

Rather than escape, as most shy people can relate to, avoiding the social situation in the first place does occur. But who wants their world to become too narrow and without hardly any social stimulation? It is important to recognize, once again, that these methods, especially direct-action (engaging in a social activity) and response prevention (stopping escape behavior), can be accomplished at your own pace. Do not let anxiety override your experience if you need to simply adjust your expectations downward a little. One thing you can do is continue with some direct-action social activities that you know will be easiest to accomplish, at least at first. By progressing from easier to more difficult social situations or unfamiliar events, success will be had and confidence will be gained.

5. Anxiety and depression often occur together or in tandem, but it is important to work on the most debilitating symptoms first, be they from anxiety or depression. With depression, hopelessness can enter the clinical picture, for which immediate psychological treatment is indicated. One perspective on hopeless feelings is that hopelessness itself could be a defense against further disappointment. When you're shy, you may feel like things may not get better socially and simply withdraw, but this often turns out to be a short-term view. Thus, whenever we feel really down and without hope, just putting one foot in front of the other may be a good way to proceed out of a significant funk or slump.

Case Vignette
Increasing Mood to Decrease Negative Thought Patterns
I recall one middle-aged adult I worked with, Jordan, who complained of being obsessed and overwhelmed by his negative thought patterns. He talked about becoming more socially isolated, which furthered his anxiety and depression, as well as hopelessness. A bright academic, Jordan commented in one therapy session, "I think it was the poet W.B. Yeats who wrote something like 'back to the foul rag-and-bone shop of the heart,'—well, that's where my thoughts go every day." Clearly, before focusing on how to participate more socially, we needed to decrease Jordan's negative preoccupations and ruminations. He agreed, yet seemed puzzled by the sequence of first increasing his mood, then social interaction following as the main goal. I offered an analogy. "It's like if you see someone who might be having a heart attack—you kneel down and start CPR. You don't stand back and suggest to the person that they should work on improving their diet." Jordan got it: eliminate symptoms that fuel hopelessness first, improve mood, and then increase social interaction.

What is sometimes referred to as an agitated depressive state is when anxiety and tension accompany a low mood. Shy individuals can relate to being both anxious and depressed when the thought of engaging in a difficult social interaction or set of circumstances presents itself. As *Successful Shyness* includes many different strategies to approach social situations, including focused breathing, PMR, and various psychological techniques, these tools can help decrease both anxiety and depression.

6. Learning to accept some degree of anxiety and distress. Without some anxiety, we may not develop enough drive or motivation to get going on our goals. Too much anxiety and tension cause us to become more hesitant and, in the extreme, immobilized. Thus, we all try to find that balance wherein we can use anxiety to move us forward, but not have it so high and discomforting that it is no longer helpful.

7. Cognitive therapy techniques are a way to help you become more aware of your own inner dialogue. In time, you can learn to create a different relationship with your thoughts by reframing them. For example, if someone says something to themselves as simple as, "I don't think I can do this," the stage is set for more anxiety and tension. If the same person restructures or reframes their doubt, as in, "I'm anxious, yet others may be understanding," things will likely go better.

8. Use behavioral activation. Being more active and putting oneself in positive situations will, in turn, promote productive thoughts and feelings. Chaquille was a bright young adult who wanted to join his college debate team. What held him back was his own acknowledgment of being shy around others. With coaching from his peers, he was encouraged to go ahead and join the debate team, and they would "have his back." With this, Chaquille was able to engage himself in a rewarding endeavor that he came to enjoy after some initial hesitation.

9. Create or enter an environment that will maximize your prosocial actions. For example, if you like music and play an instrument, getting out there and playing with a few other musicians would be a great start.

10. Promote positive self-talk. For example, "I know I can do this as I've done it before, or at least something similar, with success." The preceding statement is preferable to the more negative self-talk of "I've done this before, or something similar, I don't see how I can repeat my success."

11. Arrange postaction reinforcement. For example, "I introduced myself to the people I said I would; now it's off to the movie I promised myself as a reward."

Three Different Types of CBT Interventions

1. The first CBT strategy that can be used to decrease social anxiety focuses on modifying maladaptive cognitive processing, independent of emotion. This is referred to as working with *cold cognition* or thoughts. This approach is based on psychologist Dr. Borkovec's cognitive model and clinical research.

Case Vignette

Working with a Cold Cognition

Freda, a forty-five-year-old advertising agent, had an occasional thought of "choking it," as she put it, referencing the few times when her company presentations were subpar in her view. In working with Freda, it became apparent that even a minor slipup in her presentations, such as mispronouncing one word, qualified as choking it in her self-appraisal. She did not necessarily get that upset over the mistakes and wasn't that frustrated about them, but she felt she could do better. Freda learned to modify her cognitions regarding presentations by saying to herself, "One little mistake in speaking isn't that big a deal." This helped her modify her slightly troublesome choking it cold cognition or thought. She was able to produce the cognitive consideration that a more realistic one little mistake in a presentation isn't that consequential.

Practice Opportunity

Changing a Cold Cognition to a More Realistic Cognition

List a cold cognition on the left and a more realistic cognition one on the right.

Freda's response:

Cold Cognition
1. "Choking it"

Realistic Cognition
"One little mistake in speaking isn't that big a deal."

Place a cold cognition or thought you've had on the left. On the right side, write down a more realistic cognition you've arrived at after some consideration.

Cold Cognition
1. _____

2. _____

3. _____

Realistic Cognition
_____
_____
_____
_____
_____
_____

2. The second CBT strategy used to lower social anxiety responses focus on modifying maladaptive cognitive processing that can be influenced by emotional states. Working in this realm effectively centers on dealing with *hot cognition* or thoughts. This is a primary aspect of rational emotive behavior therapy (REBT), which has been researched and practiced by psychologist Dr. Albert Ellis and colleagues.

Case Vignette
Dealing with a Hot Cognition

Javier, a middle-aged auto worker, provided his own example of a hot cognition or thought when he explained to his vocational counselor that he would get upset. "You know, I get angry whenever someone teases me." In REBT terms, the teasing was an activating event for Javier. His counselor explained that an (A) activating event can link to Javier's (B) belief about being teased. He was able to identify that the frustration and anger that stemmed from being teased must mean he's incompetent, as judged by his peers. Not being competent came to Javier as a quick negative emotion or hot cognition. The work done in counseling then focused on his belief that he was incompetent due to peer teasing. His counselor went on to define a (C), or consequence component of Javier's belief. His consequence was the emotional upset he then had to endure. Now comes (D), or a dispute about one's unrealistic beliefs, which his counselor encouraged him to practice. He said, "Javier, when you dispute your unrealistic belief that you're incompetent just because you've been teased, you'll diminish its power and not beat yourself up over it. Get that dispute going. You can do it."

With his counselor's lead, he was able to think differently about the teasing. The A, B, and C dimensions above concerning an activating event (A), then a belief (B), followed by a consequence (C) provided a straightforward explanation for Javier's hot cognition. He was able to learn that by adding a fourth dimension to his thinking, (D) for dispute, he could challenge any unrealistically negative belief. In working with his counselor, Javier was able to develop the alternative notion that peers commonly tease one another and that it doesn't have anything to do with one's competence. A healthy dispute resulting in the elimination of the sweeping incompetent belief made Javier appreciate the power of working with his thoughts and feelings. Javier's strong emotional response lessened when he came up with a newer cognitive or thought process. After going through all four A, B ,C, and D dimensions, he was then able to modify his thinking to arrive at a more realistic self-statement: "So I'm getting teased. It happens to me and others. I think I'll just put my energies somewhere else." When I consulted with Javier's counselor, it was nice to hear him say that he was pleased that Javier could calm himself down by rethinking his response to teasing.

Practice Opportunity
Changing a Hot Cognition to a More Realistic Cognition
List a hot cognition on the left and a more realistic cognition on the right.
　　Javier's response:

Hot Cognition   Realistic Cognition

1. "You know, I get angry."   "So, I'm getting teased, it happens, I think
                                        I'll just put my energies somewhere else"

Place a hot cognition or thought you've had on the left. On the right side, write down a
more realistic cognition. Refer to the A, B, C, and D elements of REBT above for guidance.

Hot Cognition   Realistic Cognition
1. _____   _____

                                       _____
2. _____   _____

                                       _____
3. _____   _____

                                       _____

3. The third CBT strategy used to decrease social anxiety focuses on accepting
   thoughts and feelings via pursuing personal values, but not changing the content
   of thoughts. Clearly, this is a different approach and is referred to as acceptance and
   commitment therapy (ACT). Psychologist Dr. Steven Hayes and colleagues have
   conducted research demonstrating ACT's empirical research support as an effective psychotherapy method. ACT encourages engagement in activities consistent
   with your values, despite symptoms. That is, ACT focuses on the acceptance of the
   symptoms, situations, and problems borne by an individual. Reductions in avoidance can occur with the use of ACT strategies, making direct-action or exposure
   opportunities easier.

Case Vignette
Accepting Thoughts
Sofia, a thirty-four-year-old biology professor, attended brief counseling sessions with a clinical psychologist while visiting her hometown of Chicago.
The psychologist used primarily ACT strategies to help her work on the angry
thoughts and feelings she was having. She wanted to deal with her negative
emotions constructively, as she remained concerned about heading into what
would be an upcoming family reunion. Sofia explained that she got along with

most of her large family, but that two of her brothers were "losers." "They're always drinking, carrying on, and destroying our peaceful family times." With a focus on ACT, her psychologist suggested ways in which she could accept her thoughts related to anger and not wanting to show up for the reunion. This approach worked, but Sofia's long-standing social anxiety rose again at the thought of having to interact with her two loud brothers. She couldn't shake the strong tendency to avoid the whole upcoming event because of their, in her words, "mindless and disturbing antics." Sofia was able to learn that, after becoming awareness of her negative feelings toward her two siblings, she could use a present focus to calm herself down. Once more relaxed, she was able to achieve, to a large degree, acceptance of her situation.

After a measure of success in accepting her negative thoughts, Sofia next worked on the commitment part of ACT by focusing on a long-standing value of hers. Specifically, she valued keeping her family together while having some fun with one another in the process. By engaging with her family at a reunion, the value of a family connection could be maintained. But how did she lower her social anxiety related to her brothers' presence? Sofia decided that although her brothers could be a pain, saying, "Personally, I think they both belong in the loony bin, or psychiatric facility, I suppose is the proper term," she would try to stay centered. Sofia thought that she could indeed spend quality time, and be less anxious, by directing her attention and energy toward those interactions in the family that were generally positive in nature. Thus, she was able to accept several harsh thoughts and feelings while maintaining her commitment to family unity, or at least togetherness.

Practice Opportunity
Accepting Thoughts and Feelings then Making a Commitment
List a thought and feeling on the left, with a commitment on the right.
    Sofia's response:

Thoughts and Feelings   Commitment
1. Angry thoughts and feelings   Staying centered and directing attention to
                                         positive family interactions

List a thought and feeling on the left, with a commitment on the right.

Thoughts and Feelings   Commitment
1. _____   _____

                                         _____

2. _____   _____
                                          _____

3. _____   _____
                                          _____

   To summarize, each of the above three CBT-type methods, especially in combination, appears to be equally effective in treating social anxiety. I encourage the reader to further explore the different CBT, REBT, and ACT approaches that are readily available in the literature, both in books and online. Note that all three approaches come under the umbrella of CBT proper in that they use different cognitive strategies, and they all share a behavioral component.

A Simple Cognitive-Behavioral Strategy for Evaluating Your Actions

Most of us can be hard on ourselves at times. Shy individuals, particularly when self-esteem drops, can become highly self-critical. There is a simple cognitive-behavioral strategy you can use that effectively eases up on unnecessary harshness toward your own actions. In a nutshell, instead of automatically thinking, "I got it wrong" or "I screwed up," consider a likely more accurate self-statement such as, "I tried something and didn't get the result I wanted."

Case Vignette
Creating Accurate Self-Statements

Arlette, a middle-aged woman with a long career as a clothing buyer for a large retailer, described herself as a "people pleaser." In counseling, she was motivated to work on being more assertive and communicating clearly with others. She made significant strides in managing her shyness and was pleased that she had more social activities to pursue after work as a result. The one thing that she ruminated about was, as she put it, "Constant blame. I always blame myself if things don't go right and get depressed." While working with Arlette, it became clear that she tended to see things in black or white and right or wrong terms, which tended to box her in for some punishing self-criticism. We discussed using the specific self-statement of "I tried something and didn't get the result I wanted" as an accurate descriptor of her actions, but she was non-blaming.

   Due to Arlette's high motivation and strong insight capability, she was able to use this simple self-statement effectively. She stated, "Just last week I had a customer who ordered a green jacket, and when it came in, it was more of a green-blue color. Then the customer said it was 'all wrong,' so I looked at the order." She went on to comment, "I started to blame myself, then stopped, because the order actually didn't clearly specify what type of green. I concluded that I tried; it didn't work, but it wasn't exactly my fault—I just didn't get the result I wanted." This cognitive strategy helped her move through her actions at work more confidently (the behavioral part of any cognitive-behavioral strategy), and she became far less self-critical in the process.

Of course, this strategy has its limits. For example, I recall an adolescent that I was seeing in counseling who came in after an incident with his parents' car. He was speeding down a residential street and ended up hitting at least two parked cars. His response was, "I did what you said. I didn't want to blame myself or put myself down. The road was wet. I guess I just didn't get the result I wanted." My only comment was, "Remember, it should be in the realm of an accurate self-statement regarding the result."

Practice Opportunity

Negative Automatic Thoughts Turned into Accurate Alternative Self-Statements

Think of a few statements you've made to yourself that were negative or blaming but not accurate, because you were simply trying something that didn't get the result you wanted. List a negative automatic thought on the left, the result on the right, and then below it a more accurate alternative self-statement. Arlette's cognitive work in this regard is summarized below.

Arlette's response:

Negative Automatic Thought
1. "I blame myself."

Result
Depressed mood, remaining concerned about things not going right

Alternative Self-Statement
I tried something and didn't get the result I wanted.

Try this practice opportunity yourself; it can really help turn an unrealistic negative automatic thought you've had into one that is alternatively accurate, clearer, and more positive—a self-statement that is certainly not unrealistically critical or blaming. First, list a negative automatic thought on the left. Next, on the right side, briefly describe the result or response that occurred. Finally, consider (and, if reasonable, say to yourself) the standard, and usually more accurate, alternative self-statement listed below.

Negative Automatic Thought
1. _____

Result
_____

_____

Alternative Self-Statement

_____

Negative Automatic Thought
2. _____

Result
_____
_____

Alternative Self-Statement
_____

Negative Automatic Thought
3. _____

Result
_____
_____

Alternative Self-Statement
_____

Turning Thoughts from Negative to Positive

An important reason to work with your shyness as it relates to cognition or thinking is that positive versus negative self-statements can really make a difference in becoming more social. In general, many shy individuals tend to overly focus on the negative details of various social situations, often to the point of distorting the interactions. Sometimes brooding enters the picture, and a shy person can ruminate over their current situation, unrealistically viewing others as doing much better in all social situations. There are many ways to deal with negative thoughts, and the following simple cognitive strategy is worth practicing.

Case Vignette
Negative to Positive Thoughts

Take Latisha, a fifty-four-year-old successful real estate agent. At times, she complained about "freezing" when in conversation with clients over a real estate transaction. In counseling, she recalled that her parents usually wanted her to respond to a question right away, and, particularly when young, she remarked, "I was too shy to answer." In working with Latisha, I suggested that she use a phrase that was realistic, such as "I've handled difficult matters with clients before. I can do this." In fact, she could, and with focused breathing before client meetings and using a positive yet realistic self-statement, she carried the day without avoiding important transactions.

Practice Opportunity
Turning Negative Thoughts into Positive Alternative Thoughts

If you have a negative thought, write it down. Next, come up with a realistic positive thought that counters the negative one, and write this new thought out on the right. In the following example, you can get an idea of how quickly Latisha may have been able to turn around a quick or automatic negative thought. Her negative thought is listed on the left, with her positive alternative thought on the right.

Latisha's response:

Negative Thought	Positive Alternative Thought
1. "I'm too shy. I can't do this."	I've handled difficult matters with clients—I can do this"

Consider a few instances when a negative thought came to you quickly as you responded to a difficult conversation or situation. List the negative thoughts on the left, and then create positive alternative thoughts on the right.

Negative Thought	Positive Alternative Thought
1. _____	_____
	_____
2. _____	_____
	_____

In general, it is helpful for the shy person to consider more realistic alternative explanations as to what happened during a particular interaction. By being more realistic, especially in terms of self-statements, you can essentially give yourself a break from harsh brooding or rumination. We tend to go where our thoughts take us, thus being realistic and positive in our inner dialogue helps propel us to make constructive efforts.

Case Vignette
Developing Realistic and Positive Thinking

For another example, take Melody, a forty-five-year-old accountant who expressed difficulty with small talk among her coworkers or joining in on social activities with them after work. The accounting firm where she was employed was large with hundreds of staff, yet she was able to maintain everyday contact with coworkers in her department. On one occasion, her supervisor asked her and her coworkers to attend an upcoming company picnic.

Melody described in counseling that she first panicked, then calmed down, but brooded over whether or not to go to the social event. She dwelled and ruminated about how she might "mumble or tank" in conversations during such an outing. Melody focused on the negative details of what might happen, saying, "My boss always calls me Melanie, but I don't know if I should ever speak up and remind her it's Melody." "Sometimes I think it is better to stay home. And by the way—she has known me for years." In working with Melanie, I mean Melody, I let her know that one effective strategy for her could be to think of a positive detail related to the upcoming social event. She mulled things over for some time and came up with the idea of actively thinking about how some of her coworkers were genuinely nice to her. She then suggested that this imagery of "nicely responding peers," as Melody put it, could help her enter the company picnic on a positive note. I shared a quote from Theodore Roosevelt with her, one that we both felt was too dramatic yet made a good point about getting out there. "It is better to try big things, even though checkered by failure, than to rank with those poor souls who neither enjoy much nor suffer much." I was then reminded of my old baseball coach, who commonly used to say, "You can't steal second base with your foot on first," a more refreshingly concrete imagery. May we all get out there more.

4. If you find yourself having engaged in previous social interactions in which you were bullied, a forgiveness-type intervention can help. In this model, you can uncover any negative feelings about the offense and then decide whether to pursue forgiveness. Work toward understanding the offender and possibly discovering unexpected positive outcomes and empathy for the offender. Reconciliation with the offender is not part of this intervention sequence but may accompany it.

Case Vignette
Recognizing and Avoiding a Destructive Thought
Helpful CBT strategies include recognizing and avoiding destructive thoughts and behaviors. Importantly, try to recognize triggers that result in withdrawing versus connecting with others. Once recognized, the next task is to learn to avoid or manage those triggers. For example, Dominic, a recently divorced woman of thirty-eight with two young children, was having negative thoughts about her ex-husband and even fantasized about some radical behavior. She related the following in counseling: "My ex is a jerk. He is really outgoing, loud around others, and sometimes drinks a lot. He told me he quit. Anyway, I asked him if I could come by and pick up some things I'd left at his place." She added, "I'm much quieter than him, even shy around his family and friends, certainly not loud and obnoxious like him." When asked if she was going to go over and get her things, she replied, "You wouldn't believe it. I was only going to be there a minute or two, and he said any contact at his place would be a threat to his sobriety." Dominic then added, "He also told me recently that nagging was one of his 'top three strangulation triggers,' but I think he was joking."

While working with Dominic, it became clear that she was somewhat intimidated by her ex-husband, yet she also clearly understood the benefits for herself of coming across in a reasonable manner. At the same time, her destructive thoughts and fantasized behavior were going in an opposing direction and were even concerning in nature. "I thought to myself, I'll be a threat to your sobriety. Maybe I could drive through your front door to get my things." Upon reflection in session, Dominic viewed her own thoughts and fantasies as just that, mental gymnastics. "I think about these things sometimes, but of course would never do them." I suggested to Dominic that she could use the "rational override" technique as described in this book and just stay calm and clear with her ex when talking with him. Additionally, she liked the idea of bringing a friend along who her ex actually liked. We joked that a "support gorilla" wasn't necessary.

Chapter 14

Interpersonal Psychotherapy (IPT) Concepts and Strategies for Shyness

IPT Concepts

Interpersonal psychotherapy (IPT), which focuses on adaptive, constructive functioning between people, can be helpful in reducing social anxiety and avoidance. Regarding shyness, the first major goal of IPT is to learn how to stabilize interpersonal relations, or basically find ways to deal with others. For example, a shy teen may receive feedback from friends and realize that they have been running too hot and cold lately. This teen then takes some time to sort out their own moods (be they hot or cold) and ways of coming across. The positive result is that the teen develops a more even way of relating to others. Of course, as all teens traverse the demands of adolescence while changing dramatically in terms of rapid development, responding evenly to others can be a tall order.

A second major goal of IPT is that interpersonal problem solving becomes important to examine. For example, what has helped you in the past to gain friendships, and what has caused you to shrink back from contact? How have you resolved conflicts with your family members or friends over the years? You can ask yourself what has worked and when it hasn't gone so well with others. By reviewing how you've managed your interpersonal relationships, you can plot a course to continue those social behaviors that have worked for you and use them with new people you meet.

The third major goal or tenet of IPT is helping yourself through negative thoughts and feelings while gaining traction with others in terms of socially interacting. Within the IPT approach, learning to use assertion and direct communication can facilitate having a good relationship with others and resolve any role conflicts or disputes. Let's say a friend continues to want to do only the activities they want to do. You might speak up (assertion) and verbalize a compromise (direct communication). A simple statement might do the trick: "Hey, can we do this today instead?" In IPT, the forward focus is on improving the future, with no need to remain preoccupied or ruminate about past difficulties in social situations. Somewhat related, shy individuals need to be aware of the *avoidance and rumination* combination. This occurs when a shy person avoids a particular social situation, but then goes over and over it in their thoughts. They may wonder how they should have gone forward and what difficulties could have happened in the social situation if they did. One way to break the avoidance/rumination cycle is to strive to be future oriented versus past preoccupied. It is by being future oriented that you can temporarily suspend your worries and just proceed. Later, you can evaluate how you did, for example, by going over a particularly challenging social interaction experience with a trusted family member or friend. Use what insights you've gained in trying to be more social to promote future actions.

IPT Strategies

While not becoming too preoccupied can be a little difficult initially, IPT calls for individuals to first recognize any of their maladaptive personality features, then move forward and don't dwell. What's a maladaptive personality feature? Something as common as being too bold and loud in conversations can be considered problematic. Another personality feature that others might find objectionable could be passivity, which is letting others carry the load in face-to-face responding and not contributing to the discussion. Passivity due to a self-conscious stance is a prominent feature of shyness. This feature is not always problematic, especially if you're just trying to warm up socially. To proceed more actively, simply watch how others are initiating and maintaining a given conversation to get the idea. Then, by being sensitive and using direct communication skills, you will be ready to join in. This is an example of recognizing a possible interpersonal problem, namely passivity, then going about operating differently with others by talking more once you've warmed up.

Case Vignette
Mood Dependent or More Ingrained Behavior

Making a distinction between mood dependent behavior and more ingrained behavior is sometimes easy. When I saw Alfonso in counseling, he was having trouble communicating his concerns with a longtime friend that he viewed as "difficult." Alfonso, a forty-year-old building contractor, described himself as an "on time" individual, one who doesn't particularly like it when other people are late. He related a sequence with his younger sister, Maria, that he said was very frustrating. One weekend, his sister showed up late after they had agreed to meet with their father at a lumberyard around 10:00 a.m. Maria apologized to Alfonso several times, recognizing his punctuality, although she did view his behavior as being "uptight." She had explained to him that she was bummed out because a package she was waiting for hadn't yet arrived. Maria, like Alfonso, is usually on time (but not always), and she respects schedules, as he even acknowledged.

Clinically, we would describe her behavior as situational and her tension about being late mood dependent. That is, she was frustrated with herself for being late, but it was due to a delayed delivery, not her own fault. Alfonso accepted her apology and noted to himself at the time that, as he put it, "She meant no harm." In general, if we think about it, situational or mood dependent behavior can be relatively easy to forgive. Who hasn't been out of sorts from time to time over someone's "goof"? Next, though, comes a friend of Alfonso named Rogelio, who is characteristically late. In this regard, Rogelio demonstrates what psychologists refer to as a more ingrained type of behavior. Alfonso is shy and often passive, generally worried over how he is coming across to others, which he described as his "cross to bear." At the same time, he was aware of how frustrating his long-term friend's lateness had been, and he found it hard to take. Unfortunately, Rogelio's response was typically a "one-note" excuse to anyone who expressed even a hint of annoyance at his lateness. Alfonso mocked his friend's statement with a loud, "Hey, you know me. I'm always late, deal with it." While we might pause to reflect on the incredible insensitivity Rogelio's position on his lateness testifies to, the ball is now clearly back in Alfonso's court.

Whereas Alfonso forgave his sister for her unusual lateness with understanding, as he had endured only a minor dose of irritation, the situation with Rogelio was different. Alfonso, it turns out, was aware that he could and even should respond to Rogelio's repeat-offender late behavior but said he didn't know how. Alfonso had let his shyness and go-along-to-get-along demeanor get in the way of learning how to be more assertive and represent his own interests. We discussed the reasons it would be good to assertively confront his friend. I was able to explain to Alfonso that this set of circumstances is what counseling can help with, as the sessions can provide guidance on how to communicate effectively. Specifically, we worked collaboratively on the reasons it would be important for Alfonso to communicate his displeasure with his long-term friend regarding the lateness issue. He was able to conclude that the time had come, mostly because Rogelio's behavior had been causing him frustration and annoyance for far too long. Instead of Rogelio's lateness being a one-time or infrequent occurrence, it was, as mentioned, ingrained behavior. Interestingly, in working with Alfonso, I recalled a Dear Abby column written years ago in which she was giving someone the advice that "If someone is almost always late, that's rude; drop them." Clinical psychology clearly offers a less absolutistic or black-and-white approach, yet she had a point.

Once Alfonso's issue was understood, we went into problem-solving mode. If a long-term friend continues to frustrate you with some aspect of their behavior, you can manage your shyness effectively by assertively responding. For example, one assertion technique I worked on with Alfonso is what has been referred to as the "When you...I..." sequence. In a role play, Alfonso practiced saying to his friend Rogelio, "When you are late, which is often, I get frustrated, and it strains things between us." Of course, things don't always go well, so I thought I'd be Rogelio in a role play and responded, "Hey, Alfonso, what kind of bush league psychobabble are you throwing at me? You know I run late. Give me a break." I followed quickly saying, "Jeez, be on time, be on time—talk about political correctness. Alfonso, you've been watching way too many Mr. Rogers episodes." At this juncture, in helping Alfonso stay the course, I introduced the concept of the *rational override*, more commonly referred to as the voice of reason. This therapeutic communication strategy helps one remain matter-of-fact even though the other person is escalating. By the way, we psychologists expect people to escalate when they first hear news that is, in their view, negative. How is this handled? Just ride it out; people do calm down (for the most part), so don't take it too personally if you're the helper.

Back to the rational override. The next step in the role play was for Alfonso to add the *broken record technique,* wherein he simply repeats by rephrasing what he originally said, "Rogelio, I was just trying to get across my point that when you are late a lot, it does bug me, so I wonder if we can work with it a little." This demonstrates using both the rational override and being the adult in the room, combined with the broken record technique of repeating the point. The repetition strategy is useful because, when assertively (and appropriately) confronted, most of us may first respond with emotion, and so we don't always hear the sender's true message.

The "When you...I..." sequence is a simple yet powerful assertive communication technique. What it does is describe the other person's behavior (without judging it) and then help you identify the effect that behavior has had on yourself. Another example, apart from Alfonso's, could be represented by a couple. The wife says to the husband, "When you don't take your shoes off after working in the yard, I get angry because the floor was just cleaned." This is an admittedly trivial daily dust-up, but in the next example, the strategy shows how it can be effective in a more consequential way. Months go by, and the same wife says to the husband, "When you drink to the point that you forget your own name, let alone mine, I get really upset and actively consider divorce." Hopefully, the husband is listening. Note: In general, one negative feature of being shy to the point that you don't feel comfortable asserting yourself with others is the possible development of physical symptoms. For example, if you find yourself holding back from someone who is frequently annoying you, the resulting inhibition on your part can drag you down a bit, as in, you may feel worn out. So, as Alfonso was learning, speaking up when things are bothering you is generally a good idea.

To summarize the IPT approach, take time to make a commitment to actively pursue your goal of being more social. Work on being both aware and engaged in activities with others whose company you think you will enjoy. If distressful thoughts occur during a *Successful Shyness* practice opportunity, such as "I don't think I can go through with this," acknowledge the thought, yet try to proceed anyway. Learning to relate to others, sometimes referred to as "relational learning," takes time, and some amount of difficulty, including awkwardness, is to be expected. The saying "Smooth sailing never made a skilled sailor" applies in that rough going social encounters can result in learning gains. At least with a relevant practice opportunity on communication skills, it is just practice; you're allowed to make mistakes.

The goal we are striving for here is to learn how to manage any social awkwardness, not eliminate it. Who in their daily lives haven't experienced socially awkward moments? In this regard, important subgoals include:

1. Being productive socially, despite some anxiety and tension.
2. Decreasing the anguish of social withdrawal and isolation.
3. Experiencing accomplishments in social relationships.

Major Role Transitions with Implications for Shyness
1. Major role transitions, including normative progressions, occur throughout the life cycle. Childhood, adolescence, young adulthood, mature middle-age, and beyond to the elder years form major role transition periods. These forward motions are considered normative because most of us go through them, be it at a slower or quicker pace. Shy individuals tend to be shier in childhood and less so heading into adolescence and adulthood as more ways of relating to other people are learned.
2. Shyness involves both tension and inhibition, and sometimes dependent behavior can be a component. One role transition that can be recognized in most all people as we head into maturity involves the process of becoming less dependent while learning to be more independent. Allow yourself time, as this major role transition takes years.
3. Problems in social interaction can lead to withdrawal and isolation, with loneliness sometimes the result. Thus, if you identify as being lonely or separated from others that you would like to become more involved with, consider that your role transition task can be increasing social contacts one person at a time. This process will help you go from socially inept (like all of us at times) to more socially adept (for which we may all strive).
4. Turn off, or at least turn down, thinking about yourself. Instead, a self-propelled role transition can include focusing more on others. This may well lead you to interact more with others face-to-face, which will result in increased social skills while decreasing any quiet desperation from lack of contact. While you're at it, you can practice what I refer to as *intentional imperfection*. That is, recognize that we all

make mistakes and slipups in conversations, and don't worry—social interactions tend to come with fits and starts at times. Just get out there and allow yourself to have a social warm-up period, then initiate social interaction.

Case Vignette
Working Through a Role Transition

I saw Jane, an eighteen-year-old, as an outpatient who came into counseling for slight anxiety and a moderate degree of shyness. In time, she progressed well in terms of talking with more people and enjoying various social activities with her peer group. Her anxiety lessened, and Jane described feeling ready to pursue her education. She left Orange County, California, to go to college and traveled a short distance south to attend San Diego State University (SDSU) as a freshman. She first lived in the dorms and then became a member of one of the larger sororities on campus. This alone was a significant development because it brought her into contact with many other students, and she developed several friendships. When I saw Jane next, it was for a session while she was home on break. I was surprised and proud to learn that she had been elected social chair at her sorority. When I asked what prompted such a direct people contact role, she was able to describe how it would keep her "in the mix socially" versus isolating. Withdrawing was her previous defense or protection when shyness created too much internal discomfort.

Thus, therapeutic progress continued. In fact, an experience occurred after Jane returned to SDSU for the spring semester that helped her to be the helper. As social chair of her sorority, one responsibility Jane had was to set up the sorority house for a holiday party, straddling Thanksgiving and Christmas. This activity occurred right before students went on winter break. Jane acknowledged that she would initially get anxious before talking with anyone, but since she recognized that shyness management sometimes just involves simply warming up to a social situation, she was in the game. In a follow-up session, we discussed how Jane experienced her increased communication with others. She remarked that she could share more and be empathic with people because her communications were no longer strained but relaxed. Clinically, we've observed time and time again that when shy individuals are anxious, a warm-up period to social activities allows for significant decreases in tension and preoccupation. Jane did well with her new warm-up tool, which usually involved watching others in their interactions at a new social activity before she joined in.

Merging (Contact) Versus Separating (Withdrawal) in Social Interactions

Common themes that are important to discuss with adolescents and adults include merging (contact) versus separating (withdrawal). To explain, every interaction between two people usually involves two fundamental behaviors: merging (contact) or separating (withdrawal). Regarding contact versus withdrawal, a shy person can get on the front end of this dynamic by deciding when they want to merge or make contact with others. Conversely, the same individual can consider whether it is better to separate or withdraw from a particular situation or set of social circumstances. The case vignette below is meant to illustrate the merging (contact) or separating (withdrawal) psychological dynamic as it plays out in a family.

Case Vignette
Merging and Separating Behavior
Shailene was a sophomore in high school. She had good grades and a couple of close friends. But her relationship with her parents was strained. In terms of merging or contact, all was well with her peers, although she tended to distance herself (separate or withdraw) from time to time. She would separate physically from her parents by staying in her room quite a bit, and she would withdraw from conversations if any conflictual issues were discussed. In family counseling, Shailene was encouraged to maintain contact with her close friends and reach out to other peers who could then be brought into her circle of caring relationships.

Regarding her parents, the opportunity arose to have Shailene tell them in session the reason she would withdraw at times from discussions with them. At one point, she told them, "I don't like the raised voices. You two argue with each other, then with me." Clearly, this provided an example of why she would rather separate than merge or make more contact with her parents. However, her parents had a rebuttal and pointed out that Shailene was often too quiet, and this would block their appropriate attempts to make contact with her or interact with her in mutual conversation. Problem-solving included having each parent and their teen consider when they were making contact or withdrawing during the day in order to increase their interpersonal awareness. This simple intervention worked well with family members agreeing they could make contact or merge with each other more often when they kept their voices at a decent level respected one another's need for space, especially after long days at work or school.

Tips to Manage Shyness for Yourself and When Dealing with Others
1. Ask yourself what the reasons may be for feeling shy in social situations. Common responses include the social situation being too threatening or overwhelming. Also, anxiety may rise too high to comfortably approach others initially but may lower in a few minutes. On occasion, you may notice that certain people seem loud and obnoxious in an ongoing conversation, from which it is likely best to gracefully depart and engage others present.

2. If someone questions why you are being so shy, one way to respond is to say, "I'm feeling a little quiet right now, pulled back; it's been a busy day." There is an implicit cultural norm that we at least talk a little and even smile when out and about or with friends. For shy people, it is important to consider that by staying entirely quiet, you may unwittingly bring the very attention (and questioning) you don't welcome or want. This situation is akin to the teenager who comes home from high school or a part-time job and goes straight to their room without saying a word. Predictably, the parents who are standing nearby look at each other quizzically, wondering what's going on. If the teenager had simply said something short and sweet like "Hi, I'm home. How's everyone doing?" then things would go more smoothly. I suppose the communication idea is that you don't need to talk a lot, but some interaction with others makes our social world run a little easier.

3. Remind yourself that being in situations that promote mutual social trust will positively impact your physical health.

4. Smile more and remember to give direct eye contact, which can result in a more relaxed social situation overall.

5. Shyness is often an initial internal response. Once you take the first step to reach out and get to know someone, even a little, you will likely relax somewhat and feel more comfortable.

6. Tell yourself that you are "learning to avoid avoidance." Encourage yourself to stay in a given social interaction longer than you first anticipated.

7. A key strategy is to acknowledge shyness or anxiety by stating to yourself, "So what? My shyness can be an asset at times." To others, you can simply say, "I turn quiet sometimes" or "I get a little anxious at times," depending on the circumstances.

8. Avoid harsh start-ups. For example, if you feel the need to confront someone on an issue, begin with a neutral statement such as "I'd like to talk with you about something, okay?" before launching into the main issue: "I didn't appreciate it when you yelled 'Movie' when we were visiting that fire station." Try to keep emotions at a moderate versus high level of intensity.

9. Ask a friend to observe you in a variety of social situations, then give you candid feedback on their views of how you came across.

10. Yes, at times you may be awkward in a particular social interaction. Try using the technique of asking yourself, "So what?" and then, "What does this say about me?" If you conclude with a negative thought or cognition, such as "I really blew it talking with that person. I'll never be able to get it together," then working on not catastrophizing will be in order. If on the other hand, you surmise, "I was a little nervous, but that happens to everyone from time to time," you've successfully mastered the art of a more reasonable or realistic conclusion.

As mentioned previously in *Successful Shyness*, one good role-modeling example to give yourself is watching any competitive sport. For example, in football, the quarterback of a top-ranked team may throw an interception on a play or, worse, trip over his own feet. This spectacular failure is observed in front of thousands and thousands watching the game or on TV. What happens? Generally, the quarterback brushes it off, gets set for the next play, and goes on to do his best at being more effective. Sports can teach us that making mistakes, even large ones, are not only common but permissible and certainly does not need to lead to self-condemnation. In fact, there is usually another game around the corner, and during a season, suiting up again is only days away. The same goes for social activities, with even more opportunities for frequent tries in the interpersonal world. Thus, keep trying and remember—there is no need for a perfect performance.

11. Another communication prompt is to ask someone who has made a specific pronouncement or statement during a conversation, "How do you know that?" This general query or question for evidence will either deepen the conversation or be viewed as an invitation to argue. For example, one person may respond ,"Well, I'm glad you've asked. I've been researching this topic for years and written a few letters to the editor on it." More typically, though, another person might state, "I don't know. I read it somewhere." Thus, I suppose it should be a curiosity question best used with someone with whom you've already established a relationship and are on friendly bantering terms.

12. On the topic of rejection, it has been shown that shy individuals can be so-called rejection-sensitive. That is, the shy person may not even engage in asking for a date or going out with friends for fear that the answer may be no. Working this through can simply be a matter of going ahead and asking for what you would like to do, be it go out on a date or some other social activity. Through practice, anxiety generally subsides significantly, at least when asking others to do things. Yes, rejection will occur, but you are likely to get more positive acceptance than negative responses over time. While we're on the subject of rejection or hurt feelings, I found that putting one foot in front of the other is still the way to go. Take it from Ralph Waldo Emerson, who, while he did not create the following adage, popularized it: "Some of your hurts you have cured, and the sharpest you have yet survived; But what torments of grief you endured; From evils that never arrived." Emerson also offered: "Do the thing you are afraid to do, and the death of fear is certain." I think he meant, summarized that, if you keep those direct-action efforts going, things might end up much better than you anticipated.

The reverse direction in rejection is particularly important to consider but seldom discussed. I've not seen all that much in the psychological literature on the constructive rejection of others, but what a great skill to learn. Let's say someone asks you to go somewhere or do something, and they are really counting on it. You are reluctant to agree. What do you say? A blunt forget it is not constructive. A simple yet truthful "I'd like to, but I promised my family I'd spend the day with them" is both informative and constructive, not to mention more empathic. A more consequential, if humorous, example would be the sensitive firing of an employee at a company that makes World Globes for elementary schools. "Larry, you are well liked here as an employee making the stands for our globes, but unfortunately, our fit may not be too good." To which Larry responded, "What do you mean?" The employer then elaborated empathetically, "Well, we've learned that you belong to the Flat Earth Society, and we make round globes. It's nothing personal. It's just that we clearly entertain very different beliefs."

13. If you tend to blush, which likely has a genetic component in some of those who have social anxiety, simply acknowledge it. Flushing, blushing, and sweating are psychophysiological indicators or markers that are natural responses that can occur during stress. If someone starts to sweat in conversation and then blushes, a straightforward response can be helpful, such as "Looks like I'm sweating a little. I might also be blushing, which I do occasionally. It's kind of funny; the sweating I can see, the blushing I can only sense, it may be going on."

14. Shy people can benefit from learning that if they are emotionally reactive or pitched up, they can first calm themselves before trying to listen to others in busy social situations.

15. Learn to increase your self-awareness by tuning into how others are reacting or responding to your voice, body language, and general communication style. This focus will allow you to adjust how you're coming across, if needed, to be more effective in your interactions with others.

16. Strive for consistency in your personality style. That is, people get along more easily with those who tend to be reliable and dependable in both their manner of relating and the actions that they take. Individual personality features can shine when you interact with others. In fact, you can work on increasing your self-esteem by recognizing and embracing your unique characteristics, including shyness. One way to do this is by letting others know that you tend to relate in a more quiet or reserved manner, at least initially, then warm up.

Try to develop realistic expectations by not attempting to ensure that every conversation comes off without a hitch or hiccup. Conversations are dynamic, except, of course, the "Hi, then, bye" automatic type. Work through inevitable gaps or pauses in communication as par for the course. If conversations were all perfect interactions, they would come off as too robotic and not very spontaneous.

Chapter 15

Shyness, Social Anxiety, and Substance Use

Shyness and Alcohol Interventions

In many instances, a shy teen or adult may find that alcohol calms them down and relaxes them, enabling easier social responses. Because alcohol relaxes our inhibitions, it can make it easier, particularly for the shy and anxious, to speak up and interact more comfortably in social situations. There is a downside to using alcohol as a coping tool, as any overuse can be problematic. Specifically, alcohol can lower anxiety and social discomfort, but the effect is temporary and at a cost. Consider that the sober individual has the advantage of working through any anxiety experienced in social situations to get to the other side. That is, discomfort and tension may well occur at the beginning of many different social interactions, yet they often subside. When an individual can learn to ride things out in a social conversation by staying the course, confidence will build, true relaxed responding will occur, and there will be no alcohol side effects. Nevertheless, social activity and alcohol go together frequently at sporting events, weddings, and outdoor parties.

> **Case Vignette**
> *Shyness, Social Anxiety, Alcohol, and Cannabis*
> Individuals who are shy and socially anxious are more at risk of developing an alcohol use problem. Cara, a thirty-year-old high school teacher, reported being talkative enough in her classroom but would "clam up" when interacting with other teachers and administrators at her school. She remarked that she was less shy than when she was young, but sometimes the demands of teaching, and particularly parent conferences, pushed her into "retreat mode," as Cara put it. She began to use alcohol more frequently in the evening and before attending some events, adding, "I also smoke some pot to take the edge off." In counseling, Cara learned to use focused breathing and relaxation skills when at home and before any social events. She said, "It's a work in progress, but I'm finding I have more energy for the next day when I don't drink." She added that parties

and other social events didn't seem nearly as intimidating "if I've done my relaxation and breathing exercises beforehand."

One general way to look at the slippery slope of alcohol and other drug use is that for some, they can start with fun, turn to fun and problems, with the final phase detrimentally including only problems. For example, Dave, a young college student, may find that drinking and partying while watching football makes for a (fun) time. Several months later, Dave finds his grades slipping, yet he continues to enjoy the benefits of partying, including talking more easily with others when alcohol is used (fun and problems). Finally, family and friends have noticed that Dave's mood has become more depressed, and he has just learned that he's been placed on academic probation (problems).

General Issues in Substance Use and Shyness Responding

A) Substance use, be it alcohol or drugs, can be a misguided method or attempt to alleviate anxiety. It may work in the short run; someone who takes a drink may relax before a social event. Unfortunately, when used as a routine coping method, when someone is without their chemical relaxer, their anxiety may shoot through the roof. That is, alcohol or drug use has provided a crutch over the long term, and without it, there hasn't been an opportunity to learn drug-free ways of relaxing when socially anxious. The implication for those who are shy and may be socially anxious is to be careful with alcohol or any relaxing type of drug or medication.

Case Vignette
Being Social Without Alcohol

Liam had developed many friends at his personal fitness operation. Yet he was a young adult who often chose to drink when attending social events outside of his work. These social occasions would also include some of the clients he had first met as part of his job. Most others saw Liam as quiet, somewhat serious, but nice enough. Liam was, in fact, very shy outside of his role as a personal trainer. At one event, Liam found himself drinking quite a bit while being friendly and sociable with others. One of Liam's friends came up to him and said, "Why have you turned to drinking more alcohol?" In counseling, Liam related that his comeback to his friend was "Because it amplifies my personality," to which his friend retorted, "Yes, but what if your personality is that of a jerk?" As Liam related this interchange between himself and his friend, he expressed having been taken aback and then saddened. This led to a discussion about how too much alcohol use can quickly exceed its sociability-enhancing effects, and then trend right into sometimes bold and obnoxious social responses.

We discussed being social and assertive, but without using alcohol to any significant extent, if he wanted to preserve his friendships. I said, "Being tactful has its place." Liam asked what I meant about being tactful in social situations, and we both laughed at the quote I dug up on tact by Winston Churchill: "Tact is the ability to tell someone to go to hell in such a way that they look forward to the trip." Liam also wanted to know how he could have a serious conversation with someone over a heated topic without having the other person get so adamant about things. I just let Liam know, shy or not, to try and remain reasonable when engaging in hot topics. The relevant quote I thought of was: "If you argue with a jackass, no matter how smart you are, after a while, no one can tell which one is the jackass." Pleasantly assertive is a good way to go.

B) One way to learn alternative methods to alcohol or drug use to relax in social situations is to try out different approaches. This book details the popular progressive muscle relaxation (PMR) procedure, along with breathing exercises and other ways to decrease tension and anxiety. I encourage all of us to watch quality online offerings on relaxation methods, take workshops, and attend wellness-type community events to see what fits our preferences best.

C) Another useful skill to learn non-alcohol or drug ways to relate to others is to practice small, then larger social interactions with family, friends, and finally opportunities in the community at large. These activities can be valuable because, if shy or socially anxious, relying on a substance to relax can be a slippery slope. Some individuals, shy or not, can get caught up in the insistence and persistence that substance use sometimes entails. I recall a client I once saw in counseling who was in the Vietnam War. He described a friend he was with near a river. He said the locals were pointing to crocodiles as they aimed to cross over to the other side. He said his friend kept holding a cigarette and beer can high above his waist so he wouldn't get them wet as they made their way. To me, this was the very definition of the insistence and persistence substance use can hold on an individual. I did not recall him mentioning whether they were conversing with the locals, so there was no word on whether there was any shyness or social anxiety at this phase of their trek. Perhaps it would have made a great commercial as they made it to the other side, although luck was probably the largest factor.

D) Be aware that social anxiety disorder is different from simply being shy. One characteristic of social anxiety disorder is that the individual life is restricted to a small circle of friends or family or to engaging in limited social interactions overall. Unfortunately, this restricted lifestyle could make a very socially anxious individual more at risk for relaxing or calming themselves by using alcohol or drugs in new or unfamiliar social situations.

E) As avoiding social situations can limit an individual's lifestyle, it is important to consider that short-term relaxers such as alcohol or certain drugs, especially if used routinely to lower anxiety, do not help an individual learn more constructive ways to engage socially.

F) Alcohol and certain drugs decrease inhibition, so their use can be tempting to the shy. Unfortunately, the dangers of substance use can be significant, especially when it comes to changes in mood. That is, one price for a substance-induced lessening of anxiety, particularly social anxiety, is that it can ultimately affect mood negatively. For example, depression can follow a period of substance use or abuse, and the shy person hasn't used their sober self to hang in there with an anxiety producing social situation to get to the other side. I had one client, Alan, a forty-five-year-old building design specialist, who was quite insightful regarding his drinking at some parties. At one point in discussing his drinking and socializing, he said, "I had that alcohol-induced veneer of painful politeness with others." Clearly, Alan understood that when drinking a little alcohol during parties, he was able to socialize more but could also come off as more glib or superficial to others. Because this was not what he wanted, learning more non-alcohol or drug-free ways to respond to others, including using relaxation methods and focusing more on the other person first, helped him in his efforts.

Chapter 16

Medications for Social Anxiety Disorder

There are no medications specifically for shyness, which makes sense because it is not a disorder. Yet as a broad personality trait, shyness comes with its share of positive and negative features. One major asset of individuals who are shy is that they are oftentimes sensitive and caring. Another positive about shy people is that they can be good listeners. Problematic aspects of shyness call for its effective management in a variety of situations. There are medications for social anxiety disorder, which many have considered akin to extremely severe shyness, wherein daily functioning is affected. A major criterion to diagnose social anxiety disorder (SAD) using the Diagnostic and Statistical Manual of Mental Disorders (5th ed., text rev. DSM-5-TR; American Psychiatric Association, 2022) includes persistent anxiety that lasts six months or longer. The anxiety occurs in one or more social situations in which the individual is exposed to possible scrutiny by others. Further, among other criterion for SAD is the central observation that the anxiety experienced appears out of proportion to the actual threat posed by the social situation. By contrast, individuals who are shy oftentimes brave through social situations, even though anxious. Thus, there is less pervasive avoidance or escape behavior than with SAD.

This section will review medications that can decrease significant anxiety, including social anxiety. The strategies in this book as well as many other books on shyness, focus primarily on practicing social skills. The goal is for shy individuals to learn ways to be more direct in their interpersonal responses. A corollary of this goal is to help the shy in their efforts to gain greater ease in a variety of social situations. The importance of medication lies in its ability to improve symptoms such as bodily discomfort and overarousal. When needed, as may be the case for SAD, this can be a useful pharmacological intervention. Medication can be particularly effective when combined with psychological strategies, including cognitive behavioral therapy (CBT) and interpersonal psychotherapy (IPT). The practice opportunities in *Successful Shyness* will facilitate effective shyness management provided in a self-help format. Counseling or psychotherapy is also recommended for those who want or need to involve professional healthcare expertise. Medical assessment and intervention are necessary when considering any prescribed medication indications.

As discussed in earlier sections of *Successful Shyness*, CBT, IPT, and other therapeutic self-help strategies are all used to help individuals effectively manage their shyness. For those diagnosed with SAD, there are research-supported approaches for prescribed medications or drug treatment to decrease severe anxiety in social situations. The three main classes of medications to treat social anxiety include antidepressants, antianxiety medications, and a limited number of anticonvulsants. Medications referred to as beta-blockers can be helpful for specific performance concerns (e.g., public speaking). Finally, a brief section on herbal and other natural remedies is included due to their recently growing popularity for reducing social anxiety.

As mentioned above, there are several different types of medication that are used to treat SAD. In the sections below, medication is referred to by its generic name (based on the drug's chemical makeup), followed by the brand name placed in parentheses. As an example, ibuprofen is the generic name, and a common brand name is (Advil).

Shy or not, many individuals have nervous systems that are highly reactive. This type of all-hands-on-deck alertness is often accompanied by anxiety as a largely physical response in a person. The combined symptoms of high reactivity and accompanying severe anxiety are what make consulting a prescribing healthcare professional an appropriate referral. In the case of SAD, it is important to recognize that medication can help reduce symptoms that contribute to social anxiety but will not directly improve social skills or build confidence. Oftentimes, when it comes to severe social anxiety, medication can be used in combination with psychological interventions (CBT, IPT), as mentioned above and will be discussed in more detail below. This researched multimodal approach aimed at decreasing anxiety and improving daily social functioning has demonstrated effectiveness. If in need, seek consultation regarding those medications that are specifically prescribed to alleviate the symptoms of moderate to severe anxiety.

Before describing the separate classes of prescribed medications for social anxiety, it is important to know that alcohol and drug use can be dangerous ways to cope. These non-prescription substances are sometimes regarded as a form of self-medication, particularly when used as a long-term strategy. Also, prescribed medications should not be combined with alcohol or other drugs. Clearly, it's best to skip any self-medicating strategies to cope with shyness and social anxiety. This is true even though the effects of alcohol (and some other drugs) may have positive temporary social lubricant or social extroversion effects that are unfortunately chemically induced.

Thus, as is detailed in this self-help book, there are different constructive non-medication approaches to lessen physical arousal and nervous system reactivity that can be tried first. The aim is that, through practicing these techniques or procedures, you will be able to feel more comfortable in awkward social situations. *Successful Shyness* highlights two main procedures for lowering physiological distress: focused breathing and progressive muscle relaxation (PMR). Further, the practice opportunities in this book provide the vehicle you can use to implement these primarily CBT and IPT-based interventions. This psychological approach, alone or in combination with medication, can be used when it comes to severe social anxiety.

The main goal is to effectively manage your shyness. Basically, if severe social anxiety enters the picture, then medication is worth considering. In summary, by decreasing high physical reactivity and severe anxiety, prescribed medication, if needed, can be used effectively. When combined with CBT and IPT psychological interventions, the goal of uniformly calmer responding in a variety of different social situations can be reached.

Antidepressants

There are several different medications classified as antidepressants that work to decrease anxiety, in addition to treating depression. In general, antidepressants have the best research support for effectiveness with social anxiety, followed by antianxiety medications, which are also commonly used. Selective serotonin reuptake inhibitors (SSRIs) are prescribed as the first-line type of antidepressant medication for symptoms of significant and persistent social anxiety. Basically, the SSRIs work to increase serotonin levels and can decrease not only symptoms of depression but also excessive worry and other social anxiety features. Some data suggest that SSRIs may also lessen negativity by calming the amygdala. As discussed in *Successful Shyness*, the amygdala governs fear, among other emotions. Commonly used SSRIs for social anxiety include paroxetine (Paxil), the controlled-release form of fluvoxamine (Luvox CR), sertraline (Zoloft), citalopram (Celexa), and escitalopram (Lexapro). Sleepiness, sexual dysfunction, and weight gain are the most common side effects of SSRIs. Side effects often lessen with time. Prescribers monitor side effects carefully and generally agree that they are best dealt with by paying close attention to dosage, especially early on, making visits for medication management vitally important.

There is another medication, the extended-release form of venlafaxine (Effexor XR), that acts on both serotonin and a second neurotransmitter system, norepinephrine. This type of antidepressant is referred to as a selective serotonin and norepinephrine reuptake inhibitor (SNRI) and has been found to be effective in treating social anxiety disorder. Advantages of taking SSRIs or an SNRI include a relatively low price and low addiction potential. Frequently reported side effects of Effexor XR include, but are not limited to, sweating, nausea, constipation, and dizziness. To avoid significant withdrawal symptoms, this medication, as well as most others, should be discontinued gradually and under the advice of your prescribing healthcare professional.

Antianxiety agents

There are several different medications classified as benzodiazepines that can bring down anxiety relatively quickly due to their relaxant properties. Although they do work rapidly, they can be sedating as well as habit-forming. Thus, the benzodiazepine class of drugs is typically prescribed for only short-term use. Commonly prescribed benzodiazepines include alprazolam (Xanax), lorazepam (Ativan), and clonazepam (Klonopin). Different from the antidepressants, which are used on a daily basis, the benzodiazepines are often taken only as needed. Like the antidepressant types of medication, they are relatively low in price but have a higher addiction potential. Benzodiazepine type drugs should not be taken with alcohol. Some individuals report a rebound of their anxiety after stopping this type of medication, with another accompanying side effect being insomnia. Thus, the symptoms of withdrawal are best managed by gradual rather than abrupt discontinuation.

Beta-blockers

Medications known as beta-adrenergic blockers can help with specific performance concerns, such as public speaking. Beta-blockers such as propranolol (Inderal) and atenolol (Tenormin) are prescribed for angina (chest pain) and hypertension (high blood pressure). When used for these two medical conditions, they can decrease heart rate and blood pressure. Beta-blockers work largely by blocking the stimulating effect of epinephrine (adrenaline). They can also decrease physical symptoms of tremor (shakiness) and the uncomfortable feeling of tachycardia (pounding heart) when stressed. As an example, a beta-blocker could be used when an individual who has an upcoming social event leadership role becomes anxious about it. They may want to decrease their bodily symptoms associated with the anxiety and focus on the task before them. Even though this type of medication can help when used on an as-needed basis, such as for performance anxiety or jitters, beta-blockers do not appear to be effective on a regular basis for the treatment of social anxiety disorder. Relatively few side effects occur with beta-blockers, but they can cause dizziness, lightheadedness, or fatigue. Withdrawal can result from suddenly stopping this medication; thus, a slow taper is in order. Also, this class of medications, like all the others discussed, must be used under medical supervision.

Anticonvulsants

Preliminary studies have shown that one class of medications that has shown possible usefulness in treating social anxiety disorder is known as anticonvulsants (usually used to treat seizures). Gabapentin (Neurontin) has been used to reduce anxiety and has very few interactions with other medicines. Pregabalin (Lyrica) has also shown some benefit and can be prescribed as an alternative to gabapentin. The most common side effects are dizziness and drowsiness. These drugs have the advantage of not being addictive and may result in fewer withdrawal effects than benzodiazepines. Note that this class of medications has not yet been approved by the Food and Drug Administration (FDA) for the treatment of social anxiety disorder.

Herbal and Other Naturopathic Remedies

Several herbal remedies have been studied to treat anxiety, but the outcome research to date has yielded only mixed results. Kava kava (kavalactone compounds) is an herb that has been purported to have antianxiety properties. L-theanine (an amino acid), which can be found in black and green tea, is a supplement that some research has shown might also have an antianxiety effect. There are many other herbal and other natural remedies that are being marketed to an ever-increasing number of people who want to try these substances to help reduce their anxiety. Side effects of kava kava include dizziness and drowsiness as well as possible allergic skin reactions. L-theanine seems to have few side effects, but large amounts of green tea can cause irritability and GI upset due to caffeine content. Caution is in order because even though these substances are marketed as natural, they do have physiological effects on the body and can interact adversely with other medicines you may be taking. Of course, before taking any herbal or naturopathic remedies, consult with your prescribing healthcare professional to make sure of their safety.

Medication Consultation

In general, medications are prescribed for their important main effects, but side effects seem to be a constant shadow and occur when taking most medications. Thus, it is important to first consult a prescribing health care professional to be fully informed about any intended medication for the reduction of severe social anxiety. To decrease the seemingly ever-present risk of side effects, your prescriber will often start with a low dose of medication. The prescribed medication is then gradually increased to a full therapeutic dose. It is important to recognize that it may take several weeks to several months with medication treatment for your symptoms to see noticeable improvement.

Combined Medication and Psychological Treatment

As mentioned above, even if you have a specific medication on board that helps lower the physical reactivity of anxiety and helps with calmer responses, it is worth considering combined treatment. That is, medication intervention can be coupled with psychological treatment, such as CBT and IPT. Note that anxiety is more likely to return after stopping medication than with the skill-based CBT and IPT interventions, though the psychological approach can also result in anxiety returning, at least temporarily. For example, when trying out CBT and IPT based practice opportunities that encourage direct-action (or exposure) and avoidance (or response) Prevention, your anxiety may initially increase, then settle back down as you follow through. If you are considering trying one treatment or the other first, it may largely depend on personal preference. The combined approach is clinically effective for those who need it and, when experiencing severe social anxiety, is worth careful consideration. In fact, those with social anxiety disorder are often treated with both antidepressant medication (e.g., an SSRI) and psychological (e.g., CBT, IPT) interventions.

Medication helps lower the negative physiological effects of anxiety and can increase calm responses. The self-help strategies you can take advantage of in *Successful Shyness* focus on learning cognitive, behavioral, and interpersonal skills to better manage shyness and social anxiety. It will be helpful for you to pursue many other resources to explore more detail about medications and their possible combination with psychological approaches for social anxiety. As one reputable national resource, the numerous offerings published by the Anxiety and Depression Association of America (ADAA) are recommended.

Case Vignette
Medication and Therapy to Lower Social Anxiety

Aubrey, a twenty-year-old sophomore in college, came in for crisis intervention sessions while she was on winter break from her school. I had previously seen her in individual counseling several different times before she left for her fall semester. Fortunately, we had established a good working rapport. Aubrey excitedly explained to me that there was a social event at her sorority. "Well, I don't know why, but it really shook me up." She said that her sorority had a rush week during which mostly freshman students would come over to check out the place and possibly be invited to join. Apparently, one sorority prospect who attended the membership rush drank a lot of alcohol prior to reaching the sorority house. Aubrey said, "She was kind of out of it. Her face was flushed, and she spoke with a slight slur." I was somewhat surprised, likening the experience to someone who would, with poor judgment, drink before a job interview—not good.

I asked Aubrey if she knew this person, and she said that she did and that she was "really nice." I then asked if she knew the reason she drank before attending the event. Aubrey said, "I have no clue," to which I responded that I didn't have any idea either. I explained that, not knowing the individual's genetic predisposition or social experiences with drinking, I wouldn't hazard a guess. I then remarked that when someone doesn't know something, especially regarding substance use or abuse, you can consider probabilities. Aubrey asked what I meant, and I replied, "With social events, some of which can be intimidating, like joining a sorority, some individuals may drink a little to take the edge off but can go overboard not knowing their limits." This brought us to a discussion of shyness and how to cope with it, as Aubrey's experience in high school was one of pulling back and not relating to others well. She described being mainly concerned over how others might scrutinize her actions and didn't want to be judged. Aubrey said, "I don't drink, but I saw myself in this person. She seemed really nervous as soon as the sorority sisters went up to meet her. I can still get tense and anxious around others too, especially if I don't know them."

Aubrey had been pleased with her success in focused breathing and progressive muscle relaxation (PMR) routines to relax. She said, "I'm less shy and generally calmer around others, but sometimes I still get really anxious." Aubrey went on to say that she had a panic attack during the first week she was on her college campus. Beneficially, she initiated a visit to the student health center for help. A nurse practitioner there prescribed Xanax (.5 mg/prn) which she has been taking "only when I feel like I'm having a meltdown." We reviewed several of the practice opportunities that Aubrey had learned related to managing shyness. She said that she liked the ones where you take a small risk and go out and talk with people about "situational things." Aubrey said, "It helped to be more open, and these days I can usually calm down right during the conversation."

I asked how the student was doing who went to the sorority rush event, and the news was hard to hear. Aubrey said, "Yeah, well, she won't even walk by the sorority house. I think because she's embarrassed." I then asked Aubrey if she would be willing to engage in a new practice opportunity once she returned to college after break. She was game, and the task we agreed on was straightforward. Basically, I had remarked, "Because you commented that you knew this young woman and that she was really nice, why not ask her to study together or go out for some coffee." Aubrey liked the idea and said she would. Clinically, in the best spirit of the interpersonal psychotherapy therapy (IPT) aspect of Aubrey's treatment, we discussed the benefits gained from making a genuine social connection. I said, "By helping someone interpersonally, a person you could relate to and empathize with, you'll both benefit." We concluded our last session before Aubrey's return to campus by going over a quote I had heard somewhere before that seemed applicable to her current set of circumstances: "May we have the ability to distinguish an individual's problems from their value as a human being." Aubrey responded, "Yeah, she may have drunk too much that one time because she was visibly uptight, but she really is a nice person. I will ask her to do something together."

Chapter 17

How to Manage Stress in a Variety of Social Situations and Problem Areas

General Treatment Strategies for Dealing with Stress in Social Situations

1. Call people you know but haven't talked to in a while. Start with someone who you are most familiar with and have had pleasant conversations with previously. Family members or friends are a good place to begin. You can keep the conversation short and discuss anything relevant that you want—an upcoming family reunion, a time in high school with an old friend, you name it. The point is to learn to converse in measured ways to manage your stress, then go ahead with longer talks with different people.

2. Shift attention from yourself to others and the social situation. Think of the phrase "shift happens" to guide the effort. To expand, consider that many shy individuals are generally self-conscious in social situations. To what degree self-consciousness is experienced by an individual depends on the specific interaction, be it with another person or group of people. It makes sense then, if you want to be more engaged yet relaxed in a social situation, that a constructive goal is to be more other-conscious. That is, focus on the other person or people with whom you are interacting, and you will likely become less self-conscious as a result.

3. Make a prediction before you enter a social situation. Try thinking, what is the worst thing that can happen? Then ask yourself what is a more realistic outcome that will likely happen. For example, Nadia, a senior in high school, predicted that many people would laugh at her prom dress, which she had made herself, and she wouldn't know how to respond. She thought about a more realistic outcome after talking with her mom. Recognizing that her friends really liked her dress, most at the prom would probably say it's at least okay, enabling her to relax and talk freely with others.

4. Develop tools to initiate conversation. Basically, come up with ways in which to make a good faith effort. For example, Avril was an experienced stockbroker who liked to work behind the scenes. She was competent and likable, yet shy and reticent. Her coworkers would invite her out for social hour after work, which she

usually turned down. One day her closest friend told her that she needed to get out more and that her coworkers "deserve the honor of your presence from time to time." Avril took the feedback to heart but felt that her biggest obstacle would be how to initiate dialogue. In work with her in-house Employee Assistance Program (EAP) counselor, she learned that small talk was the answer. Her EAP counselor advised Avril that something as simple as a mention of the day's news or, in her line of financial work, how a high-flying stock was performing would get things off to a good start.

This scenario brings up a good point, which is that shy and withdrawn individuals are sometimes pulled back simply because they want to say the right thing. They feel that they could be subjected to criticism if they don't. In other words, something important needs to be said, or nothing at all, is how many shy individuals have self-reported that they operate. Once learning that small talk is a valuable asset and is enjoyed by many people to break the ice in conversations, shy people can often feel liberated. Try it at your next opportunity. There is one caveat, which is, don't dwell on the weather, as it is an overused opener, as in "Boy, it looks like rain again," after it has been raining continuously for the last seven days.

5. Shyness can be due to overfocusing. In some cases, shyness and its isolating effect can be due to an individual's strong focus on other matters. Like any other person, a shy individual may bury themselves in constructive pursuits or productive hobbies. Take Noah, a twenty-year-old self-described shy college student who did little but study for four years, completing a bachelor's degree in chemistry. In counseling, he said that after graduation, it hit him. "The dawn of recognition came to me—I've concentrated all my energies on my studies, not interacting with others." One realistic initial goal was set for Noah, who was willing to engage in small talk with others. He asked for suggestions. I said, "It can be initiating a conversation about virtually anything. You can try situational issues, something like 'It appears that the economy is slowing again, but it seems like that happens a lot in the early part of the year.'" Noah reached out to others with some immediate success and was encouraged to keep situational talk in mind anytime he was out and about.

6. How to handle vigilance and hypersensitivity. Shy individuals are sometimes concerned about not wanting to be a nuisance" to others, however mistakenly, and will withdraw from interpersonal contact as a result. Thus, it can be helpful to learn ways to dial down this type of hypersensitivity. With a less vigilant approach and not over worrying about how others may respond, communications will flow more rewardingly. For example, I saw a young man in counseling, Vladimir, who came from a strict Russian family background. He was concerned about being too "wordy" when talking with others and felt it would be annoying to even his closest friends. Interestingly, given his mother's sentiment regarding casual conversation, he had a point. Vladimir told me that she would often comment, "Saying more

than hi or bye is elaborating. Let the other person speak." Because no one likes totally one-sided conversations, Vladimir could improve his communication style by lowering his worry level and starting with a few comments or questions to others, then seeing how it goes. He tried some short sentences and added various small talk conversation starters, and it worked. In fact, "Hi, how are you?" was Vladimir's first try at elaboration, and things got better from there.

7. Use behavioral rehearsal with social-evaluative feedback. In anticipating many social situations, you can first rehearse what you want to say and how you want to say it. Following a social situation, you can ask for social-evaluative feedback. A good place to start for feedback comes from friends or family on how you communicated. Importantly, don't worry if you tend to talk a lot, or are briefer in what you say. Basically, you are looking for feedback on the quality of your verbal and nonverbal communication style, not the quantity of words spoken. As an analogy, I used to watch birds gather on a telephone wire when I was young, and I suppose I still do from time to time. It appears that some birds are quite outgoing and enjoy each other's company ("birds of a feather flock together"). At the same time, there are other birds that enjoy sharing space, but do so at a distance from the others. These distanced birds that are on the same wire but further away from one another seem more cautious. I don't think birds are necessarily shy, but they can act like they are, or maybe they just want less stimulation.

Sound familiar? People seem to behave much the same way. Outgoing individuals like to mingle, sometimes in close quarters and with a variety of people. The shy tends to hang back some distance from others, even though they seem to want to be a part of the social activity. What stops the shy centers on concern and discomfort over how they might be perceived and whether they will be criticized or judged. This interpersonal trepidation is in reality based on social inhibition and can be emotionally painful. Thus, beginning with short interpersonal interactions is a good way to start. Basically, shorter versus longer socializing will help lower any personal distress before trying more complex or challenging situations.

Dealing Constructively with Problem Areas in Managing Shyness

Difficulties that shy people can experience include interpersonal anxiety combined with a strong self-focus or preoccupation. This inward orientation in the shy isn't so much about putting oneself first—it centers more on concern about being criticized or judged in social situations. To become more other-focused, begin by practicing "situational talk," preferably with a variety of people. As stated in different sections of this book, by starting conversations with situational talk, or small talk, as it is sometimes called, interactions can move along more smoothly. Take the pressure off yourself, recognizing that situational talk is about whatever is happening around you. Comments do not have to be regarding anything all that important—you're just trying to build rapport and find commonality.

If you're shy, what you will experience over time will likely be decreased anxiety and tension. Basically, you've been able to interrupt your own self-focused behavior in favor of being more other-focused. When we are other-focused, we can actively listen to what the other person has to say, and it becomes easier to find common ground or shared interests. For example, Darnell, an eighteen-year-old from the suburbs of Austin, Texas, found it difficult to speak with people he did not know. When his father drove him to several college campuses for a prefreshman visit, he wanted his dad to do all the talking. Fortunately, his dad knew his son was having trouble speaking up and wanted him to take the initiative more often. Darnell was hesitant at first, but when it was suggested that he start by talking with anyone he chose, such as a store clerk, college librarian, or the ever-smiling assistant admissions director, he stepped up. By talking more often to near random people in his current life, Darnell's anxiety and strong self-focus began to subside. The situational talk he would begin conversations with ranged from what the person he was speaking with felt about the university to how a store clerk liked their job. His dad was proud of him, and Darnell himself felt more at ease, with a corresponding increase in confidence.

After some experiences with being other-focused, another dimension to consider is not letting initial resistance stop you from pursuing your social goals. This term refers to initially not really wanting to engage in a social interaction or communicate with someone else. Yet, if your goal is to move forward and participate in a given dialogue with someone, you'll find that your initial resistance can melt away. In fact, the relatively quick drop in this type of resistance can occur after only a few minutes in a conversation or social activity. Once initial resistance fades, your anxiety and tension will decrease on their own, and your comfort level will go up. Another example, involving a group social activity, is having some initial resistance to going out and playing tennis since you haven't picked up a racket in a long time. Let's say you muster your energy and go. After a short period of time, you sense that the initial resistance is fading away. Your tennis skills may still be off, but you're enjoying yourself with others.

Bullying and Shyness

If we make the reasonable assumption that shy individuals are oftentimes sensitive, particularly in social interactions, then being bullied is a truly relevant issue. One form of bullying involves verbal intimidation, which is when someone becomes hostile or belligerent in their communication with you. As is discussed in the section on assertion, there are ways to handle such verbally challenging behavior by others. It is a myth that only weaklings can get bullied. In fact, strong people who are quite capable, intelligent, and well-liked can also find themselves targeted by bullies. An example of unwanted direct social aggression is when someone calls another person a derogatory name or, worse, initiates a physical altercation.

There can also be so-called indirect aggression. For example, another common form of bullying is someone gossiping about you. Such roundabout behavior makes it important for the shy (or non-shy, for that matter) to speak up for themselves and counter any misperceptions that might be occurring as the result of gossip. Another example is when a shy person is excluded from a group of friends and doesn't speak up about it. Yet another example of the indirect expression of aggression has as its source the newer world of cyberbullying. In this instance, the bully doesn't even need to be face-to-face. Many people, if not most, have had their feelings hurt because of online antics. A familiar complaint is when false rumors are spread. Bullying can threaten a person's self-esteem, confidence, and overall well-being. One effective problem-solving strategy is to actively seek support from friends and family. Find the helpers in the world, as Mr. Rogers of television fame suggests.

An immediate way to respond to a bully is to be matter-of-fact and not overreact to their actions, if possible. The reason for this is that bullies generally hope to get a reaction from you. If they don't get a response from you, they may, regrettable as it sounds, move on to another easier target. Alternatively, and sometimes the more appropriate way to respond depending on the situation, is to stand up to a bully by being assertive. By directly responding to the bully with a firm and even tone, you can point out their behaviors and how they have affected you. For example, a straightforward "You're pointing out my faults almost daily. It makes me feel sad. Perhaps our friendship has run its course" would hopefully have some purposeful impact. Ironically, bullying (if not too harsh) can help shy and more sensitive individuals learn to constructively defend themselves. Others, who are already more direct in their social interactions, may already know how to confront a bully from the get-go.

Shyness and Anger Expression or Suppression

1. Learn to manage your own anger and stress responses by nurturing yourself. For example, reward yourself with a pleasant activity you would enjoy for having controlled your temper in a difficult social interaction. Overall, self-care behaviors can help calm us from the potentially negative effects of escalating anger. People who take care of themselves generally experience higher self-worth and are more likely to be more satisfied on a daily basis. After taking care of yourself, recognize that sometimes just changing the communication environment can help. For example, I had one client who enjoyed the company of a friend, but he learned not to go with him to sporting events because, in his words, "his loud voice was too annoying." Another example comes to mind that I would term a "changed communication environment fail." I had a shy client, a young adult female, who related a "poor-timing episode" in her words. She described having had too much to drink one night and said, "I had thought about it and decided at 2:00 a.m. that it would be a terrific time to call my ex and let him know all the faults he had." This individual regretted her action and was able to gain insight as to how alcohol can hurt rather than help communication in many different situations.
2. There are constructive ways in which to manage anger, shy or not. One effective way, while seeming obvious, involves learning to control your reactions. But how? First, try to improve your frustration tolerance by taking some things, especially small issues, in stride. Second, practice responding openly and directly with others.

Third, learn and practice relaxation techniques as described in this book, such as focused breathing and progressive muscle relaxation (PMR). Relaxation techniques can be especially useful whenever you notice your anger rising. Finally, calling up pleasant imagery or visualizing a calm scene can go a long way in helping you tolerate momentary frustration or stress.

3. If you become irritated or angry in a social situation, try to calm down by consciously using a matter-of-fact tone. Next, acknowledge your feelings when in a conversation. For example, you can state something like, "I'm getting frustrated here. Let's slow this discussion down a bit" or "I've noticed my irritation, but it's just that we're talking about a controversial subject." Basically, it can be helpful to say anything that references your feelings as long as it's delivered constructively. Notice that the above statements use "I" versus "you." When you reference yourself, it is taking responsibility as opposed to "If you'd just lower your tone, we can get along better here."

4. In general, how do you handle your anger when interacting with others? Shy individuals sometimes hold anger rather than openly express this strong emotion. Although, regarding the expression of anger, it is sometimes a good idea to take a break in a social situation. This is particularly true if there is an interaction that is turning emotionally charged, if not explosive. Backing away and engaging in a contrasting (enjoyable vs. stressful) activity for as little as a few minutes can be helpful. Many people find that taking a brief walk, practicing meditation, listening to music, and spending time in nature can lower stress and tension.

5. Review your own angry reaction to certain things. As referenced above, has shyness influenced your anger in the sense that you've held on to feelings at times rather than expressing them openly to others? Take some time to go over what the favorable and unfavorable consequences of the anger you've had have been. Anger in and of itself has been considered a necessary emotion. If someone nearly hits you with their car as you're walking across the street in the crosswalk, it would be perfectly natural to react with anger. On the other hand, if being quiet and not challenging an individual on their verbally abusive behavior for months occurs, it is time to watch out. Some shy individuals may end up over responding to a bully due to pent up emotion. Should this occur, it would be a good time to review your anger suppression versus expression balance.

Case Vignette
Working with Anger Expression versus Suppression
Ramona, a thirty-one-year-old paralegal, came in for counseling sessions to learn how to express her anger constructively. As she put it, "I flew off the handle" with a colleague and was regretful afterward. We discussed one immediate intervention she could use at her work. The clinical explanation was that we

can all learn to modulate the outward expression of angry feelings. I let Ramona know that she could take her "anger temperature," and if it was too high in a situation, she could calm herself first, then respond. Clearly, this is not always easy to do, but it is worth the effort. Ramona learned to slow her breathing, think of what she wanted to say, then proceed. Learning that you don't always have to act on your thoughts is a powerful insight indeed. Ramona said, "I was so angry at first. I wanted to kick her ass; I even pictured it. But then I calmed down before I made any confrontation." This was good initial progress. Usually shy and reserved. Ramona was sometimes astonished at how angry she could feel.

The next step in counseling was an exploration of the impact shyness can have on anger. That is, even though angry, the shy tends to control their responses. You may see a flash of anger from a shy individual, then observe that there isn't a lot of emotion behind it; the expression is muted. Ramona recognized that she tended to let anger build up, then suppress it. She said, "I just don't want to be judged for 'losing it.'" Ramona and I took a look at what to do when you find yourself being too reserved or reticent following an appropriately angry feeling rising. I mentioned first trying to identify the feeling and rating it as a low, medium, or high level of anger or frustration. Next, respond with the internal recognition that anger is usually modulated best when it isn't too high. If it is too high, as Ramona agreed, it may be best to wait awhile. The expression "cooler heads prevail" came to mind, and Ramona decided that she would repeat this phrase to herself "unless I'm too angry to recall it." These things take time, and she agreed that yet another expression, "Rome wasn't built in a day," could form the basis for some soothing self-compassion.

F) Try changing the way you think to be more logical or rational when angry. A thought occurs, you then interpret the thought, and an emotion follows. The choice point is at the interpretation, wherein you can shift perspective (develop cognitive flexibility). For example, instead of thinking that a friend always disappoints you when the evidence suggests that it's just occasionally, learn to leave out the inaccurate *always* word. If you do, you'll have practiced cognitive flexibility and, in the process, become more accurate in your appraisals or viewpoints. If you're getting criticized, try to step back. Instead of responding immediately, hear the other person out first, then respond. Thinking things through in and of itself can slow an angry response and allow you a more rational, effective reaction. As a bonus we generally feel better when we respond calmly when possible. Things may not always go well in our daily conversations or discussions, but the overall communication success rate will go up. For somewhat of a humorous take, a truthful exchange occurred between a prison psychologist and a violent offender inmate. The psychologist had asked the young man, following his release, "What did you learn while you were in prison?" His response was telling. "I learned that I don't always have to act on my thoughts."

G) To be effective in the moment, use emotion regulation. That is, use your emotions as a resource. For example, if you can estimate that your emotion is running high in a frustrating social interaction in which you're getting angry—let's say it's at seven or eight on a scale of one to ten—self-talk can help. You can say something to yourself like, "I know I'm getting uptight; I'll try to dial it back to a five or six in this conversation I'm having with my internet customer rep." The ability to picture the scale in your mind, slow down breathing, and then pick a lower number on the scale allows you to respond better when frustrated or angry. In general, one major component of emotion regulation is our perceived ability to handle an event, which can range from shaky to confident. Resetting the dial from one to ten if it is trending too high in a difficult interaction will help you find steadier emotional responses.

Cynical Shyness—The Good, the Bad, and the Ugly

As discussed in the Assessment section of Successful Shyness, cynical shyness can occur when a shy student, for example, develops a darker type of shy and withdrawn response, the source of which is building anger and hostility. Prominent psychologist and shyness researcher, the late Dr. Carducci, commented that with repeated social rejection comes hurt, then anger. These individuals, usually in high school or older and predominantly male, create what Dr. Carducci descriptively terms a "cult of one." So where is the good? Most shy individuals, especially adolescents, can develop a somewhat cynical outlook from time to time, given the complexities of the world. Yet this type of cynicism may simply originate from a sensitive and discerning cognitive outlook that recognizes not all things are peaches and cream out there. When people are cynical at times but not significantly angry and hostile, we may all be able to relate to their stance,

Importantly, as shyness is not in and of itself inherently bad in any way, there should be no inaccurate dramatic messaging of cynical shyness alone leading to aggressive action. To me, it is not at all certain that cynical shyness, or what has also been termed pathological shyness, may be the most accurate descriptor for such an isolated, angry, and withdrawn individual's response. There is a broader label to describe "the bad," which must include a combination of not only shyness, but significant detachment along with increasing impulsivity, meanness, and boldness. These negative behaviors, along with other disturbing ("the ugly") ones, such as violating the rights of others, are covered by the label antisocial personality disorder.

With individuals who manifest antisocial tendencies, there is often an isolative stance, with impulsive behavior and poor social skills that can come across as "Oh, he's just shy." Not so. This is an inaccurate label because the personality of someone who is antisocial is clearly callous and interpersonally disregarding. This is a vastly different clinical picture than someone who comes to counseling and is simply shy and likely interpersonally sensitive. Nonetheless, cynical shyness is certainly an area that deserves more comprehensive research because some shy people can turn extremely negative over continued thwarted tries or attempts to be more social. If the accompanying rejection of being "on the outs" with peers becomes too repetitive, some shy individuals could find it demoralizing and hard to take. Support from family, friends, and the community at large is crucial for these individuals to stay the course and remain proactive in their daily lives.

Case Vignette
A Cynical Side to Shyness

Consider the case of Robert, who, according to family members and friends, was long considered shy and withdrawn. He was also viewed as an overly sensitive child who would cry if forced into any unfamiliar situations or circumstances. As he grew older, Robert was viewed by others as the kid who stood apart and would not socialize. He was considered slightly different and not that approachable. Robert was thin, insecure, and quite possibly had attention deficit hyperactivity disorder. His peers remained apart from him throughout most of his school years, and he acted like he didn't care. This was true, even though Robert secretly wanted to socialize with others and have a good time. Robert grew frustrated and angry while maintaining a lone wolf approach to life. As a teenager, he became interested in solo hobbies and developed a good deal of musical skill on the piano. He was able to date and liked socializing, with slightly more ease evident during his high school years. In time, Robert's anger at not being fully accepted, combined with an internal sense that he did not meet the expectations of others, fueled his frustration and disappointment with life in general.

Robert turned to alcohol and drugs to lower his tension, with little regard for the probable negative side effects that might occur both physiologically and psychologically in relation to others. His cynicism grew, and as he treated himself negatively through his self-defeating behavior, he began to externalize his problems. Robert ended up blaming everyone and everything for his current problems. He dropped out of individual counseling, explaining that shrinks couldn't help him, adding an oddly philosophical viewpoint that he needed "expansion not shrinkage." Robert would episodically rage and give others a hard time. He did reenter counseling while attending a local community college and learned that by reaching out more socially, he was able to develop several supportive friendships.

With those relatively few who are shy but turn significantly negative or cynical, it is possible that they may have initially been motivated to move toward others, even trying to engage repeatedly. Sadly, there could oftentimes be rejection. In turn, this creates a problematic combination of feelings. First, these individuals become anxious about most social situations. Second, the cynically shy may then develop a corresponding hostility toward others if they perceive they're being negatively judged. There is more reason to reach out to these individuals as early as possible. With family, friends, and community support, they can learn the ways of effective shyness as detailed in this book and so many others. There are also quality online resources at hand and professional help if desired or needed. For those who are not shy, one way to intervene is to reach out to those shy individuals whose shyness is a source of anger and hostility. Our local communities can do a lot by offering many different types of social activities and encouraging all to attend. With connection comes closeness. The goal is that no one is left outside in the cold.

The next case vignette also considers a cynically shy individual. Through friendship and bonding, there is hope for a more proactive set of lifestyle changes.

Case Vignette
Isolated and Cynical Turning to More Social

Elijah was a senior in high school when his family and friends noticed he was becoming more detached, cynical in his outlook, and seemingly angry. He was always shy and avoidant, but this was different. Elijah would make a conscious effort to stare anyone down who tried to approach him, which was off-putting to others. He was caught one day at school with a screwdriver in his backpack. The screwdriver was found and confiscated after a classmate saw it and reported him. Elijah, known for his street smarts and seemingly limitless capacity to make excuses, simply said, "It's not a weapon. I was just going around and tightening all the door hinges on the bathrooms because they were squeaking." To which he added, "When you think about it, I was really trying to help the school out." He was expelled for three days. News traveled through the school's grapevine fast, and upon his return to classes, most of his peers gave him a wide berth, and a few outright ignored him. Elijah did agree to meet with the school psychologist.

Hope springs eternal, and one peer, Simone, reached out to him and described her own troubles with authority and "being told too many rules to follow." At first, Elijah ignored her, saying he wanted to be alone. Simone persisted, and one day asked him if he would like to meet her at the school's cafeteria to eat lunch. Elijah responded with, "I guess, if you don't have anything better to do." The statement he made expresses some reserved approachability as it was a sort of invitation, one mixed with the reflection of his low self-esteem. His school psychologist endeavored to work with Elijah's emotional difficulties early on, as it was easily recognizable that they needed some shoring up.

Turns out Elijah grew up in an abusive household. His frustration and anger were building because his own shyness created a hesitancy to talk with others. He did not want to be criticized or, worse, rejected. Detachment and cynicism about the world around him were growing. Young as she was, Simone recognized his vulnerability, and they became friends. They seemed to share a distain for the sometimes-arbitrary rules of society and what Holden Caufield derisively referred to in *The Catcher in the Rye* novel as "phony" adults. These two teenagers were able to connect socially, with one reaching out and the other taking a risk to accept the gesture. They were both better off for the experience and, without consciously processing it at the time, learned more effective social skills.

To summarize, those shy individuals who become isolated and cynical, as well as generally negative, can be helped by learning how to engage with others more effectively. In a sense, they can learn to cope better socially and create a sense of community for themselves (versus remaining a cult of one). This stands in contrast to most young people, who are shy and may become frustrated with their own pulling back, but do not necessarily experience their shyness as a source of anger and hostility.

Strategies to Effectively Deal with Rejection

Rejection is a fundamental law of the (social) universe. Not surprisingly, rejection sensitivity is common and likely occurs in many of us for one important reason. Rejection sensitivity is discussed in the chapter on helping children and adolescents when it can be so intense for young ones, but it is also true for adults. Basically, it is because the drive to bond is deep in our DNA, making rejection painful. Because rejection does have an emotional pain pathway, it can be experienced like physical pain; it hurts. Being ditched by your best friend, for example, can be as threatening to your well-being as touching a hot stove. Thus, scanning the social environment does have an evolutionary advantage in remaining vigilant to the reactions of others. Such keen awareness has helped us remain on top of things because, for most of our ancestral history ,we depended on small group involvement, largely for survival.

What specifically does all of this have to do with our deep-seated DNA? Sociologists who study such matters consider it a kind of altered follow-the-leader mentality. Celebrity popularity, or even worship, somehow approximates being a part of a larger societal group. That is, we don't want to be left out of the group, and in many parts of the world, that group apparently includes famous celebrities. Following what these individuals wear, what trends they follow, and how they present themselves gives many people a feeling of belonging.

There is a downside to social wariness, which is that a highly tuned rejection-detection mechanism in an individual, particularly if they are very shy or socially anxious, can backfire. This occurs because detached, shy, or socially anxious responses may bring about a self-fulfilling prophecy. What can happen is that other individuals may end up rejecting the shy person because of the shy individual's tense and narrow stance. There is a strategy that can be helpful to use. I call it the "average acceptance/rejection frequency model." Take, for instance, a prospective dating set of circumstances. There are reasonable expectations you can operate on, given the law of averages and your own motivation. For example, in asking ten different people out over the next several months, five may say they are already in a committed relationship right at the outset. Three more people may say yes, and the last two will give an interminably vague response. This approach will let you know that in the dynamic world of relationships, particularly dating, risk is involved. Yes, rejection may likely occur, but not all the time. The more people you ask out, the more individuals with yes replies will present themselves sooner or later.

An associated goal would be to buffer yourself against the effects of being rejected, stung, or hurt by developing emotional muscle. In this strategy, gaining emotional muscle is simply the discipline you can achieve in following through with your social interaction goals. By moving on from those situations that aren't working and proceeding with those that are, you will enjoy the rewards of your efforts. It takes work, yet in time you will find those who want to be caring and supportive of you, as well as loyal in your daily life. According to prominent psychologist Dr. Robert Leahy, an increased general sense of uncertainty concerning performance can make us more vulnerable to rejection. This can take place when our emotional muscles seem to be taking a break. Public life tends to shrink quickly with less social interaction activity. Sorry to say, we may be headed toward an even more performance-based culture. In this type of society, individuals may ramp-up their rejection radar even further because of the harsh judgmental aspect a strong self-performance focus can have when in public.

As Dr. Leahy draws out his clinical perceptions, one can find a silver-lining. That is, he states that overreading signs of rejection may be preferable to underreading. This can be the case in terms of emotional protection in that significant disappointment can be avoided by putting energy into those who do reciprocate with us, as opposed to those who are distancing. One psychologist colleague of mine has an interesting view on rejection, with her pithy conclusion being that the earlier someone rejects you, the better, as it allows you to move on quicker to more satisfying relationship possibilities. I suppose that works unless you really wanted that person to accept you. From my viewpoint, we don't want society to pay the continuing price of sensitive, shy, and socially anxious people pulling back because of concern over their public behavior or performance. We benefit when the shy, reserved, and quiet people in our communities share their positive assets. These assets include particularly good listening skills, strong knowledge on a variety of topics, along with the ability to be loyal and trustworthy when it counts.

Chapter 18

More Strategies and Techniques to Effectively Manage Shyness

1. It's okay to beat a "strategic retreat" at times; just recognize that you want to make it very temporary." As applied to shyness, this phrase best refers to dwelling on a safety behavior for too long. Safety behaviors, such as staying in your room instead of going out to socialize, sometimes get a bad name. To me, resorting to safety behavior is not necessarily negative. In other words, safety means just what it says—being safe. If you use a safety behavior akin to any port in a storm, just know that it is best to make it a quick, temporary stay. Otherwise, a safety behavior that is frequently used will be so automatically reinforced that it may be hard to stay in the direct-action mode. If you move out of a safety behavior quickly and get back into direct-action, there are great benefits. You can join in with others more quickly and easily, and your new-found confidence will remain intact. As Robert Frost aptly put it, "The best way out is always through," which we can interpret with regard to shyness to mean the best way out of avoidance is to go through it, as in a social activity.

2. Increase self-monitoring. One way to increase your social awareness is to take note of your own actions and monitor how you're coming across during or right after a social interaction. The only caveat is that you're self-monitoring for a purpose—to take note of how you did in a social interaction. This type of self-appraisal is fine, but otherwise don't self-monitor during, say, a conversation, as this just reinforces preoccupation. Pay more attention to the other person and actively listen to be assured of better results.

3. As related to 2) above, resist analysis paralysis, that is move forward with direct-action. I remember taking one of my first CPR classes years ago, and the instructor made it clear that "Yes, you want to learn the procedure, but, in reality, doing something, anything you can think of to help, is much better than freezing and doing nothing at all."

4. Ask, "Where's the evidence?" and "What do I need to do next?" Both are cognitive strategies in the form of constructive self-statements you can make. For example,

Drake, a young adult chemical engineer, expressed concern over the prospect of having to make a presentation to other engineers at his workplace. He was anxious and shared a fantasy in his weekly counseling session that was unsettling. Drake said the fantasy involved an image that if one of his colleagues asked him a question during his presentation, he would not be able to answer and would faint, slumping to the floor. I asked him if this, or anything like it, had ever happened to him before, and he responded simply, "No." Next, I asked Drake what evidence he had that would indicate the fantasy could be realistic at all. He had no evidence, and both he and I then had a chuckle over how our minds often play tricks on us when we anticipate challenging assignments.

At this point in treatment, the strategy used to redirect Drake's attention away from the negative fantasy was a straightforward "I want you to ask yourself what you need to do next in this situation." This young, scientifically minded adult reflected a bit and came up with what he needed to do next to make a meaningful presentation. He said, "I think I can do what most people do—prepare." While wordiness was not Drake's preference, I did ask him to expand on his "what to do next strategy." He explained that reviewing material and asking others to listen to a draft of his presentation would occupy his attention and direct his focus. Drake's talk went well, and he was pleased that several attendees asked relevant questions. And no, he did not faint, although he was somewhat anxious. As a psychologist once said, "Anxiety is the price we pay for planning." As mentioned earlier in this book, anxiety and associated tension aren't necessarily bad things (in smaller doses), as they can get us mobilized. The downside is that too much anxiety can do the opposite, which is to immobilize us. Thus, it is best to try to find a balance.

5. Do not confuse a thought with a fact. Thoughts are fluid; they come and go. Facts, on the other hand, are hard data and do not change (unless, of course, they are revised and updated with new information).

6. Try not to think in all-or-none terms; instead, look for the gray area in-between. For example, if you say to yourself, "I'm reserved, and everyone else is outgoing," you're not looking at a more moderate (and accurate) middle ground. That is, some people are likely to be more reserved than yourself, and not all other people are outgoing. The phrase we learned in graduate psychology training was "don't be absolutistic," which to me was when my mom would say, "It's not just black or white."

7. Distinguish low-probability events from high-probability events. Evan was convinced that if he so much as asked a single question in class, he would be laughed at (a low-probability event). On the other hand, he was equally sure that if he never asked any questions in class, his participation grade would be lower (a high-probability event). In terms of problem solving, Evan would do well by taking a chance and asking a few questions. His realistic hope would then be that his fellow students would likely be supportive.

8. Are you assuming every situation is the same? In other words, if you found it difficult to speak up at one meeting, does that mean you'll never be able to speak up at any future meetings? Doubtful. One helpful technique for shy and non-shy people alike is to use the law of averages. That is, let's say you have seven meaningful conversations with people over the course of a week. Using the law of averages alone, it is likely that a couple of those conversations may have indeed gone well, a few not as well, and, for several, you would like to have had a do-over. The point is that rarely are our actions all successful or the opposite, all poor performances. Seek flexibility and accuracy in your perceptions of how you've really done in different social activities. Finally, as John Wooden, the famous basketball couch, would say, "Never try to be better than someone else." He went on to discuss how you can do well by just measuring any progress you've made from where you were weeks or months ago. In other words, compare yourself to your own performance, not others.'

9. What has worked for you in the past? It can be a helpful, strength-based exercise to consider those things that have helped you through a shyness episode in the past. Were you initially hesitant to go out with a friend that you hadn't seen in a while, then decided you would go ahead and found that your tension level dropped as soon as you engaged in an activity together? Once you've found an example or two of what helped in the past, you can repeat the same strategies again and again to successfully manage shyness. Here's a short and simple practice opportunity to help you recall a couple of effective behaviors that helped you through a shyness episode.

Practice Opportunity

List one or two behaviors that have helped you through a shyness episode in the past:

1. _____
2. _____

10. Don't jump to conclusions. For example, if you find yourself having difficulty choosing the right words in a conversation, does this mean you will always have such difficulty? Not likely. Again, use the law of averages method detailed in number eight above to be flexible and accurate in how you've handled many different conversations. Some conversations may have been nearly flawless, along with a few others where you were tongue-tied. Everybody has had both kinds.

11. Ask yourself what difference an event will make in a week, a month, or a year? For example, it is doubtful that anyone will remember or care a year later that you made a silly remark at a holiday party. Actually, a few people may remember, but they're not usually your friends or even friendly peers.

12. Focus on any strengths and competencies you have already learned in successfully managing your shyness. For example, I've had many clients in individual counseling who have said initiating short conversations was easier than they thought. So-called

small talk can work well to get the communication going. Situational talk is an element of small talk wherein you can bring up a topic, such as an upcoming local community event or how you're doing at school or work, and often get a receptive reply. Also, shy individuals self-report that once they've learned to use more direct eye contact, conversations tend to last longer and are more mutually satisfying.

13. Use direct-action and response prevention. As discussed throughout *Successful Shyness*, a recommended CBT-type ingredient for treating social anxiety is taking direct-action (or exposure) regarding the feared situation or circumstances. In addition to behavioral activation, challenging one's maladaptive thoughts to be more positive goes a long way. For example, taking direct-action while being more realistic and using an "I can get through this" thought will prevent the response of avoiding or escaping a social situation.

Motivational Interviewing

Helpful motivational interviewing strategies include recognizing the difference between how you are interacting with others now and how you would like to do so differently in the future. The following case vignette details how a shy individual can quickly develop a more active goal-oriented stance by using motivational interviewing techniques. Once basic relaxation skills are employed to bring down anxiety, a shy individual can then orient toward interacting more socially versus remaining detached. The components of motivational interviewing, discussed within Zara's case, can be used to jump start self-identified social goals.

Case Vignette
Using Motivational Interviewing to be More Social

Zara, a thirty-three-year-old graduate student in civil engineering, described in counseling how she was shy and anxious when talking with several alumni of her university's engineering department. She wanted to interact more with the recent graduates, especially the women; as she said, it's still a male-dominated field. Her main interest was in future employment opportunities. In terms of motivational interviewing, the focus was on how Zara was currently detached regarding conversing with others but that she wanted to interact more in the near future. The discrepancy between her present self-described shyness and her wanting to be more social resulted in a goal to work on, namely, to get more social.

As Zara valued getting along with others and wanted to reach out more, so she agreed that she could develop the necessary motivation to do more socially. In counseling, Zara learned focused breathing and progressive muscle relaxation (PMR) techniques. Once equipped with these methods to lower her anxiety, she took steps to talk with her fellow students and alumni more often. Asking motivational interview-type questions about her main goal of wanting to be more social allowed this method to take hold. In time, she felt more confident in dealing with others socially, and her interaction skills improved as a result. Every time we're more social with others, it can really be interpreted as engagement in a "live" practice opportunity because we are developing our interactional skills. Maybe politicians are sometimes described as smooth talkers because they've learned how to be persuasive through their near constant public appearances. I suppose it could be the other way around, wherein some smooth talkers get into politics because they like to persuade others, but I digress.

Developing Frustration Tolerance

Be careful of detaching socially or withdrawing too often. This can result in built-up frustration, especially if you desire more social contact. Pent-up tension can result in escalating and overreacting to small things, which, of course, is not desirable. There are things you can do to cope with frustration, namely, increase your frustration tolerance. Frustration tolerance is the ability to deal with obstacles effectively to better withstand stressful events.

Increasing frustration tolerance can be done by using several of the skills outlined in this book, including focused breathing, progressive muscle relaxation (PMR), and mindfulness. Also, "doing nothing instead of doing something" has been a helpful clinical strategy I've used, depending on the situation and circumstances. For example, because frustration is a normal human emotion, simply accepting the feelings of frustration is sometimes enough, as might be useful in a traffic jam. While you're busy doing nothing while sitting in your car during snarled traffic, you can always engage in a spontaneous passive activity such as slowing your breathing down. Breathing in through your nose, a little more deeply than usual, and then exhaling through your mouth can calm down the mind and body. Some people include a mantra while exhaling, such as "this too shall pass." I have better luck with "I hope this is the last traffic jam I'll be in for a while."

Another example is if you're shy and getting frustrated because you would like to be more social at, say, a large gathering. If you sense you're being inhibited, you may want to slow down instead of speeding up. That is, frustration can be hardest to tolerate when we are pushing ourselves against a sea of resistance. In other words, you may want to be more social, but your inhibitions are holding you back. Don't fight it—just slow down a tad, breath more deeply, and allow yourself to warm up with no self-demands on speaking with others right away. You can survey the room and look for a friendly face. Sometimes it can be helpful to ask someone who has set up the event relevant questions, such as "How many people usually come to these?" or "Do you like working large venues?" The point is that most people are happy to answer a few questions if you're showing true interest. Who knows? If they notice you're a little nervous, they might be even more receptive to putting you at ease.

Summary of Effective Treatment Modalities for Shyness and Social Anxiety

1. Cognitive-behavioral therapy (CBT). Focus on positive and realistic cognitions and adaptive behavior.
2. Social skills training. Social and emotional learning programs are designed to increase social skills. A straightforward example of social skills training is to have the individual focus their attention on others, ask questions that express interest, and make sure to use direct eye contact.
3. Stress inoculation training. Desensitization to maladaptive stress responses.
4. Exposure training. Direct-action by staying in situations without avoidance or escape.
5. Anxiety management training. Relaxation and tension reduction strategies help decrease physiological reactivity (learning to calm the mind and body).
6. Self-instructional training. Used to self-pace any of the therapy and training above.
7. Significant avoidance is more associated with social anxiety disorder than shyness, yet shy individuals can benefit from learning to stay in sometimes uncomfortable situations. Avoiding a situation stemming from the shy individual's inhibition is something that can be improved.

    By staying in various social interactions and not avoiding events in the first place, the shy will experience the reward of gaining interpersonal contact. Besides, as a shy person becomes more aware of others, watch what happens. That is, by careful observation, notice what occurs in most social interactions—people will initially pay some attention to you, but mostly to themselves. It seems that actors, who look and act dramatic as routine job requirements, recognize that if they don't act boldly, less attention will be paid. Interestingly, many actors report being shy when the cameras aren't rolling.
8. Do not let acute situations, such as occasional avoidance, turn into a chronic problem.
9. Through practice with direct-action, staying in social situations longer, and developing positive coping strategies, both confidence and hope for the future will follow.
10. Reflect on how you make changes. What do you believe happens? An example would be when a shy person speaks up more and ends up enjoying others company. They may conclude accurately that it was their behavior of voice modulation (slightly louder) that did the trick.
11. Learn ways to be empathic toward others. A particularly important sentiment for all of us to embrace is "the ability to distinguish an individual's problems from their value as a human being." For instance, you may find someone on their way to the loud side and highly boastful, both interpersonal problems. Yet, you know this person has a kind heart and is very loyal, thus their value as a human being remains intact. Such an individual just has a few social issues to work on for self-improvement.

Another way to look at it is that, in general, you want to "judge the problem and not the person."

12. Mindfulness-based stress reduction (MBSR). An effective meditation-based treatment for anxiety and depression.

13. Motivational interviewing (MI). These strategies can be effective in treating social anxiety, including increasing empathy, developing discrepancy, rolling with resistance, and supporting self-efficacy. You are the expert on yourself.

Summary of Anxiety Management Skills and Overall Positive Change

1. Focused breathing. Basically, just breathe slower so that you can take some deeper breaths, which will help you relax.

2. Progressive muscle relaxation (PMR). As discussed throughout *Successful Shyness*, this is a simple procedure where you can tense and then relax different major muscle groups throughout the body. The results are less muscular tension and a feeling of calm.

3. Thought stopping. It's just what it states, that you can stop a negative thought. Next, you can replace it with a more realistic, positive one. For example, someone might say to themselves, "Not another presentation. I'm not very good at these." Alternatively, and likely more realistically, the positive thought instead could be, "These presentations make me somewhat anxious, but I've done them before, and generally they work out well enough."

4. Covert rehearsal. Similar to allowing yourself to make realistic positive self-statements, in covert rehearsal, you simply go over what you would like to say in a given social interaction and picture yourself going through the process, including body language, voice modulation, and good eye contact.

5. Role playing. After you've run through some covert rehearsals of how you want to interact in a certain situation, try out responding live with a friend who can give you feedback in what is essentially a dress rehearsal. Feedback can be a great aid before you go "live."

6. Exercise daily. This can include any activity that is cardiovascular. For example, walking, running, aerobics, swimming, and the like.

7. Maintain a healthy diet overall while decreasing caffeine and sugar intake.

8. Set up a short (fifteen to thirty minutes) worry time, which will allow you to go over any concerns you've recently had. Assigning a specified time and place is important. This strategy gives you some measure of control over your worries or preoccupations. Indeed, you will likely find that your concerns won't pop up randomly as often. Should any worries occur that don't need immediate attention, you can tell yourself, "I'll be going over that problem during my 'worry time.'"

9. Establish a healthy lifestyle routine that works for you and stick with it. Allow for flexibility given the unanticipated events in your schedule.
10. Maintain healthy sleep patterns, which include a calming nighttime routine (it's a good idea to cycle down on electronics and screen time), and try to wake up at roughly the same time each day. One often overlooked physiological factor everyone can benefit from identifying in themselves is the circadian rhythm. Basically, this is your twenty-four-hour clock, and, as it turns out, some of us are at our maximum energy level in the morning (larks, as in the bird) and some of us are at our peak in the later hours of the day (owls, again a bird comparison). In planning before you give a student report or work presentation, for example, you can practice at your peak energy and concentration periods, be it in the morning or evening. Whenever your talk occurs, it will now come off better than if you tried to prepare while tired or at a low attention/concentration point during the day.
11. Allow for any setbacks you may have in working toward effective shyness responses. Take stock in maintaining the gains you've made in confidence and social skills along the way.

What better way to end the topics in this book than by outlining the key areas of positive change strategies, stress inoculation strategies, , creative problem solving, and, finally, a pleasant activities list=?

Positive Change Strategies
1. Encourage a greater range and comfort in emotional expression.
2. Promote self-awareness and insight.
3. Work on improving self-esteem, social skills, and hopefulness.
4. Learn new behaviors, including problem-solving and conflict resolution.

As a general recommendation, it is important to recognize that as you implement positive change strategies, you can monitor your progress and make any adjustments you feel might help. A solid approach to positive change involves starting with an identifiable target problem you would like to change, then setting an easy goal to measure your progress.

Case Vignette
Identifying a Target Problem and Measuring Progress
Eduardo, a forty-five-year-old pharmaceutical executive, entered counseling to deal with speaking up at work. He had previously been a pharmaceutical salesperson and had no problem visiting doctors and hospitals to explain how his company's medications could be helpful. When it came to supervising his employees in his new role, he tended to "clam up and become shy," in his words. It turned out that Eduardo had a difficult time letting his employees know when

they weren't doing things right or according to policy and procedure. We discussed how his orientation toward people was moving toward, meaning being pleasant and going-along-to-get-along doesn't always work when in a management role. He identified a target problem to work on that had the focus of learning to be more assertive.

Basically, based on the feedback he received at work, Eduardo decided that he needed to be more direct with others. He set it as his goal to be more definite with employees and speak openly to them if they needed any guidance as to how they should proceed in their roles. The target problem then was being too indirect and passive, with the goal of using assertions to allow for more directness with his employees. Eduardo measured his goal by estimating how many times he was able to interact with his employees. He included in his measurement how and when he was able to provide direct guidance and constructive feedback using assertion techniques. Eduardo was pleased with his communication skills. At the same time, he felt tired the first week of being more direct because it was a new way of relating to others in a work situation. In time, he grew more comfortable and was pleased that he was less hesitant to approach his employees.

Stress Inoculation Strategies

1. Assess the probability of a negative event occurring in a social situation. Next, visualize what a positive event could look like.
2. Consider becoming involved rather than avoiding the social situation.
3. Use universal self-acceptance (U.S.A.) rather than self-criticism before you even act.
4. Engage in the social situation that has caused you some initial hesitation.
5. Reinforce or reward yourself for having followed through with the social situation, and take some time to evaluate how you did.

Creative Problem-Solving

1. Stop and think about how you want to proceed in a particular social encounter.
2. Consider all aspects of the situation that are relevant and begin to problem solve.
3. Think about it, and come up with a few different ways you may want to respond.
4. Anticipate how things might turn out with the alternative you choose to proceed with.
5. Carry out the course of action you've selected. For example, it can be as simple as initiating a conversation with a specific person you would like to meet.

Pleasant Activities List

By increasing time spent in pleasant activities, you will likely find yourself becoming more relaxed and, at times, ending up in spontaneous conversation with more people. Below is a list in menu format that you can choose from when contemplating what might be a pleasant or fun activity to join in on:

1. Thinking about something good in the future
2. Thinking about people I like
3. Being with friends
4. Watching people
5. Having an open conversation with a friend
6. Listening to music
7. Complimenting or praising someone
8. Enjoying TV, the computer, and the phone
9. Taking a nature walk or hike
10. Exercise
11. In general, enjoying people, places, and things
12. Other:_____

Conclusion

The practice opportunities in this book are designed to help you build confidence and learn ways in which to communicate with others more easily. By working through any problems that you've had with any problematic shyness behaviors, you'll be on your way to learning how to be successfully shy. Building confidence and effective social skills are important goals that can be gained more readily when you're able to step out of your comfort zone at your own pace. *Successful Shyness* has also focused on bringing your shyness assets to the fore; these include active listening capability, interpersonal sensitivity, and quiet determination. The saying "If at first you don't succeed, try, try, again" definitely applies to becoming successfully shy. Psychologists call it "successive approximation." This term means that as we get closer to our social interaction goals, detours—sometimes accompanied by awkwardness—may occur. Basically, it's the two-step forward and one-step back progress format.

Speaking of awkwardness, most everyone has experienced it. The practice opportunities have been constructed in such a way as to take steps forward, a little at a time and at your own pace. Getting a little awkward along the way is okay as you learn to be successfully shy. Once again, consider and hopefully take to heart the words of Winston Churchill, "Success consists of going from failure to failure without losing enthusiasm." Thus, make room for some temporary emotional disruption to be felt from time to time on the road to building confidence and effective social skills.

Finally, I'll be brief and to the point. May your success with shyness continue to grow while your worries and concerns recede. Thanks for picking up and reading some or all of *Successful Shyness*. The practice opportunities included are meant to provide you with a basis or foundation for significant positive change. If you think any of your peers, friends, or loved ones would benefit, please let them know about the book. Finally, I welcome any feedback.

About the Author

Dr. Marc Skelton is a licensed psychologist as well as a marriage and family therapist. He also earned board certification as a Diplomate in Clinical Psychology from the American Board of Professional Psychology (ABPP).

Dr. Skelton received his B.S. in psychology from the University of Iowa and an M.A. in psychology from Pepperdine University. Following a predoctoral internship at Capistrano by the Sea Hospital, he earned a PsyD in psychology, with a specialization in marriage and family therapy from the United States International University (USIU). After a postdoctoral internship at the same facility and years of private practice, Dr. Skelton returned to USIU (now Alliant International University or AIU) to complete a second doctorate, a PhD, in psychology.

Over time, a combination of hospital and office-independent practice facilitated a thorough clinical experience base. Dr. Skelton has published in the area of adolescent assessment and treatment and has also been involved in teaching psychology courses at several local universities, including Pepperdine, USIU, AIU, and most recently Brandman University—Chapman University System (through 2013).

In 1998, Dr. Skelton served as president of the Orange County Psychological Association. In 2001, he was elected to the position of chair for the Division of Clinical and Professional Practice of the California Psychological Association (CPA) for a one-year term. Annual professional memberships include the American Psychological Association (APA) and the Orange County Psychological Association (OCPA). For the past forty years, he has maintained a private practice, with the bulk of the time (1983–2018) located in Laguna Niguel, California.

Selected References

American Psychiatric Association. (2022). *Diagnostic and statistical manual of mental disorders* (5th ed., text rev.). https://doi.org/10.1176/appi.books.9780890425787

Bernstein, D.A., & Borkovec, T.D. (1973). *Progressive relaxation training: A manual for the helping professions.* Champaign: Research Press.

Cain, S. (2012). *Quiet: The power of introverts in a world that can't stop talking.* New York: Random House.

Carducci, B.J. (1999). *Shyness: A bold new approach.* New York: Harper-Collins.

Lazarus, A.A. (1997). *Brief but comprehensive psychotherapy: The multimodal way.* New York: Springer.

Neff, K. (2003). Self-compassion: An alternative conceptualization of a healthy attitude toward oneself. *Self and Identity, 2,* 85-101.

Prochaska, J.O., DiClemente, C.C., & Norcross, J. (1992). In search of how people change: Applications to addictive behaviors. *American Psychologist, 47*(9), 1102-1114.

Skelton, M.D. (2022). *Skelton Shyness Survey.* Unpublished, Private Practice, Laguna Niguel, California.

Weiner, B. (1985*).* An attributional theory of achievement motivation and emotion. *Psychological Review, 92,* 548-573.

Resources

Anxiety and Depression Association of America (ADAA). https://adaa.org

National Institutes of Health: Social Anxiety Disorder. www.nimh.nih.gov

Shyness Institute. www.shyness.com

Milton Keynes UK
Ingram Content Group UK Ltd.
UKHW050831111223
434160UK00011B/747